The state and industry in South Korea

The economic success of East Asia is often attributed to the relationship between state and business. In *The State and Industry in South Korea – The Limits of the Authoritarian State*, Jong-Chan Rhee presents a more balanced view of Korea's 'industrial miracle'.

The book examines the limits of a strong authoritarian state as a vehicle for intervening in the market or for sponsoring liberal reform. In so doing the author focuses on why and how state-controlled industrial adjustment in Korea has succeeded and failed. This is clearly illustrated by an examination of unsuccessful state intervention in the heavy and chemical industrial sectors which led to the breakdown of the state–big business governing coalition. This is contrasted to the successful transformation of these same industries in the 1970s. However, the mid-1980s unsuccessful attempts at liberalization led to the failure of business-led industrial adjustment. Further insights into these limitations are provided by a comparison with state-industry relations in Japan and France. His new institutional approach gives a fresh theoretical framework beyond existing state theories by analytically integrating structure and agent in institutional arrangements.

Jong-Chan Rhee teaches in the Department of Political Science at Kyung Hee University, Seoul. He is particularly interested in the comparative financial politics of Korea, Japan and France.

D0208530

The state and industry in South Korea

The limits of the authoritarian state

Jong-Chan Rhee

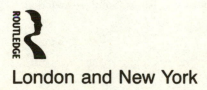

London and New York

First published 1994
by Routledge
11 New Fetter Lane, London EC4P 4EE

Simultaneously published in the USA and Canada
by Routledge
29 West 35th Street, New York NY 10001

© 1994 Jong-Chan Rhee

Typeset in Garamond by Intype, London

Printed and bound in Great Britain by
Mackays of Chatham PLC, Chatham, Kent

British Library Cataloguing in Publication Data
A catalogue record for this book is available from the British Library

Library of Congress Cataloging in Publication Data
Rhee, Jong-Chan, 1957–
    The state and industry in South Korea: the limits of the
authoritarian state / Jong-Chan Rhee.
        p. cm.
    Includes bibliographical references and index.
    ISBN 0–415–11102–1
    1. Industry and state—Korea (South) 2. Korea (South)—Economic
policy. I. Title.
HD3616.K853R48 1994
338.95195—dc20   93–43156
ISBN 0–415–11102–1   CIP

To my parents Hyung-Sung Rhee and Keum (Hu) Rhee

Contents

Figures and tables

FIGURES

TABLES

Abbreviations

ALA	Administration of Labour Affairs
CMES	Comprehensive Measures for Economic Stabilization
CMIC	Changwon Machinery Industry Corporation
DFIFs	Disposals of Financially Ill-Managed Firms
DJP	Democratic Justice Party
DRP	Democratic Republican Party
EPB	Economic Planning Board
FKI	Federation of Korean Industries
FKTU	Federation of Korean Trade Unions
HCIs	Heavy and Chemical Industries
HCIIA	Heavy and Chemical Industrial Investment Adjustment
HCIPC	Heavy and Chemical Industry Promotion Committee
HMC	Hyundai Motor Company
IDL	Industrial Development Law
IPDC	Industrial Policy Deliberation Council
KCCI	Korean Chamber of Commerce and Industry
KDB	Korea Development Bank
KDI	Korea Development Institute
KEA	Korean Employers' Association
KEPC	Korean Electric Power Corporation
KFSMB	Korean Federation of Small–Medium Business
KFTA	Korean Foreign Traders' Association
KIET	Korea Institute for Economics and Technology
KSC	Korean Shipping Corporation
MCI	Ministry of Commerce and Industry
MF	Ministry of Finance
MPR	Ministry of Power and Resources
NDP	New Democratic Party

NIF	National Investment Fund
OBSE	Office of Bank Supervision and Examination
POSCO	Pohang Iron and Steel Company
SCIR	Subcommittee of Commerce, Industry and Resources
SCNSM	Special Committee for National Security Measures
SHMC	Shinjin Motor Corporation
SMC	Saehan Motor Company
WWPDC	Worker's Welfare Policy Deliberation Committee

Preface

The purpose of this research is to solve the puzzle of why the so-called 'strong' authoritarian state failed to impose the heavy and chemical industrial investment adjustments and to achieve the market-oriented reform by restricting big business dominance. The major theme of this study is the limits of authoritarian state capacities either for state intervention in the market or for liberal market reform; the authoritarian state became fragile without a supporting coalition with big business.

In order to prove this theme, this study will explain why and how the state-controlled industrial adjustments in Korea succeeded or failed – why and how state managers could or could not create capitalist collective action for industrial adjustment. My major focus will be on the unsuccessful policy implementation of the state-controlled heavy and chemical industrial investment adjustments during the period of 1979-80. My minor focuses will be both on the successful heavy and chemical industrial transformation in the early 1970s, and on the disposals of financially ill-managed firms in the mid-1980s as a result of the failure of liberal market reform. In addition, in order to supplement my arguments, this study will compare these Korean industrial adjustments with the Japanese and French state-led industrial adjustments. A synthesis of new institutional approaches will form a theoretical framework beyond existing state theories by means of an analytical integration of structure and agent in institutional arrangements, including state institutions for economic policy-making and implementation, institutional linkages between the state and big business, and the financial system.

This study uses documentary research and survey interview research during two field researches. Primary sources are collected from newspapers, the government's documents and publications, National Assembly Records, business associations' and labor unions' publications, and business groups' publications. The field works for the primary sources were done in the following places: the National Assembly Library in Korea and the Library of Congress in Washington; the Government Archives in Korea; the internal libraries of the Ministry of Commerce and Industry, the Economic Planning Board, and the Ministry of Finance in Korea; the Federation of Korean Trade Unions, the Federation of Korean Industries, the Korean Chamber of Commerce and Industry, the Korean Foreign Traders' Association, the Korean Federation of Small–Medium Business, and the Korean Employers' Association; and the internal data centers of the Korea Herald, the Dong-A Daily News, the Chosun Daily News, the Joong-Ang Daily News, the Maeil Kyungje Daily News, and the Hankook (Hyundai) Kyungje Daily News.

Secondary sources, including books, journals, working papers, and Ph.D. dissertations, were collected at the following places: the Van Pelt Library of the University of Pennsylvania, the Institute of East Asian Studies of the University of California, Berkeley, the World Bank, the Library of Congress in the United States, the Library of the Seoul National University, the Korean Research Institute of Christianity and Social Problems, Korea Development Institute, and Korea Institute for Economics and Technology.

I interviewed high government officials, big businessmen, and a banker in order to generate data in regard to the policy processes of the economic stabilization measures and the heavy and chemical industrial investment adjustments. Most of the interviewees were directly involved in the process of policy-making and implementation: Woun-Gie Kim, a former Deputy Prime Minister of the Economic Planning Board; Moon-Young Kwon, a former Chief of the Section of Investment Investigation in the Economic Planning Board; Kyong-Shik Kang, a former Minister of the Ministry of Finance; Gak-Kyu Choi, a former Minister of the Ministry of Commerce and Industry; Soo Myung Cha, a former Assistant Minister of the Ministry of Commerce and Industry; Choon Lim Lee, one of the Chairmen in the Hyundai Business Group; Myung-Kul Choi, one of the Chairmen in the Daewoo Business Group; and Soo-Kon Pae, a former President of the Office of Bank Supervision and Examination. Their careers are presented in the appendix.

I could not have completed this book without many people's encouragement, support, and valuable comments. First of all, I owe a special debt of gratitude to my advisers at the University of Pennsylvania: Thomas M. Callaghy, Chong-sik Lee, Edwin T. Haefele, Fred Block, and Peter A. Swenson. I also thank the following scholars for their advice or comments: Robert Bianchi, Jose E. Campos, Inwon Choue, Hilary Conroy, Stephan Haggard, Yong-Ho Kim, Margaret Levi, Chung-in Moon, Lisa Moore, Jack H. Nagel, Hak-Soon Paek, Paul Pierson, Hyuk-Sang Son, Jung-en Woo, and Jung-Dong Yuh. In addition, I owe much more than I can gracefully express to my interviewees who generously shared their valuable time and exclusive experiences and offered their sincere opinions. They should not take any responsibility for my own interpretation. I am grateful to editors of Routledge Alison Kirk and Rebecca Garland for their sincere and excellent editorship.

Finally, my deep gratitude goes to my family. My father Hyung-Sung Rhee and my mother Keum (Hu) Rhee have given me their endless encouragement and support for my study over many years. This book is dedicated to my parents. My father-in-law Jung-Kyu Lim and my mother-in-law Kyung-Sook (Lee) Lim also supported my study with warm encouragement and assistance to my field research. My wife Young-Mee (Lim) Rhee has played a patient triple role of wife, mother, and lecturer. I was always sorry to my son Jae-June that I could not take good care of him. Her warm-hearted support and his behaviour as a good boy made it possible for me to complete this book.

Jong-Chan Rhee
Seoul, Korea

Introduction

THE PROBLEM SETTING

During the late 1960s and the early 1970s, a slowdown of Korean economic growth occurred as a result of the limits of export-oriented light industrialization. The relative economic crisis became one of the causes leading to the rise of the bureaucratic authoritarian regime (the *Yushin* [Revitalizing] System) of 1972. It coincided with the socio-political crisis that had resulted from labour disputes and a rigged election.[1] In March 1973, shortly after the emergence of the authoritarian regime, President Park declared an ambitious industrial transition programme that shifted emphasis from export-oriented light industries to export-oriented heavy and chemical industries.[2] The industrial policy was a sectoral development strategy focusing on heavy and chemical industries (HCIs): iron and steel, non-ferrous metals, shipbuilding, machinery, automobiles, electronics, and petrochemicals. During the 1970s, the HCI sectors had been promoted by a broad range of policy instruments including privileged policy loans, subsidies, and tax reduction and exemption. Without such strong government supports, few big business firms would have been willing to bear the risks. The HCI sectors required massive investments and a long gestation period of profits. The industries had an uncertain comparative advantage in international competition and in the small domestic market.

The overemphasis on the HCIs resulted in an overheated economy from 1976 to 1978.[3] During this period, the sharp increase in heavy and chemical investments heightened the ratio of fixed investment of expenditure on gross national product. It rose from 26 percent in 1976 to an unprecedented 37 percent in 1978. During the same period, more than 77 percent of all manufacturing equipment investment was put into the HCIs. To support these investments, the share of HCIs in total manufacturing bank credit reached 60 percent in 1978. Investments in the HCIs exceeded the potential demand even before the second oil-shock of 1979, when heavy and chemical products lacked international comparative advantages.

The rate of inflation had been more than 10 percent per year since 1960. Policy-makers as well as the general public tended to regard inflation as an inevitable price to pay for high economic growth. From 1976 to 1978, the high inflation triggered by the investment boom was accompanied by a rapid increase in wages, at an annual rate of 34.2 percent, which surpassed the growth of labour productivity. The wage increases resulted not from the government's welfare policy for workers but from workers' increasing wage struggles and some sectoral labour shortages. As an effect of inflation, weakening export competitiveness led to slow growth in the Korean export-oriented area. The export growth of Korea had been declining since 1977. In addition, the financial status of corporations became more fragile because external borrowing was rapidly increasing at a rate that was much greater than the internal financing of investment during the period. Consequently, to improve the financial condition, businessmen became obsessed with unproductive businesses and speculations in real estate.

In response to this situation, the government announced the comprehensive stabilization programme on 17 April 1979,[4] which led to decisive policy changes. The major components of the programme included restrictive fiscal and monetary management, price stabilization for daily necessities, and investment adjustment in the HCIs. However, the stabilization policy had not been implemented in an effective and consistent manner during the years of 1979–80. The economic situation had been aggravated by the second oil-shock and political turmoil during the economic crisis, which was characterized by high inflation, overinvestment (surplus capacity), and low capital utilization (low operation). During the 1970s, the Korean economic policy had emphasized economic growth based on strict labour control while ignoring income distribution.

In the late 1970s, labour disputes became vehement and began to reflect workers' political demands. About 200 women in the bankrupted Y.H. company staged a protest to demand their salaries. They continued the protest at the headquarters of the New Democratic Party (the major opposition party). The government brutally suppressed the protesting coalition of workers and opposition lawmakers. It conspired to bring about the dismissal of the president of the opposition party, which in tu·n triggered the anti-government uprisings in the cities of Pusan and Masan. Within the power bloc of Park's regime, power struggles occurred between hardliners and softliners who tried to cope with the socio-political crisis. The power skirmishes led to the breakdown of the authoritarian regime through Park's assassination.

Acting President Kyu Ha Choy, of the Interim Government, was elected President in his own right by the rubber-stamp electoral college of the National Conference for Unification. Leading politicians competed for political power while drafting a new constitution. However, President Choy was unable to coordinate negotiations between the ruling and opposition parties. A conspiracy for political intervention occurred among military hardliners who had already grasped power by staging the coup within the military on 12 December 1979. Widespread student demonstrations and the Kwangju uprising of May 1980 demanding democratization provided a good opportunity of implementing the planned military takeover. With the resignation of President Choy, former General Doo Hwan Chun, one of the coup leaders, was elected President in August 1980. In the end, the economic and political crisis resulted in the first negative rate of economic growth (–5.2 percent) in 1980 since the emergence of Park's regime (1961–79). Inflation also soared to 28.7 percent, as measured in consumer prices, and to 38.9 percent, as measured in wholesale prices.[5]

Economic adjustment strategies for economic stabilization and crisis management included a tight monetary and fiscal policy along with investment adjustments in the HCI sectors, in the short term, and policy changes for liberal reform in economic planning and goals, in the long term. During the period of 1979–80, heavy and chemical industrial investment adjustments (HCIIAs) were compulsory decisions imposed by state managers. The investment adjustments had been attempted through strong state intervention without voluntary agreements of big businessmen. Ironically, the long-term programme of economic policy emphasized reducing the role of the state in the economy by pursuing market-oriented economic management. The direction of policy goals was expressed in the drafting of the Fifth Economic Plan (1982–86), which would seek a long-term change of economic priorities – from economic growth, unbalanced industrial policy, and the 'state-led economy' to economic stability, balanced industrial policy, and a 'private-initiated economy'.[6]

In the early 1980s, the new authoritarian government (Chun's regime) attempted to make liberal economic reforms towards economic stabilization and liberalization, and to prevent big business dominance in the market by cutting off the state-big business ruling coalition under Park's regime. In the mid-1980s, however, Chun's regime failed to achieve these reform policies. Along with the unstable regime security, the government intervened deeply in rescuing financially depressed large firms in declining industries. In the end, it returned to the symbiotic alliance between the state and big business under Park's regime; then, it succeeded in attaining the compulsory industrial adjustment under the collusive state –big business governing coalition.

THE RESEARCH PURPOSE AND QUESTIONS

The research purpose is to solve the puzzle of why the so-called 'strong' authoritarian state failed to impose the HCIIAs and to achieve the market-oriented reform by restricting big business dominance. The major theme of this study is the limits of authoritarian state capacities either for state intervention in the market or for liberal market reform; the authoritarian state became fragile without a supporting coalition with big business. In order to prove this theme, this study will explain why and how the state-controlled industrial adjustments in Korea succeeded or failed – why and how state managers could or could not create capitalist collective action for industrial adjustment. My major focus will be on the unsuccessful policy implementation of the state-controlled heavy and chemical industrial investment adjustments under state-big business conflicts or the breakdown of the state-big business governing coalition. My minor focuses will be both on the successful heavy and chemical industrial transformation in the early 1970s, and on the disposals of financially ill-managed firms (DFIFs) in the mid-1980s as a result of the failure of liberal market reform. In addition, in order to supplement my arguments, this study will compare these Korean industrial adjustments with the Japanese and French state-led industrial adjustments: the comparative chapter will focus on the limits of both so-called strong state capacities and state-big business governing coalition.

My major parts in the empirical chapters will explain why and how the policy of the HCIIAs failed despite strong state intervention. This major question will be answered within the context of exploring what kind of industrial adjustment was adopted and implemented in response to the economic crisis during the fall and rise of authoritarian regimes. Minor questions are why and how the state-controlled heavy and chemical industrial transition and the disposals of financially depressed large firms worked. My major research questions are:

1 How could the authoritarian government facilitate, in the early 1970s, the capitalist collective action of investing in the HCI sectors by building new institutional arrangements within the state (state institutions for economic policy-making and implementation), between state and society (institutional linkages between the state and big business), and between state and market (the financial system)?

2 Why and how had these effective institutions for high economic growth run into the situation of decay in the late 1970s, and disorder in the period of 1979–80?

3 How had changing institutions affected interests and bargaining power of state managers and big businessmen in policy formulation and implementation, and in what ways and to what extent did state-big business conflicts or the breakdown of state-big business governing coalition impinge on the policy failures?

4 Why did the authoritarian regimes in South Korea fail to create the state-controlled capitalist collective action of investment adjustment through mergers in the heavy and chemical industrial major fields?

5 How had the new authoritarian regime attempted to build new institutions for market-oriented reforms, and why and how was the liberal economic reform aborted? Then, why did the authoritarian government return to the collusive state-big business ruling coalition?

6 Finally, why and how could the Chun government create the state-controlled capitalist collective action of acquisitions and/ or mergers for disposals of financially weak large firms in the structurally depressed industries?

Chapter 1 will discuss theoretical approaches and briefly mention major arguments in the analytical framework. Chapter 2 will compare these Korean industrial adjustments with the Japanese and French industrial adjustments according to the stages of high economic growth and economic stabilization and liberalization. Chapter 3 will explain the industrial adjustment for heavy and chemical industrial promotion and then the process of decay in the institutional arrangements for high economic growth in the HCIs. Chapters 4, 5, and 6 will deal with the policy failures of heavy and chemical investment adjustments. Chapters 7 and 8 will explain the failure of liberal economic reform and the industrial adjustment for the disposals of financially depressed firms. The Conclusion will explain theoretical implications and the major theme. It will also briefly mention the decline of government capacities for capitalist collective action in the process of the Korean democratic transition.

NOTES

1 I use the concept of bureaucratic authoritarianism according to O'Donnell's basic argument: political exclusion of political access to the popular sector, economic exclusion of economic benefits to the popular sector, and depoliticization of social and political issues in the deepening process of dependent development (Guillermo O'Donnell, 'Reflections on the Patterns of Change in the Bureaucratic Authoritarian State', *Latin American Research Review* 13 [No. 1, 1978], p. 6).

2 For the politics of industrial transition, see Inwon Choue, 'The Politics of Industrial Restructuring: South Korea's Turn towards Export-Led Heavy and Chemical Industrialization, 1964–74', Ph.D. Diss., University of Pennsylvania, 1988.

3 For the overheated economy, see Paul W. Kuznets, 'The Dramatic Reversal of 1979–80: Contemporary Economic Development in Korea', *Journal of Northeast Asian Studies* 1 (No. 3, 1982); and Sang-Woo Nam, 'Korea's Stabilization Efforts since the Late 1970s', in Joong-woong Kim, ed., *Financial Development Policies and Issues* (Seoul: Korea Development Institute, 1986).

4 See Korea Development Institute (KDI), *Collection of Documents and Study Reports Related to Economic Stabilization Policies, Vol. 1* (Seoul: KDI, 1981), Chaps. 1, 2, and 3 (in Korean).

5 Kihwan Kim, *The Korean Economy: Past Performance, Current Reforms, and Future Prospects* (Seoul: Korea Development Institute, 1985), p. 19.

6 See the Federation of Korean Industries (FKI), *A Survey of the Korean*

Economic Development (Seoul: FKI, 1987) (in Korean); and Kyung-Sik Kang, *Beyond Economic Stability* (Seoul: Korean Economic Daily News Press, 1987) (in Korean).

Chapter 1

Institutional change and capitalist collective action
The analytical framework and arguments

This chapter will discuss how to analyse the politics of industrial adjustment. It will deal with theoretical variables (state capacity, big business firms' choice, and institutional arrangements) and frameworks to explain the mechanism of state intervention in industrial adjustment.

THE POLITICS OF INDUSTRIAL ADJUSTMENT

Industrial adjustment (restructuring) is the core of economic adjustment. Herein lies the critical problem of why market forces may fail to produce necessary restructuring and how state interventions may help to achieve this. The issue of government policy towards industrial adjustment has been increasingly raised in most countries. During the 1980s recession, especially, industrial policy placed governments in the position of intervening actively and consciously in specific firms, industries, or sectors. This strategy is distinguished from macroeconomic policy that merely influences a general level of savings and investment. In terms of scope or context of industrial policy, government policy may become directly involved in a restructuring process even at the level of an individual company. Governments offer incentives to emerging industries or sectors and upgrade or reduce declining industries or sectors.[1] The politics of industrial adjustment will be approached within a fundamental logic of political economy: 'Politics determines the framework of economic activity and channels it in directions which tend to serve the political objectives of dominant political groups and organizations.'[2] The important questions related to industrial adjustment are: What is the purpose of the adjustment? What is to be adjusted? What are the means (policy instruments) for adjustment? Who are involved in the adjustment? Who benefit or lose as a result? How does the adjustment occur in terms of policy changes, institutional changes, changing relationships among agents, and market or government intervention? Why does the adjustment work or not?[3]

The purpose and policy instruments of industrial adjustment

As for the purpose of adjustment and what is adjusted, the Korean industrial adjustments were to achieve industrial promotion for high economic growth or to stabilize the industrial sectors in response to the general or sectoral industry crisis in both the domestic and international economies. In this study, the Korean economic adjustments will include the following: the industrial transition for heavy and chemical industrial promotion; the industrial adjustment composed not only of the heavy and chemical industrial investment realignments in the short term, but also of the major economic policy changes and the installation of new institutional arrangements towards a market-oriented economy in the long term; and the industrial restructuring for disposals of financially depressed firms in the declining industries. These industrial adjustments were also parts of state managers' strategic responses to the political crises in the wake of the rise and fall of the authoritarian regimes.

The Korean state had used industrial policy instruments for inducement and constraint. The instruments for constraint provided coercive enforcement of punishment for business firms' noncompliance: economic penalties (suspending new loans, withdrawing old loans, and tax investigation) and political revenge. The instruments for inducement offered financial incentives to reward firms' compliance: preferential interest rates, tax reduction and exemption, direct and indirect government subsidies, privileged access to policy loans, and mono-oligopolized rights of production and sale. These types of policy instruments had been used in such policy measures as investment designation and allocation, credit allocation, and acquisitions and/or mergers.

The dimensions of these industrial policy instruments are both 'discretionary field manipulation' and 'discretionary command'.[4] Korea had depended heavily on both discretion and command, especially in the investment adjustments and the disposals of financially depressed firms. Obviously, the authoritarian regimes imposed policy decisions. They enforced mandatory obligations both with the implicit sticks (threats) of withdrawing privileged benefits as well as with the carrots (inducements) of offering financial incentives.

How industrial adjustment works

The questions of how and why adjustment succeeds or fails are important in analysing the economic adjustment. In view of how it works, we can compare differences and similarities with regard to the types of adjustment that occur among developed or developing countries and even between developed and developing countries. This question also includes who are agents of adjustment and for whose benefits or losses the adjustment is chosen and implemented. Expected answers are given to what a governing coalition for adjustment is, who are excluded from adjustment, and who are the winners and losers in sharing in the benefits of adjustment. The question of why adjustment succeeds or fails allows us to compare successful and unsuccessful cases in terms of the determinants of policy formulation and implementation. The problem of how it works is closely related to that of why it works or not, because the former represents institutional structures of adjustment and the latter indicates causal relations between policy choices and outcomes (success or failure) within these institutional constraints.[5]

This study will focus on domestic political structures for industrial management, instead of the dichotomous explanations for economic growth, in order to show how and why state intervention does or does not work. From this point, we have to explore in what ways the state has intervened in market failures and to what extent such state intervention has been effective. The phenomenon of state intervention is more visible in industrial policy than in macroeconomic policy. The politics of industrial and macroeconomic adjustment is deeply embedded in economic performance (economic stabilization or growth). Institutional arrangements of different types of adjustment form constraints and opportunities in policy formulation and implementation.

In order to devise a specific explanatory mechanism, scholars have analysed different characteristics of state institutions, financial systems, or relationships between state and society at the structural level. The variable of state institutions constrains or facilitates state autonomy *vis-à-vis* socio-political forces. It also affects state capacities to formulate and implement policies. State institutions are usually measured by the coherence and coordination of the decision-making structure in the bureaucracy and by an independent power of technocrats from political leaders. Financial systems are analysed in terms of the roles of government and banks in setting interest rates and allocating credits. Institutional linkages between state and society shape and limit patterns of interest representation, policy-making involving interest groups, a governing coalition, and direct interactions between the state and individual firms. In addition, they use such explanatory factors as agenda and perceptions of economic crisis, relations with external financial agencies, regime types, regime change, political cycles (elections), and international political and economic relations.

Zysman classified types (institutional arrangements) of economic adjustment as 'company-led', 'negotiated', and 'state-led' in terms of financial systems that correspond to Katzenstein's 'liberalism', 'corporatism', and 'statism', respectively – the three forms of contemporary capitalism.[6] Company-led adjustment is represented by the United States; negotiated adjustment is most visible in the small European states (Switzerland, Sweden, Norway, the Netherlands, Denmark, and Austria); and state-led adjustment is found in Japan and France. Liberalism usually relies on macroeconomic policies and market management; corporatism leads to flexible and incremental adjustment of industry through a coalition among the state, business, and labour that sometimes includes political parties; and statism pursues planning and administrative guidance through a structural transformation of their economies.

In the Korean case, a general type of state-controlled adjustment in an authoritarian regime can be added to Zysman's three types. As I mentioned above, the state-controlled adjustment in South Korea has been characterized by discretionary field manipulation and discretionary command. The means of command had been used, in many cases, without enactment of concerned laws: they were heavily based on administrative orders and presidential decrees, and even informal orders without official government orders. Policy measures through discretionary command were more frequently used in the economic crises. In contrast to the Korean cases, the state-led adjustments in Japan and France relied mainly on discretionary field manipulation for industrial adjustment. In South Korea, policy-makers adopted compulsory measures, instead of a possible state-led adjustment with a sufficient agreement of business groups, a negotiated adjustment among the state, business, and labour, or a company-led adjustment through the market.

In particular, institutional arrangements for industrial adjustment tend to change in crisis situations. The politics of Korean industrial adjustment was associated with changes in institutional arrangements under the general or sectoral industry crisis, along with the rise and fall of the authoritarian regimes. During the period of economic crisis that was accompanied by political crisis, existing institutions within the state, between state and society, and between state and market, began to weaken or broke down. The economic and political crisis resulted in changes not only in state managers' and social groups' interests but also in power relationships among them, which had been shaped and constrained by the existing institutions. In the end, not only did these policy changes occur, but also there were changes of institutions for policy formulation and implementation (state institutions for economic policy-making and implementation, the financial system, and institutional linkages between the state and social groups).

Until now, we have examined institutional constraints for industrial adjustment in revealing how adjustment works. Here, institutional constraints facilitate or prohibit successful or unsuccessful policy implementation – why adjustment works or not. The following two sections will discuss theoretical approaches as to why state-led or state-controlled industrial adjustment works or not. The former will focus on state capacities and big business influence in analysing government-business relationships. The latter will examine how institutional arrangements affect state managers' and big businessmen's interests and bargaining power and how state intervention solves market failures that result from unsuccessful capitalist collective action.

THE LIMITS OF STATE THEORIES

Block and Skocpol emphasized the 'potential autonomy' beyond Poulantzas's relative autonomy of the state in economic or political situations.[7] The relative autonomy of the state from instrumental control by the capitalist class may exist in opposition to specific factions of the dominant class if state actions serve the interests of general capital. Furthermore, Block and Skocpol found the potential autonomy of the state in exercising economic reforms to oppose even the general interests of capitalists and grant concessions to workers without being reduced to class struggles during the period of the New Deal.

During the economic crisis of 1980, the Korean authoritarian governments tried to restore and establish state autonomy from social groups after losing control over the big business and labour sectors. The regimes continued to adopt monetary and fiscal austerity policies for economic stabilization against general business demands for economic activation. Chun's regime attempted to restructure big business by means of 'business ethics' movements as part of social purification, the strengthening of the financial status of business groups,[8] and an anti-monopoly law. For a stricter labour control, the regime passed new labour laws in the Legislative Council on National Security in late 1980. The major goals of labour laws were to prevent third-party intervention in labour disputes and labour-management bargaining and to reinforce existing labour regulations. Only the government could take part in settling labour disputes between workers and employers. The Federation of Korean Trade Unions (FKTU) and Industrial Labour Unions, as its subunits, were also interpreted as third parties. Chun's government tried to overcome the limits of state corporatist control over the above federations under Park's regime. The system of labour control changed from the industrial labour union system to a business enterprise labour union system.

From the cases of Korea and the United States, we can assume that the state may have greater autonomy with regard to business during crisis situations than at normal times, although they showed the different responses to labour demands. In the cases of the Korean HCIIAs, the state could not successfully implement the policies even though the state managers were able to choose compulsory mergers with greater autonomy from big business. Here, the policies of investment adjustments show us typical cases in which state autonomy over social groups is not a sufficient prerequisite for state capacities to implement government policies. The policy failures came from aborted implementations.

State capacity is affected not only by state autonomy from social groups but also by state institutions. In this study, the concept of the state is understood as an 'administrative apparatus', including a bureaucracy, with an 'institutional legal order'.[9] Scholars, who emphasize state institutional structures, usually analyse the coherence of, and the coordination within, a public bureaucracy and the power relationships between political parties and the executive.[10]

In the case of the New Deal, Skocpol criticized Block's arguments about structural relationships among state managers, capitalists, and workers in terms of state institutional structures that included governmental institutions and political parties. She argued that Block's causal mechanism could not explain why the National Recovery Act failed to achieve its policy objectives. She contended that Block did not examine the internal institutional constraints affecting state managers' interests and capacities.[11] In response to Skocpol's arguments, Block accepted her institutional explanations of state managers' conflicts and abilities. However, he clearly pointed out a limit of her approach in that strong autonomous administrative institutions do not necessarily produce effective state actions, which depend on specific interactions between state institutions and societal forces.[12]

As I mentioned previously, this study will consider not only state institutions but also institutions both between state and society and between state and market in order to explain the Korean state-controlled industrial adjustments. In the cases of investment adjustments, the policy failures were considerably influenced by weakening institutional arrangements both in the state-controlled financial system and in the mode of direct interactions between the state and business groups that bypassed business associations. Just as the reduced coherence and coordination of state institutions resulted in a lack of efficiency in policy implementation, so too did the withering institutional capabilities of the state in dealing with business groups lead to big business competition and opposition. The state was unable to adjust business groups' interests and competition both in the inefficient financial system and in direct (non-corporatist) channels between the state and business groups. Therefore, the policy failures cannot be completely explained without analysing both the financial system and the interactions between the state and business firms.

In the next section, 'new institutional' approaches will be discussed as alternatives to state-centred approaches for dealing with state capacity.

NEW INSTITUTIONAL APPROACHES

This section will explore how to combine state-big business relationships (state capacity and big business influence) with institutional arrangements within a theoretical framework.

The 'institution-based' new institutional approach

Traditional institutional approaches were not able to link structural (macro-level) variables to actors' (micro-level) intentional interactions. In order to formulate a more convincing approach to clarify causal connections between institutional variables and policy choices and outcomes, it is imperative to analyse how institutional variables not only shape and limit actors' interests and capacities but also interact with one another through mediating actors. Another group of scholars made an effort to synthesize state-centred and/or society-centred and/or market-centred approaches in terms of institutional analyses.[13] Their approach clearly showed how institutional variables shape and constrain preferences and abilities not only of state managers but of social groups by facilitating or inhibiting access to foreign or domestic economic policy-making.

According to these new institutional approaches, there are distinct characteristics of institutional explanations.[14] First, individual interests (or preferences) and abilities (or capabilities) are conditioned by institutional structures. They understand institutions as structural characteristics defined by practices, norms, rules, organizational structures, and organizations that guide both internal relationships within groups and interactions among actors. This study focuses on such formal institutions as rules, organizational structures, and organizations. Institutions shape and constrain actors' interests and also facilitate or prohibit actors' capabilities. Therefore, institutional structures limit the range of policy-making and implementation options available to policymakers. Second, institutional arrangements at a point in time are 'both a dependent variable at time t and an independent variable at time $t + 1$'. In other words, prior institutional choices condition future options and institutional capacities are 'a product of choices made during some earlier period'.[15] Finally, institutional continuity (persistence) may be found even when more efficient alternatives exist at normal times. However, in general, during economic or political crisis, prior institutions break down, interests (goals) change, and actors then attempt to form new institutions.

However, most of their analyses could not suggest a theoretical framework of overall institutional change, which would provide an explicit causal mechanism for the following questions, even though they recognized institutional changes in crisis situations or institutional reforms.[16] Thus, this study will also answer the following questions: (i) Why and how had institutional capacities of the state weakened in terms of state institutional structures and relationships of the state with society and market? (ii) How did interests and capacities of state managers, supporting actors, and excluded actors remain undetermined within weakening institutional structures? (iii) In what ways did concerned actors, including state managers, change their interests and conflict with one another, and how did actors' capacities change? (iv) How did a governing coalition (winning groups through power struggles) build new institutional arrangements in accordance with its policy choice after an economic and/or political crisis?

This early new institutional approach focused on how existing institutions affect policy choices and outcomes. In particular, thus, this approach could not explain microfoundations (actors' choices and strategic interactions) of institutional origins (intentional design of institutional change).[17]

The 'rational choice-based' new institutional approach: the politics of institutional change (intentional design)

Recently, in order to uncover a concrete mechanism between politics and economy, economists, sociologists, and political scientists in the field of political economy began to pay attention to how institutional constraints matter with the market in two different ways. One way, as I mentioned in the previous subsection, is to analyse how institutions affect economic policy choice and capabilities. The other, as I will discuss in this subsection, is to explain institutional origins (design) – why and how institutions evolve in order to solve market problems. I will call the former the 'institution-based' new institutional approach (which explains policy choices [micro-level outcomes] in terms of institutional arrangements [macro-level variables]) and the latter the 'rational choice-based' new institutional approach (which explores institutional change or constraints [macro-level outcomes] in terms of actors' intentional interactions [micro-level variables]).

The group of scholars who developed this kind of new institutional approach created the field of 'positive political economy'.[18] The core questions of their approach are: 'How do institutions evolve in response to individual incentives, strategies, and choices, and how do institutions affect the performance of political and economic systems?'[19] Their core theoretical arguments are as follows:

> Its [positive political economy] focus is on microfoundations, and it is grounded in the rational-actor methodology of microeconomics . . . positive political economy emphasizes both economic behaviour in political processes and political behaviour in the marketplace. In emphasizing the former it uses an economic approach – constrained maximizing and strategic behaviour by self-interested agents – to explain the origins and maintenance of political institutions and the formulation and implementation of public policies. In emphasizing the latter it stresses the political context in which market phenomena take place. By focusing on how political and economic institutions constrain, direct, and reflect individual behaviour, positive political economy attempts to explain in a unified fashion social outcomes such as production, resource allocation, and public policy.[20]

The rational choice-based new institutional approach focuses on individual choices within the constraints institutions impose on choice sets while the institution-based new institutional approach concentrates on choices (particularly, policy choices) of groups, including state managers and social groups. In addition, the analytical concern of the former is how institutional changes affect cooperation (collective action) of individual actors as a result of individual choices, whereas that of the latter is how institutional arrangements influence groups' capacities in making and implementing choices.

By synthesizing institutional constraints and rational choices in the field of political economy, one of the key arguments the rational choice-based new institutional approach has made is that institutions may solve collective action dilemmas among individual behaviours within a group.[21] We can apply this basic argument both to capitalist competition in the market and to businessmen's opposition or resistance to state intervention. Competition among business firms creates collective action problems: 'In most cases, the interests of individual firms in high profits and economic survival can best be achieved if they cooperate with their competitors and act in concert but each individual firm has an incentive to "free-ride" on the cooperation of other firms.'[22] In general, additionally, businessmen oppose or resist state intervention in their investment decision-making, which would lead to their non-compliance with state managers' policy choices. As a result, the state cannot create capitalist collective action of cooperation with economic policy choices.

In these problematic areas of collective action, a critical issue is how to solve collective action dilemmas in the market. Olson argued for requirements of 'selective incentives' (coercion or rewards) in order to solve difficulty of collective action in a large group.[23] Another issue is how to provide businessmen with selective incentives that create capitalist collective action. There may be different kinds of mechanisms to offer incentives.[24] Among them, the mechanism of state intervention may give business firms the strongest incentives (coercive enforcement and financial incentives). The state determines the basic structure of property rights and reduces transaction costs of capitalist collective action by means of institutional changes (design) that will offer selective incentives. State managers' institutional design reflects the preferences of the governing coalition (the state's and dominant social groups' interests).

My study will focus on state intervention in industrial adjustment in the so-called 'strong states' – mainly in the Korean authoritarian state, among developing countries and partially in Japan and France, among developed countries, in comparative perspective. In these countries, in general, the state intervened frequently and intensively in the industry in order to solve capitalist collective action problems that occurred as it strongly promoted economic growth and tried to efficiently implement the economic stabilization policy. The next section will set up the analytical framework and discuss the major arguments about the state-controlled industrial adjustments under the Korean authoritarian regimes.

A SYNTHESIS OF THE INSTITUTION-BASED AND RATIONAL CHOICE-BASED NEW INSTITUTIONAL APPROACHES

There is a question of how to synthesize the two new institutional approaches in order to analyse both institutional capacities of the

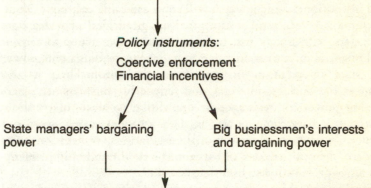

Institutional arrangements:
- State institutions for economic policy-making and implementation
- Institutional linkages between the state and big business (governing coalition and policy networks)
- Institutions between state and market (the financial system)

Institutional change (decay, disorder, and new building)

Institutional capacities of the state: state managers' policy choice and an unsuccessful or successful institutional design for issue-areas of collective action dilemma

Policy instruments:

Coercive enforcement
Financial incentives

State managers' bargaining power

Big businessmen's interests and bargaining power

Big business responses (rational choices: non-compliance or compliance): the unsuccessful or successful capitalist collective action for industrial adjustment

Figure 1 The analytical framework: the state-controlled industrial adjustment

state and capitalist collective action. That is, a synthesis of the new institutional approaches is to explain why and how state intervention through institutional design (change) can stir up capitalist collective action in the market. The rational choice-based approach will explore why new institutional arrangements evolve and how they solve a capitalist collective action dilemma. The institution-based approach will show how institutional capacities of the state (which are based on institutional design) affect both state managers' and big businessmen's bargaining power. The latter approach will focus on power relationships between state managers and big business firms, whereas the former approach will concentrate on collective cooperation among large firms.

On the whole, the analytical framework for the state-controlled industrial adjustment is divided into three parts (see Figure 1). The first part is composed of institutional variables (state institutions for economic policy-making and implementation, institutions of state-big business relationships [the governing coalition and policy networks], and institutions of state-market relationships [the financial system]). These institutional variables shape or constrain institutional capacities of the state. These institutional arrangements are changing through decay, disorder, and new building. Accordingly, institutional capacities of the state are fluctuating.

The second part is to explore how these changing institutional arrangements facilitate or prohibit state managers' policy choices and institutional design, which will solve capitalist collective action dilemmas. A successful institutional design, which provides state managers with policy instruments of both coercive enforcement and financial incentives, increases state managers' bargaining power for state intervention in investment decision-making; it also changes big business interests, and reduce big businessmen's bargaining power for resistance or opposition to state intervention. The state's bargaining power is high when state managers can reduce, by means of institutional installations, transaction costs that are 'the positive costs of bargaining a policy and of implementing a policy once it has been bargained'.[25]

Finally, the third part is a game-like situation of industrial adjustment among big business firms: it shows whether or not capitalist collective action occurs through cooperation among large firms or through big businessmen's compliance with state managers' industrial policy choices. Here, state managers can bring about individual firms' compliance with industrial adjustment, by changing payoff structures, which determine firms' responses (rational choices between cooperation and non-cooperation), by means of institutional design. Thus, they can create state-controlled capitalist collective action. This part examines policy outcomes – successful or unsuccessful implementation of policy choices.

More specifically, we can explain collective action dilemmas by means of the 'prisoners' dilemma' game and the 'deadlock' game and collective action solutions by the 'assurance' game and the 'cooperative' game.[26] In this study, the prisoners' dilemma game and the assurance game will be applied to collective action dilemmas and solutions among big business firms in the market competition, respectively. The deadlock game and the cooperative game will be used to explain collective non-compliance (defection) and compliance with state managers' policy choices, respectively.

Here, critical points are whether or not state managers can transform both the prisoners' dilemma game (the dominant strategy of defection) into the assurance game (mutual assurance of cooperation), and the deadlock game into the cooperative game (the dominant strategy of cooperation), by changing the payoff structure through institutional design. Individual firms' collective cooperation in accordance with the government's policy choice, in the cooperative game and their mutual cooperation, in the assurance game are the best choices for state interests and give state managers the highest payoff.

MAJOR ARGUMENTS

This study will deal with the three cases of Korean state-controlled industrial adjustment: the transformation of industrial strategy from the export-oriented light industries to the export-oriented HCIs in the early 1970s (heavy and chemical industrial promotion: HCIP); the investment adjustments in the HCI sectors during the period of 1979–80 (heavy and chemical industrial investment adjustments: HCIIAs); and the disposals of financially ill-managed firms (DFIFs) in the declining industries during the period of 1985–87. The major focus of analysis will be on the policy failure of HCIIAs (the second industrial adjustment: the aborted state-controlled capitalist collective actions); minor focuses will be on the policy successes of industrial promotion in the HCIs and of industrial rationalization in the declining industries (the first and third industrial adjustments: the successful state-controlled capitalist collective actions).

The HCIIAs

Institutional capacities of the state

The Korean investment adjustments took place in the context of these relationships between crisis and institutional change. The institutional capacities of the state were, to a large extent, determined by state institutions for economic policy-making and implementation, institutional linkage between the state and big business, and the state-controlled financial system. As a result of the malfunctions of the ambitious and untimely heavy and chemical industrialization during the 1970s, the existing institutional arrangements between state and market, particularly the state-controlled financial system, began to crumble. The institutional decay, disorder, and breakdown of the other two variables also occurred. The new authoritarian state institutions emerged after the interim government, and, subsequently, it built new institutions of society and market. These changing institutions had affected the interests and capacities of state managers and social groups.

Since the beginning of the economic crisis, a small group of bureaucrats had attempted to change policy goals in order to pursue economic stabilization, whereas big businessmen, as the governing partner of the state, persisted in keeping their own privileges in the market as a result of high economic growth. The institutional capacities of the state had declined, which conditioned the policy failures of the HCIIAs.

The economic crisis in the late 1970s resulted in interest conflicts not only between state managers and big businessmen but also among big businessmen within the state-controlled financial system and the existing institutions of state-big business relationships. State managers persisted in their vested rights of control over big business in discretionary credit and investment allocations. That is, bureaucrats continued to keep monopoly or oligopoly in the industrial structure of heavy and chemical industrial projects for the economies of scale in the small domestic market. On the other hand, big businessmen made every effort to invest in a competitive manner in as many projects as possible. This competition created rapidly increasing demands for enormous credit amounts and made credit allocations at an optimal level impossible. Such conflicting interests facilitated a decline of the government-controlled financial system and unstable state-big business relationships to such an extent that state managers lost, to a large extent, credit and investment controls.

As a whole, the deepening institutional decay of the late 1970s had decreased the state capacities for economic management and increased big business influence on decision-making and policy implementation. Serious conflicts within the bureaucracy and between state managers and big businessmen occurred in the process of policy-making and implementation for economic stabilization and investment adjustment. Consequently, the weakening institutions of the state, between state and society, and between state and market, led to the policy failures of HCIIAs during the crisis period.

The unsuccessful state-controlled capitalist collective action

During the late 1970s, the government had recommended that heavy and chemical industrial firms reduce their ongoing and planned investments by means of voluntary cooperation of investment adjustment among concerned large firms in the HCI sectors. These large firms, however, ignored the government's industrial guidelines, arguing that the problem of overcapacity in the HCIs would be temporary and disappear in the long term as a result of the export-oriented economies of scale, which would enhance the international competitiveness. During the period of economic crisis accompanied by political crisis, the state attempted to solve, in a compulsory manner, overlapped investments in the major heavy and chemical industrial projects under planning or construction by creating collective actions of big business compromises for investment adjustment.

However, the governments were not able to make an efficient institutional design for strong coercive enforcement and financial incentives because they lacked institutional capacities. The state managers in the HCIIAs had weak bargaining power over big businessmen due to the institutional decay or disorder. In the HCIIAs, the planned takeover large firms exerted strong bargaining power over the state managers by requiring privileged financial supports: the large firms to be merged indirectly resisted the compulsory mergers by means of foot-dragging on implementation through conflicts with planned takeover companies and the foreign actors' opposition. (See Figure 2.)

The HCIP

Institutional capacities of the state

In the early 1970s, the Korean authoritarian government set up new institutions for heavy and chemical industrial promotion. That is, the government centralized the administrative system of heavy and chemical industrial policy-making and implementation in order to enhance the coherence and coordination among concerned ministries. It also took advantage of direct interactions between the state and big business firms, which would reinforce the state-big business governing coalition, by bypassing business organizations in order to promote big business participation in the HCIs.

The prisoners' dilemma game (the capitalist competition for profit maximization): the failure of voluntary self-heavy and chemical investment adjustment

		X	Y	the state	
	1	D	C	2	
X's payoff order	2	C	C	1	the state's prefer-
against Y	3	D	D	3	ence order
	4	C	D	2	

C: Cooperation: capacity reduction for investment adjustment
D: Defection: free riding
X and Y: Concerned big business firms
The dominant strategy: Defection
Payoff: Profit maximization in market competition

The assurance game: Collective investment adjustment through compulsory mergers

		X	Y	the state	
	1	C	C	1	
X's payoff order	2	D	C	2	the state's prefer-
against Y	3	D	D	3	ence order
	4	C	D	2	

C: Cooperation: compliance with mergers for investment adjustment
D: Defection: non-compliance
X: Takeover big business firms
Y: Big business firms to be merged
X's payoff: Maximization of financial rewards
Y's payoff: Minimization of economic penalties (punishments)

The unsuccessful state-controlled capitalist collective action

State managers' selective incentives: insufficient coercive enforcement and/or weak financial incentives

The prisoners' dilemma game ———— X ————▶ The assurance game

Figure 2 The policy failure of heavy and chemical investment adjustment (mergers)

Finally, the government tightened the state-controlled financial system in order to mobilize huge capital, which would offer privileged financial benefits for large business firms.

The successful state-controlled capitalist collective action

Shortly after President Park's declaration of heavy and chemical industrial promotion in 1973, big businessmen resisted heavy and chemical industrial investment because they did not want to take the risk of participating actively in the HCIs. They were sceptical about the ambitious policy of state-led heavy and chemical industrial promotion, since their firms did not have capabilities of huge capital mobilization and advanced technological accumulation.

Afterwards, however, the authoritarian government made it possible for large firms to participate actively in the state-led heavy and chemical industrial promotion by means of coercive enforcement and financial incentives. The state managers changed the firms' payoff structure by lowering the transaction costs of industrial adjustment in favour of heavy and chemical industrial firms. The reduced transaction costs shifted big-business interests from the labour-intensive light industries to the HCIs. The policy instruments of the state managers were both threats of punishment through economic penalties for big business non-compliance and incentives of reward through privileged financial benefits for big business compliance. Thus, the state was able to create the collective action of big business participation in the HCIs by breaking through the deadlock game-like situation of the large firms' foot-dragging resistance. (See Figure 3.)

The DFIFs

Institutional capacities of the state

During the period of 1985–87, the politicized institutions (which meant that institutional operations were heavily based on political decision-making rather than economic logic [rational criteria]) had brought the state-controlled disposals of financially ill-managed large firms in line with industrial adjustment. The failure of economic reform under Chun's government to achieve credit control over conglomerates as well as financial liberalization, resulted in politicized state intervention in businessmen's investment decision-making by means of massive disposals of financially depressed large firms. The authoritarian government politicized and then exploited the financial system in order to cover both the economic cost of the state-controlled industrial adjustment and the political

The deadlock game: big business resistance (opposition) to state intervention in investment decision-making

		X	Y	the state	
	1	D	C	2	
X's payoff order	2	D	D	3	the state's prefer-
against Y	3	C	C	1	ence order
	4	C	D	2	

C: Cooperation: participation in heavy and chemical industrial investment
D: Defection: non-participation: non-compliance with the state's policy choice
X and Y: Individual big business firms
The dominant strategy: Defection
Payoff: Profit maximization, mainly in the labour-intensive light industries and partly in labour-intensive HCI sectors.

The cooperative game: Compliance (cooperation) with the policy of state-led heavy and chemical industrial promotion

		X	Y	the state	
	1	C	D	2	
X's payoff order	2	C	C	1	the state's prefer-
against Y	3	D	D	3	ence order
	4	D	C	2	

C: Cooperation: active investment in the HCIs
D: Defection: non-investment in the HCIs
X and Y: Individual big business firms
The dominant strategy: Cooperation
Payoff: Maximization of financial benefits and minimization of economic penalites
X's payoff against Y is larger in C–D than in C–C: big business firms invested competitively in the HCIs in order to dominate the domestic markets.

The successful state-controlled capitalist collective action

State managers' selective incentives: strong coercive enforcement and sufficient financial support

The deadlock game ───────────────► The cooperative game

Figure 3 The state-led heavy and chemical industrial promotion (capital-intensive HCI sectors, particularly the machinery industry)

cost of regime maintenance under the collusive state-big business governing coalition.

The state institutions for economic policy-making and implementation were politicized. The political power elite became deeply involved in industrial policy, and policy measures for industrial adjustment were largely made as a result of political decisions rather than in accordance with economic rules and criteria. Finally, the institutional channels between the government and business groups were politicized; in order to represent big business interests and to demand individual conglomerates' interests, the business groups' owners had frequent, direct contacts with the political leaders (particularly President Chun) of the regime by bypassing the top-level bureaucrats.

The successful state-controlled capitalist collective action

During the period of 1984–85, the Chun government recommended voluntary investment adjustment (acquisitions and/or mergers, or groupings according to business lines) among financially weak large firms in the structurally depressed industries of shipbuilding, shipping, and overseas construction.

However, the large firms concerned were still obsessed with profit maximization even in the depressed situation and they failed to adjust and reduce their investment. Thus, in order to reduce surplus capacities from overcompetition in these declining industries, the government intervened heavily in the big businessmen's investment decisions by means of designated and compulsory disposals of financially ill-managed firms.

The state managers used highly coercive instruments for disposing of financially depressed firms, which were designated by the government, and financial instruments of enormously privileged benefits for the takeover business firms. The financially troubled firms had no choice but to accept their dissolution in the face of economic threats of bankruptcy and/or political threats to noncompliance. The large takeover (acquisition and/or merger) firms requested that the government offer huge financial supports and benefits in return for their risk-taking in acquiring the highly indebted firms. As the general economy was doing well, the state managers provided these financial rewards in exchange for kickbacks of political donations, which paid for the increasing political cost of maintaining the authoritarian regime. (See Figure 4.)

The prisoners' dilemma game (the capitalist competition for profit maximization): the failure of voluntary self-investment adjustment

		X	Y	the state	
	1	D	C	2	
X's payoff order	2	C	C	1	the state's prefer-
against Y	3	D	D	3	ence order
	4	C	D	2	

C: Cooperation: voluntary self-adjustment (mergers, groupings in business lines, or capacity reduction)
D: Defection: free riding
X and Y: Concerned big business firms
The dominant strategy: Defection
Payoff: Profit maximization in overcompetition

The assurance game: collective investment adjustment through compulsory disposals of financially ill-managed firms (acquisitions and/or mergers)

		X	Y	the state	
	1	C	C	1	
X's payoff order	2	D	C	2	the state's prefer-
against Y	3	D	D	3	ence order
	4	C	D	2	

C: Cooperation: compliance with acquisitions and/or mergers
D: Defection: non-compliance
X: Takeover large firms (or business groups)
Y: Designated financially depressed large firms
X's payoff: Maximization of financial rewards
Y's payoff: Prevention either of bankruptcy or of political revenge.

The successful state-controlled capitalist collective action

State managers' selective incentives: highly coercive enforcement and highly privileged financial rewards

The prisoners' dilemma game ⟶ The assurance game

Figure 4 The disposals of financially ill-managed large firms in the declining industries

Chapter 2 will compare these Korean state-controlled industrial adjustments (the case of the so-called strong authoritarian state among the developing countries) with the Japanese and French state-led industrial adjustments (the cases of the so-called strong state among the advanced countries). These comparisons will be analysed in the following categories: industrial promotion for high

Table 1 The comparative analysis of the three industrial adjustments

Industrial adjustment		HCIP 1973–78	HCIIAs 1979–80	DFIFs 1985–87
Institutional arrangements	State institutions	The centralized administrative system of heavy and chemical industrial policy-making and implementation	The institutional decay or disorder of state institutions for HCIP (conflicts within the bureaucracy)	The politicized and centralized administrative system for state intervention in investment decision-making
	Institutional linkages between the state and big business	The state–big business governing coalition; direct interactions between the government and big business firms by bypassing business organizations	Conflicts within or the brekadown of state–big business governing coalition; inefficient direct channels between the government and big business firms	The return to state–big business governing coalition; the politicized direct channels between the government and big business firms
	The financial system	The reinforced state-controlled financial system (investment and credit control)	The inefficient state-controlled financial system (the failure of investment and credit control)	The politicized financial system for investment and credit control
Policy instruments		Highly coercive enforcement and strong financial incentives	Insufficient coercive enforcement and/or weak financial incentives	Highly coercive enforcement and highly privileged financial incentives

(continued on next page)

Table 1 Continued

Industrial adjustment	HCIP 1973–78	HCIIAs 1979–80	DFIFs 1985–87
Bargaining power	State managers' bargaining power > big businessmen's bargaining power	State managers' bargaining power < big businessmen's bargaining power	State managers' bargaining power > big businessmen's bargaining power
Capitalist collective action	From big business resistance to voluntary compliance (heavy and chemical industrial investments)	The unsuccessful investment adjustment (the policy failure of mergers)	Acquisitions and/or mergers between big business firms

economic growth, investment adjustment for international competitiveness in order to solve overcapacity and overcompetition in the domestic market, and investment adjustment for restructuring declining industries.

Chapters 5 and 6 will explain the unsuccessful state-controlled industrial adjustment of HCIIAs. Chapters 3 and 8 will explore the successful state-controlled industrial adjustments of the state-led heavy and chemical industrial promotion and the disposals of financially ill-managed firms, respectively.

NOTES

1 See Alan R. Roe, 'Industrial Restructuring: Issues and Experiences in Selected Developed Economies', *World Bank Technical Paper* No. 21 (1984); and George C. Eads and Kozo Yamamura, 'The Future of Industrial Policy', in Kozo Yamamura and Yasukichi Yasuba, *The Political Economy of Japan, Vol. 1: The Domestic Transformation* (Stanford: Stanford University Press, 1987).
2 Robert Gilpin, 'The Politics of Transnational Economic Relations', in Robert O. Keohane and Joseph S. Nye, eds., *Transnational Relations and World Politics* (Cambridge, MA: Harvard University Press, 1972), p. 53.
3 I added more questions to Streeten's classification (see Paul Streeten,

'Structural Adjustment': A Survey of the Issues and Options', *World Development* 15 [No. 12, 1987].

4 In synthesizing the classifications of Dahl and Lindblom, and Myrdal, Leory P. Jones and Il Sakong classified the theoretical dimensions of government intervention: non-discretionary field manipulation, discretionary field manipulation, non-discretionary command, and discretionary command (see Leory P. Jones and Il Sakong, op. cit., [this chapter, note 8] chap. 4). According to Dahl and Lindblom, there are four broad socio-political techniques: spontaneous field control, manipulated field control, command, and reciprocity. Here, government interventions are represented through manipulated field control or command. The former is defined as the 'intentional alteration of another's opportunity set so as to stimulate a desired response' and the latter as 'hierarchical direction enforced by expectations of penalties for non-compliance' (see Robert A. Dahl and Charles E. Lindblom, *Politics, Economics, and Welfare: Planning and Politic-Economic Processes Resolved into Basic Social Processes* [New York: 1953], pp. 99–109). Concerned actors either comply with or object to field manipulation while command imposes concerned actors' compliance regardless of their own advantages or disadvantages under an explicit or implicit threat for non-compliance. With regard to operational controls, Myrdal separated 'non-discretionary control' from 'discretionary control'. The former is a control in which 'application follows automatically from the laying down of a definite rule, or from induced changes in prices, the imposition of tariff duties, or the giving of subsidies to a particular branch of industry without the possibility of discrimination in favor of particular firms'. The latter is a control which 'involve an individual decision by an administrative authority with power to act at its own discretion' (Gunnar Myrdal, *Asian Drama: An Inquiry into the Poverty of Nations* [New York: Pantheon, 1968], p.904).

5 In this study, the meaning of policy success or failure is not used in terms of economic rationality – successful or unsuccessful economic outcomes. Successful or unsuccessful policy outcomes depend on state managers' abilities; thus, they mean whether state managers can implement their policy choices or not in accordance with their preferences – more specifically, whether state managers can create capitalist collective action for industrial adjustment or not.

6 See Peter J. Katzenstein, *Small States in World Markets* (Ithaca: Cornell University Press, 1985), p. 20; and John Zysman, *Governments, Markets and Growth: Financial Systems and the Politics of Industrial Change* (Ithaca: Cornell University Press, 1983), Chaps. 1, 2.

7 See Fred Block, 'The Ruling Class Does Not Rule: Notes on the Marxist Theory of the State', *Socialist Revolution* 33 (1977); Fred Block, 'Beyond Relative Autonomy: State Managers as Historical Subjects', *The Socialist Register* (1980); Theda Skocpol, 'Political Response to Capitalist Crisis: Neomarxist Theories of the State and the Case of the New Deal', *Politics and Society* 10 (No. 2, 1980); Theda Skocpol, *States and Social Revolutions* (Cambridge: Cambridge University

Press, 1979), pp. 27–31; and Nicos Poulantzas, 'The Problems of the Capitalist State', *New Left Review* No. 58 (1969).

8 I distinguish business interest associations (business interest groups, or business organizations) from business groups (industrial groups, conglomerates, or *Jaebols* [in Korean]). Korea's *Jaebols* (business groups) are similar to Japan's *Zaibatsu*. A *Jaebol* is defined as a family-based conglomerate composed of big companies. More specifically, a business group in the Korean context is a highly centralized and diversified family-owned conglomerate whose holding company controls its subsidiaries in various industries through financial linkages. See Leroy P. Jones and Sakong Il, *Government, Business and Entrepreneurship in Economic Development: The Korean Case* (Cambridge, MA: Harvard University Press, 1980), pp. 259–60.

9 Roger Benjamin and Raymond Duvall, 'The Capitalist State in Context', in Roger Benjamin and Stephen L. Elkin, *The Democratic State* (Lawrence: University of Kansas Press, 1985); Stephen D. Krasner, 'Approaches to the State: Alternative Conceptions and Historical Dynamics', *Comparative Politics* (January 1984), p. 224; Stephen D. Krasner, op. cit. (1978), pp. 8–10; and Theda Skocpol, 'Bring the State Back In: Strategies of Analysis in Current Research', in Peter Evans *et al.*, eds, *op. cit.* (1985).

10 See ibid.

11 See Theda Skocpol, op. cit. (1980), pp. 182–201.

12 See Fred Block, op. cit. (1987), pp. 20–22. For other critiques on state-centred approaches, see Gabriel A. Almond, 'The Return to the State', *American Political Science Review* 82 (No. 3, 1988); James N. Rosenau, 'The State in an Era of Cascading Politics: Wavering Concept, Widening Competence, Withering Colossus, or Weathering Change?' *Comparative Political Studies* 21 (No. 1, 1988); and Ezra N. Suleiman, op. cit., Chap. 14.

13 See G. John Ikenberry, 'Conclusion: An Institutional Approach to American Foreign Economic Policy', *International Organization* 42 (Winter 1988); G. John Ikenberry *Reasons of State: Oil Politics and the Capacities of American Government* (Ithaca: Cornell University Press, 1988); Peter A. Hall, *Governing the Economy: Politics of State Intervention in Britain and France* (New York: Oxford University Press, 1986); John L. Campbell, *Collapse of an Industry: Nuclear Power and the Contradictions of U.S. Policy* (Ithaca: Cornell University Press, 1988); Douglas C. Bennett and Kenneth E. Sharpe, *Transnational Corporations versus the State: The Political Economy of the Mexican Auto Industry* (Princeton: Princeton University Press, 1985); Stephan Haggard and Chung-in Moon, 'Institutions and Economic Policy: Theory and a Korean Case Study', *World Politics* XLII (January 1990); Stephan Haggard, Byung-Kook Kim, and Chung-in Moon, 'The Transition to Export-Led Growth in South Korea, 1954–66', *World Bank Working Paper* (November 1990); and John Zysman, op. cit.

14 For basic arguments about 'new institutionalism', see G. John Ikenberry, op. cit. (1988); and James G. March and Johan P. Olsen, 'The

New Institutionalism: Organizational Factors in Political Life', *American Political Science Review* 78 (September 1984); and James G. March and Johan P. Olsen, *Rediscovering Institutions: The Organizational Basis of Politics* (New York: The Free Press, 1989).

15 Stephen D. Krasner, Sovereignty: An Institutional Perspective', *Comparative Political Studies* 21 (No. 1, 1988), pp. 71–72.

16 Exceptionally, James G. March and Johan P. Olsen explained institutional reforms (transformation of political institutions) (see James G. March and Johan P. Olsen, *op. cit.* [1989], Chaps. 4, 5, and 6.

17 In this study, the concept of institutional change is used in two meanings. In a broad sense, one is structural transformation of institutions (institutional decay, institutional disorder, and new institutional building). In a narrow sense, the other is institutional design to solve collective action problems in policy issue-areas.

18 See James E. Alt and Kenneth A. Shepsle, eds., *Perspective on Positive Political Economy* (Cambridge: Cambridge University Press, 1990); Robert H. Bates, *Beyond the Miracle of the Market: The Political Economy of Agrarian Development in Kenya* (Cambridge: Cambridge University Press, 1989); Karen Schweers Cook and Margaret Levi, *The Limits of Rationality* (Chicago: University of Chicago Press, 1990), Part III; Michael Hecher, ed., *The Microfoundations of Macrosociology* (Philadelphia: Temple University Press, 1983); Margaret Levi, *Of Rule and Revenue* (Berkeley: University of California Press, 1988); Douglass C. North, *Structure and Change in Economic History* (New York: Norton, 1981); Douglass C. North, *Institutions, Institutional Change and Economic Performance* (Cambridge: Cambridge University Press, 1990); Elinor Ostrom, *Governing the Commons: The Evolution of Institutions for Collective Action* (Cambridge: Cambridge University Press, 1990); and Sharon Zukin and Paul Dimaggio, eds., *Structures of Capital: The Social Organization of the Economy* (Cambridge: Cambridge University Press, 1990). For this approach in comparative politics, see George Tsebelis, *Nested Games: Rational Choice in Comparative Politics* (Berkeley: University of California Press, 1990).

19 James E. Alt and Kenneth A. Shepsle, op. cit., p. ix.

20 Ibid., p. 1.

21 See Robert H. Bates, 'Macropolitical Economy in the Field of Development', in ibid.; Robert H. Bates, *op. cit.* (1989); and Robert H. Bates, 'Contra Contractarianism: Some Reflections on the New Institutionalism', *Politics and Society* 16 (Nos. 2–3, 1988).

22 John R. Bowman, *Capitalist Collective Action: Competition, Cooperation and Conflict in the Coal Industry* (Cambridge: Cambridge University Press, 1989), p. xii.

23 Mancur Olson, *The Logic of Collective Action: Public Goods and the Theory of Groups* (Cambridge, MA: Harvard University Press, 1965), pp. 44, 51.

24 As for capitalist competition in the market, Bowman found 'non-organizational solutions' (mergers) and organizational mechanisms to facilitate the capitalist collective action: organizational solutions are

'internal organizational mechanisms' (a formal price-fixing agreement, business organizations, etc.), 'external organizational mechanisms' (enforcements from suppliers, buyers, creditors, and workers), and 'public organizational mechanisms' (the state) (see John R. Bowman, *op. cit.*, Chap. 2).

25 Margaret Levi, *op. cit.*, p. 23.

26 Levi and Tsebelis applied game-theoretical analysis to tax policy and party politics, respectively, in terms of effects of institutional change (Margaret Levi, *op. cit.* [1988]; and George Tsebelis, *op. cit.*). 'The prisoners' dilemma game had two characteristics. First, defection is the dominant strategy for each player. Dominant is the technical term used to indicate that following this strategy leaves each player better off no matter what the opponent does. Thus, defection is unconditionally the best strategy for each player. Second, by choosing the dominant strategy and defecting, both players find themselves in a suboptimal outcome, that is, they find themselves worse off than if they had chosen the cooperative strategy' (George Tsebelis, op. cit., p. 62). Thus, the payoff order of player X against player Y is DC-CC-DD-CD (X:Y; D: defection; C: cooperation). In the deadlock game, there is also the dominant strategy of defection: both players are better off with mutual defection than with mutual cooperation. Thus, the payoff order of player X against player Y is DC-DD-CC-CD (X:Y). The cooperative game has two characteristics. First, in contrast to the prisoners' dilemma game, cooperation is the dominant strategy for each player. Second, by choosing the dominant strategy of cooperation, players are better off than if they had chosen the strategy of defection. The payoff order of player X against player Y is CD-CC-DD-DC (X:Y). Here, X's payoff against Y is larger in CD than in CC. This game is different from the 'assurance game'. The assurance game has no dominant strategy, but two equilibria of the game (CC and DD in player X's payoff order of CC-DC-DD-CD), which are 'stable outcomes because no player has the incentive to deviate in strategy if the opponent does not change strategy' (ibid., p. 64).

Chapter 2

The state-led industrial adjustments in comparative perspective
Japan and France

This chapter will present theoretical arguments based on the comparative analysis of the Japanese and French state-led industrial adjustments and the Korean state-controlled industrial adjustments.

As I mentioned in Chapter 1, the Korean authoritarian governments adopted and enforced industrial promotion, compulsory acquisitions and/or mergers, and investment designations without sufficient business consent or despite business opposition; they did not choose to pursue a state-led industrial adjustment with a sufficient agreement of business firms, a negotiated industrial adjustment among the state, business, and labour, or a company-led industrial adjustment through the market. The policy instruments for the state-controlled industrial adjustments in South Korea had been characterized by discretionary field manipulation, mainly in credit allocation, and discretionary command, mainly in dealing with financially ill-managed firms. The government had depended heavily on discretionary command.

On the other hand, the state-led industrial adjustments in Japan and France relied heavily on discretionary field manipulation as an effective industrial policy instrument. More importantly, these so-called strong countries among advanced countries made and implemented policy choices based on businessmen's agreement and voluntary compliance.

This chapter will briefly analyse how and why the state-led industrial adjustments succeeded or failed during the three stages of industrial adjustment (industrial promotion, investment adjustment for international competitiveness, and industrial adjustment for financially depressed firms), in which this study analysed the Korean cases. Additionally, this analysis will show the similarities and differences between the Korean state-controlled industrial adjustments and the Japanese and French state-led industrial adjustments.

THE INDUSTRIAL PROMOTION FOR HIGH ECONOMIC GROWTH: BIG BUSINESS PARTICIPATION IN THE TARGETED INDUSTRIES

The Japanese case

Institutional arrangements for industrial promotion

During the era of U.S. occupation (1945–52), the Supreme Command for the Allied Powers (SCAP) had executed drastic economic reforms for economic recovery: the dissolution of monopoly capitalist powers (*Zaibatsus*: family-based conglomerates), the enactment of anti-monopoly law, and the land reform. These reforms aimed to prevent 'rent-seeking' activities and facilitate 'profit-seeking' activities in the market, by reshuffling the old structure of property rights.[1] The breakdown of old economic organizations resulted in low transaction costs for business activities aimed at industrial promotion in the market competition.

During the late 1940s and the 1950s, institutional arrangements for industrial promotion had been built within state institutions, between the state and the business circle, and between state and market. First, in 1949, the Ministry of International Trade and Industry was established to increase exports and propel industrial policy. The ministry's major policies were to choose specific target industries and to restructure the targeted industries for the economies of scale. The bureaucrats' policy instruments for these administrative guidances were financial incentives, including tax exemptions and preferential funding, and coercive enforcements through administrative order or law.[2] Furthermore, the consolidation between the Liberal Democratic Party and the Japan Socialist Party in 1955 greatly reduced policy agenda conflicts between the conservative ruling group and the left-oriented opposition group. The former group's goal was to achieve high economic growth based on cooperative relationships between government assistance and private initiative, whereas the latter's goal was to nationalize banks and key industries for economic redistribution.[3]

Second, the emergence of the dominant conservative party

enabled ruling political leaders to fully support the bureaucrats' industrial promotion, which would work within the framework of the state-big business governing coalition. The ruling party's political support also depoliticized economic policy issues by nullifying other social groups' opposition and pressures. During the occupation era, the peak business organizations had been reorganized to increase big business influence on the economic policy agenda. In particular, the Federation of Economic Organizations (FEO) was established to encompass and represent, in an effective manner, big business interests and demands.[4] In contrast to the weak role of business organizations in the French industrial promotion, the big business-oriented business organizations, including national and industrial business associations, played an important role in industrial policy formulation and implementation.

Finally, under the American occupation, the Bank Law and the Securities and Exchange Law provided the basic legislative framework, which would empower the Ministry of Finance to control the private banking and securities activities. In the early 1950s, the Japanese government established such public financial institutions as the Japan Development Bank and the Export and Import Bank of Japan in order to channel state funds into industrial projects favoured by the government.

Under the 'credit-based' financial system, the securities markets did not play an important role in supplying funds for industry. Until the early 1960s, the volume of state funds had declined along with the increasing private city bank loans. These banks were also under the control of the Bank of Japan and the Ministry of Finance:

> ... private financial institutions were placed under the strict control of the Ministry of Finance. While tacitly establishing a principle that banks would neither be bankrupted nor go bankrupt, it regulated and directed financial activities so as to conform to industrial policy. A significant point in this policy of concentrating and distributing funds is that, in giving out industrial loans, private financial institutions decided on strategic industries and growth enterprises, most fundamentally along the judgment of MITI.[5]

Big business participation in industrial promotion

Originally, the business circle's position was to reopen and expand production through private self-adjustment.[6] However, the institutional capacities of the state enabled the state managers to offer financial incentives; they then brought about big business compromises that were in line with the government policy choices. The big businessmen tried to comply with the administrative guidance accompanied by financial incentives, and to resist state interventions followed by coercive enforcement. Big business firms opposed the government's direct intervention in investment decision-making. In general, big business firms accepted the government's industrial promotion policies, which would facilitate business investment in the targeted industries, under the close cooperation between the state and big business.

In the end, in 1960, the Japanese government announced its strategy for promoting high economic growth: 'the Plan to Double the National Income in Ten Years'. The contents of the plan explicitly presented the government officials' industrial strategy and policy instruments. They designated heavy and chemical industries as targeted industries for economic growth; they refrained from 'direct control measures', and favoured 'such indirect means as financial and monetary policies and appropriate inducement-measures designed to help private enterprises develop in a desirable direction'.[7]

The French case

Shortly after World War II, during the period of 1945–46, the French government, under socialist influence, pursued the policy of nationalization in some major industrial sectors. A political motive for nationalization was patriotic retaliation against big businessmen's opportunistic and unpatriotic activities during the occupation period. The economic motives were to achieve economic recovery and independence and to eliminate capitalist monopolies. In the meantime, the liberal political and technocratic leadership for economic policy emerged and gave priority to the economic objectives of modernization and reconstruction based on planning, instead of the political objectives.[8]

Institutional capacities of the state

In 1947, under Jean Monnet's initiative, the plan became an investment programme (a Plan de Modernisation et d'Equipement
[PME]) nourished by American aid. In the period of the Monnet
Plan (1945–52) and the Second Plan (1953–57), the planners made
an effort to enhance the institutional capacities of the state in
order to successfully push the plan. That is, the process of new
institutional building for planning-oriented growth was to prevent
bureaucratic conflicts and political leaders' intervention as well as
businessmen's hesitance and resistance.[9]

First of all, the planners tried to avoid ministerial jurisdictional
struggles and parliamentary supervision by changing the state institutional structure of plan-making and implementation. As a result,
the Commissariat Général du Plan (CGP) and the Planning Council were attached to the head of the government. The commissariat
absorbed the bureau for economic planning from the Ministre de
l'Economie Nationale.

Second, the state-led financial system emerged, along with the
nationalization of the Bank of France and the major deposit banks;
such semi-public lending institutions as the Crédit National and
Caisse des Dépôts et Consignations were established. In particular,
in 1955, the Fonds de Dévelopment Economique et Social (FDES)
was formed to fund planned projects. In fact, the CGP by itself
could not exercise direct enforcement power over firms. The planners were able to impose financially coercive enforcement over
business by way of the Ministry of Finance, in particular. This
ministry had controls over foreign exchange, credit allocation, and
interest rates under the financial system.[10]

Finally, as for institutional linkage between the state and business, the planners advocated state contracts with sectoral trade
associations, or occasionally with individual enterprises, instead of
with peak business organizations. Later, however, they preferred
highly concentrated industries and large firms because it was much
easier to manage small groups of big business firms in implementing planned projects.[11] Their goal was to create giant firms through
the promotion of mergers and specialization. As a result, the economic policy began to be based on the state-big business governing
coalition that resulted from an informal process among planners,
officials of the Ministry of Finance and big businessmen.

The successful state-led capitalist collective action

Until the early 1950s, businessmen had shown ambivalent, hesitant, or resistant responses to the industrial management of planning. Basically, they worried about state managers' coercive policy instruments, including the threats of nationalization, financial disadvantages for non-compliance, and economic penalties for non-fulfilment of assigned targets, while they supported the measures of state funding.[12] The government relied heavily on such financial incentives as government orders and purchasing through nationalized firms, tax exemptions, and state funds.[13] Since the Second Plan (1954–57), coercive enforcement had been minimal and financial incentives in favour of big business had been effective. Thus, financial rewards, rather than economic penalties through financial control, changed big businessmen's attitudes from hesitance or resistance to compliance and their participation in the plans.

In comparative perspective, Japan, France, and Korea had built new institutional arrangements for rapid industrial promotion, which would enhance state capacities to intervene in the targeted industries. The institutional capacities of these states enabled their state managers to initiate industrial policy-making and implementation in order to achieve high economic growth. The Korean government shifted big businessmen's reaction from resistance to, to competitive participation in, the state-led rapid industrial promotion. The Korean state managers used the policy instruments of strong coercive enforcement and highly privileged financial supports. In contrast to the Korean state-controlled industrial promotion, the Japanese and French governments changed the businessmen's unfavourable responses and facilitated big business participation in rapid industrialization mainly by means of financial rewards and partially by weak coercive enforcement.

THE INVESTMENT ADJUSTMENT DURING THE PERIOD OF HIGH ECONOMIC GROWTH: MERGERS FOR INTERNATIONAL COMPETITIVENESS

The Japanese case

During the 1960s, the Japanese government had pursued the economies of scale through investment adjustment in order to enhance international competitiveness and to prevent expected overcapacity in the heavy and chemical industrial sectors. The government had instigated and supported investment in these sectors by means of state and private funds and by tax incentives. As a result, many firms, particularly big business firms, had invested actively in the strategic industries. The MITI's government officials worried about overcompetition in the heavy and chemical industrial sectors, which would create the problem of overcapacity in weakening international comparative advantage. Thus, in order to restructure the industrial organization, the ministry strongly recommended mergers and groupings through investment designation.[14] Many small- and medium-sized firms had been merged into large firms under the guidance of administrative order. Under the MITI, the Industrial Structure Investigation Committee, the Industrial Structure Deliberation Council, and the Roundtable of Bureaucrat-Civilian Cooperation were established to take charge of investment adjustment. But, in contrast to the French case, mergers between large firms were unsuccessful, despite the MITI's attempted enforcement through law.

The similarities and differences between Korea's HCIIAs and Japan's HCIIAs

In Japan, the government had helped big businessmen to expand scales and upgrade the international competitiveness of HCIs with subsidies and selective credit allocations during the 1960s. Under the administrative guidance, many small- and medium-sized companies merged into large firms in order to improve HCIs. Some firms were supposed to belong to one group and to produce one item. Such groupings were used to limit a firm's entire production to one item, to concentrate a product line, and, eventually, to eliminate small producers.

The Japanese case had some different practices from the Korean case of the investment adjustments in the HCIs. First, the Japanese government respected the autonomy of big business in making investment decisions. It offered only objective criteria of investment licensing in the fields of HCIs. Thus, firms satisfying the criteria could invest in some fields at their own risk. Second, the guidelines of investment adjustment were announced after adequate state-led agreements were attained between state managers and big businessmen. Basically, the government lacked the

authority to force the firms involved to agree to unacceptable
solutions. The Japanese government did not announce programmes, nor did it propose laws and regulations without reaching
a consensus with the business sector that was most likely to be
influenced by government actions. Final decisions for mergers and
groupings ultimately depended on the investment decisions of the
concerned companies. On the other hand, the Korean government
took advantage of discretionary commands to enforce mergers and
groupings, regardless of big business views.

Third, the Korean adjustment was managed by the governing
coalition between the state and big business, which had dominated
policy formulation and implementation during the period of high
economic growth. Similarly, during the 1960s, the Japanese industrial adjustment had been led by the state-big business governing
coalition. Finally, the Korean case gave priority to rescuing financially depressed companies in the HCIs, in the short term, while
the Japanese case focused on achieving international competitive
superiority and on preventing expected overcapacity due to overcompetition, in the long term.

The unsuccessful state-led capitalist collective action: the failure of institutional design for mergers between large firms

The Japanese government aimed to achieve not only mergers of
small- and medium-sized firms into large firms but also those
between large firms, in order to create industrial giants in the HCI
sectors. In the early 1960s, the MITI tenaciously attempted to
establish the Special Measures Law for the Promotion of Designated Industries,[15] which would facilitate mergers between large
firms in an authoritarian manner. According to the planned law,
the government officials were supposed to designate industries in
consultation with business firms in order to reduce overcompetition by promoting mergers. They planned to provide merger-
related tax, financial, and fiscal incentives and to intervene directly
in business investment decision-making.

Even strong financial incentives for mergers could not incur big
business compliance among the large firms concerned. First of all,
the bureaucracy had a lack of consensus on the special measures.
In particular, the Ministry of Finance opposed the plan because
overloans would be given to the largest firms, and thus because
these firms would suffer from highly indebted financial structures.

Additionally, the Fair Trade Commission strongly objected to the possible existence of monopoly companies. The FEO strongly protested against coercive elements of the planned measures and state intervention in business autonomy: the business circle said that the government would probably determine designated industries in an authoritarian way. Furthermore, big business firms did not regard the financial benefits as attractive incentives for mergers, for they were not in serious financial shortage (urgency). In the end, in 1964, the bill died in the Diet.

The French case

In France, in order to effectively achieve the plans of high economic growth, industrial policy-makers formed an alliance with the largest enterprises in the growing industrial sectors during the latter half of the 1950s and in the 1960s. In order to achieve high economic growth, France, like Japan and South Korea, had pursued the policy of industrial management within the framework of a state-big business governing coalition. The planners' original goal of 'économie concertée' was social groups' broad participation in the making and implementation of the plan, but the real process of industrial promotion was based on symbiotic cooperation between state managers and big businessmen.[16]

Institutional capacities of the state

During the period of high economic growth, the institutional arrangements for industrial promotion based on planning had been changing. First of all, the state institutions of planning became politicized:

> What had begun as a relatively technical operation, managed by civil servants with some distance from the political parties in power, became increasingly politicized. Throughout the 1950s the planners had skillfully maintained their autonomy from the legislature and from the rather weak political executive of the Fourth Republic. The Modernization Commissions emerged as non-partisan institutions, capable of bridging the social divisions in French society where the politicians had failed. During this period it was unusual for the National Assembly even to review the Plan. By their very success, the planners preserved a

certain technical credibility and independence. With the advent of the Fifth Republic in 1958, however, the political context of planning changed. The Constitution conferred substantial new powers on the political executive. It replaced the legislature as the principal political threat to the planners; and a united Gaullist party under a strong President began to enjoy some continuity in office. The President himself embraced the Plan as if it were his own, and began to give it a high political profile. These developments enhanced the control that the political executive could exercise over the planners, and encouraged both the Government and the electorate to see the Plan as a programme for which the Government bore direct responsibility.[17]

In addition, during the 1960s, the growth-oriented economic policy had focused on industrial management rather than on planning itself. As a result, the institutional structure within the bureaucracy was changing. The Planning Commissions, which had been designed to enhance the coherence and coordination of the bureaucracy to formulate and implement the economic policy, played a smaller role in industrial promotion and adjustment; the Ministry of Finance became more involved in industrial management by using the policy instruments of financial and fiscal control over individual large firms.[18]

Second, the institutional linkage between the state and social groups had been characterized by direct negotiation and bargaining between the state and the large firms. These interactions bypassed trade associations that had represented the industrial firms' interests in planning during the 1950s.[19] Trade unions, peasants, and small- and medium-sized firms had little participation in planning and industrial adjustment. Furthermore, the new Pompidou government (1969–74) strengthened the state–big business governing coalition in order to enhance the large firms' international competitiveness in the name of 'industrial imperative' (L'Imperatif Industriel), even after the May labour and student strikes in 1968, which had resulted from the growth-oriented economic policy.[20]

Finally, the state-led financial system allowed state managers to finance funds to favoured industries and firms. Public banks and long-term credit institutions (para-public financial institutions) strongly influenced credit allocations. The pattern of corporate loans was changing from state financing to bank financing. French companies had relied heavily on external financing from banks and special credit institutions due to the weakness of the securities markets (stocks and bonds).[21] Under this financial system, the industrial promotion focused on the competitiveness of individual firms in the targeted sectors (particularly, heavy and chemical industrial sectors) rather than in the growth of entire sectors. The government had offered financial support for big business firms and promoted the mergers of small- and medium-sized firms into individual giants. During the 1960s, France had had the highest rate of mergers in Western Europe. More importantly, particularly during the period of 1969–74, these institutional capacities of the state enabled the state managers to facilitate the big businessmen's collective action of supermerger between large firms.

The successful capitalist collective action: Mergers between big business firms

In order to maintain high economic growth, the Pompidou government had facilitated supermergers between large firms in order to achieve the international competitiveness in the opening of the European Common Market. In contrast to the Japanese case, 'national champions' had been created as a result of the state-led mergers between large firms in many leading industrial sectors (mainly in the heavy and chemical industrial sectors: Saint Gobain-Pont à Mousson in building materials; Rhône-Poulenc in chemicals; Pechiney-Ugine-Kuhlmann in non-ferrous metals and chemicals; CGE-Alsthom, Thomson-Brandt in electrical engineering; Berliet-Saviem-Renault in automobiles; Sacilor in steel; etc.).[22]

The government provided merging large firms with direct and indirect financial incentives in three ways: state loans to facilitate mergers, and financial supports for exports and industrial investments; reduction of merged companies' income tax; and assisting state-led mergers in the nationalized sector. More importantly, the state managers had hardly used coercive enforcements because many industrial leaders were aware of the necessity of supermergers for enhancing the international competitiveness. In many cases, big businessmen complied voluntarily with the policy of national champion.[23] These mergers occurred with the large firms' complete compliance through bilateral negotiations between government officials and big businessmen. Thus, the government-initiated policy was successfully implemented by means of the policy instruments of moderate financial incentives and very weak coercive enforcement.

During the period of high economic growth, the Japanese and French governments had relied heavily on financial incentives, rather than coercive enforcement of administrative law, by respecting individual firms' autonomy in investment decisions. The French industrial adjustment depended on relatively more coercive elements within the direct bilateral interaction between the state and big business firms. On the other hand, Japan's well-organized business, which was composed of national and industrial business associations, and corporate groupings (*Keiretsu*), greatly influenced (supported or resisted) the policy formulation and implementation of the state-led industrial adjustment.

In contrast to the French and Japanese merger cases, the Korean authoritarian government attempted to take advantage of both highly coercive enforcement and privileged financial incentives, mainly based on discretionary command, by neglecting business autonomy. In Korea, state managers attempted to rescue the distorted heavy and chemical industries, even to the extent of opposing big business interests. In the Korean cases of the HCIIAs during the period of 1979–80, the decline of institutional state capacities brought about the policy failures in the mergers and groupings within the power-generating equipment and passenger car fields. Because of the government's insufficient coercive enforcement and/or financial incentives, the big businessmen's competition and resistance provoked state-big business conflicts, which had a decisive effect on the policy failure.

The state interventions both in the Japanese state-led and in the Korean state-controlled investment adjustment for mergers between large firms in the HCIs faced the failures of policy implementation without the big businessmen's voluntary or quasi-voluntary compliance (even under the state-big business governing coalition in Japan, and within state-big business conflicts or the breakdown of the state-big business governing coalition in South Korea).

THE INDUSTRIAL ADJUSTMENT IN THE STRUCTURALLY DEPRESSED INDUSTRIES

The Japanese case

The decay of institutional arrangements for high economic growth

In Japan, the ruling-triad of the Liberal Democratic Party, the bureaucracy, and big business was no longer efficient in terms of economic management, both just before and after the first oil-shock. The Japanese government's institutional capacities for formulating and implementing industrial policy had decreased.

First, decelerated economic growth with high inflation, the decline of the dominant party, the increasing politicization of policy-making, and the international liberalization of the Japanese economy made the efficient operation of the governing coalition difficult.[24] Such neglected groups as rural and urban workers and small- and medium-sized business firms began to participate actively in the policy-making process in order to represent their interests in opposition to the high-growth-oriented economic management of the 1960s.

Under the public pressure, the Liberal Democratic Party could no longer remain merely a supporter of the bureaucracy in making and implementing economic policies. It had to be a catch-all party in order to satisfy as many voter and interest group demands as possible. The state-big business governing coalition began to dissolve as a result of this economic and political situation. In the situation of high inflation, shortly after the first oil-shock, the business community was harshly criticized by the public because business firms had attempted to acquire huge profits by hoarding products and restricting their supply. In response to this anti-business public sentiment, the Liberal Democratic Party (LDP) in January 1974 strongly warned businessmen that '... if a large number of companies registered huge profits at the end of the fiscal year in March and failed to recycle those profits to consumers through price reductions, the LDP would take strong action against the business community in the form of the Special Temporary Corporate Tax . . .'.[25]

Second, since the late 1960s, the Japanese government had begun to lose financial control over large firms in the HCIs. As in the French and Korean cases, the Japanese state-led rapid heavy and chemical industrial promotion resulted in the large firms' competitive investments and failed to maintain efficient investment allocations. Thus, rapidly increasing investment led to the problem of overcapacity in the HCI sectors. The state managers' weakening investment control over big business firms was accompanied by their decreasing control over the credit ceiling and allocation.

During the period of high economic growth, the phenomena of 'overloan' and 'overborrowing' were characteristic of the Japanese state-led financial system. In the late 1960s, the commercial banks could not satisfy the increasing demands of the industrial firms. Afterwards, as in the Korean case, the financial shortage had been filled with the city banks' direct loans from the Bank of Japan. As in the French and Korean cases, the Japanese business firms, in the condition of underdeveloped capital markets, had relied heavily on external financing from banks. As a result, overborrowing by the firms was prevalent. Since the overinvestment of the late 1960s, the flow of funds resulting from increased overloan and overborrowing had aggravated the financial structure of highly indebted banks and firms.

Furthermore, during the 1970s, after the oil-shock, the efficient financial system, geared to high economic growth, was faltering under the changing domestic and international economic environment. Both internal and external pressures of financial market liberalization decreased the leverage of government control over interest rates and credit allocation. The internationalization of finance ignited domestic financial liberalization; firms depended relatively more on direct financing through stock and bond markets than before; and the diversified demand for finance services was increasing, thereby reducing the importance of bank loans.[26]

Thus, both the ineffective financial control and the economic environment forced the state managers to adopt liberal financial reforms – deregulation of interest rates, liberalization of financial markets, and liberalization of banking administration (from direct credit control to indirect monetary control).

Finally, however, bureaucratic conflicts between the MITI, which was in favour of liberalization, and the Ministry of Finance, which had the vested rights of financial control, slowed down the speed of financial liberalization and confused its policy orientation.[27] There were conflicts over financial liberalization even within the MITI and the Ministry of Finance. The Bank of Japan supported the liberal reform of the financial system in opposition to the conservative position of the Ministry of Finance. The bank's position was aimed at enhancing the bank's autonomy from the Ministry of Finance in the process of implementing the monetary policy.[28] As in the case of financial liberalization, the existing cohesiveness and coordination of the bureaucracy decreased as doubts about the pro-growth consensus and the aforementioned demands of interest groups led to conflicts over economic policy goals and means within and between the ministries.

The successful state-led capitalist collective action: The institutional design for limited state intervention

After the first oil-shock, the Japanese government changed the strategic industries from the HCIs to knowledge- and technology-intensive industries. In general, the administrative guidance and financial incentives established by the industrial policy instruments had been ineffectively worked, reduced, and limited due to the weakening institutional capacities of the state. As a whole, the state managers were moving towards market-oriented policies for economic stabilization and liberalization.

In this policy environment, the government became involved in rescuing and revitalizing the so-called 'structurally depressed' industries – electric steel, non-ferrous metals, aluminium, chemical fertilizers, machinery, shipbuilding, and synthetic fibres.[29] In the late 1970s, the business community faced the serious problems of financial depression and overcapacity, mainly in the HCIs. The business firms failed to achieve self-adjustment to solve the problem of overcapacity that resulted from overcompetition in the declining industries. The capitalist collective action for self-industrial adjustment was aborted because of conflicts among the firms concerned; financially weak firms were prepared to accept collective adjustments of investment (facilities), production, and price, but financially stronger firms resisted and opposed the adjustments, and tried to swallow up the entire market in accordance with the principle of survival of the fittest.

The FEO had recognized the problem of the declining industries earlier than the government and had intervened in the industrial adjustment. The peak business organization strongly demanded that the government undertake adequate measures for the depressed industries. Other national organizations joined in the issue of industrial adjustment. The national business organizations met the Liberal Democratic Party's leaders and represented mainly big business interests pertaining to the issue of the industrial adjustment.

Finally, the MITI took over the issue of industrial policy and attempted to take specific measures, including the designation of structurally depressed industries, mergers to reduce facilities, anti-recession cartels, and an 'industrial-adjustment-finance system', by means of high financial incentives and high coercive enforcement. The Ministry of Finance and the Fair Trade Commission opposed the measures of financial intervention and cartel formation, respectively. The former ministry did not want high business dependence on external funds, in consideration of monetary control. The latter ministry tried to reduce possible mono-oligopoly outcomes by objecting to the MITI's right to order cartel formation. More importantly, the business circle strongly opposed the coercive way in which the policy measures were imposed.

As a matter of fact, the MITI reluctantly intervened to restructure the depressed industries in response to business demands. The ministry fully recognized that it would have difficulty in establishing an institutional design to facilitate state intervention within the framework of the market-oriented economic policy-making and implementation. The MITI's bureaucrats did not intend to impose the original measures at the risk of resistance and opposition, unlike the case of the Special Measures Law for the Promotion of Designated Industries in the early 1960s.

In the face of the other ministries' and businessmen's opposition, the MITI eliminated such coercive elements as designation, order, and merger, and reduced financial incentives. The revised Special Measures Law for the Stabilization of Designated Depressed Industries, which was enacted in 1978, was supposed to be applied to the industrial adjustment in full compliance with the requests of the business firms concerned. Under the law, industries would be eligible for government assistance when 'more than two-thirds of the firms signed a petition seeking designation under the law'; the law called for the 'collective implementation of the capacity reduction plan by all companies in the designated industry and establishment of a joint credit fund to purchase scrapped facilities and guarantee the loans that the relevant firms borrowed from banks for the disposal of facilities'.[30] As a result, successful capitalist collective actions for industrial adjustment in response to limited state intervention were guided and precipitated by the government's weak financial support and very low coercive enforcement. Additionally, industrial trade associations and corporate groupings in the designated industries played an important role in establishing a risk-sharing system in close cooperation with the government assistance policy.

The French case

The decay of institutional arrangements for high economic growth

The industrial policy itself of state intervention in the industries (which had been a resource for rapid industrial promotion) along with the decline of planning during the 1960s began to undermine the existing institutions for economic growth in the late 1960s.[31] In particular, the state institutions for economic policy formulation and implementation, the direct bilateral institutions between the state and big business, and the state-led financial system in favour of industrial giants and the strategic industries had been crumbling and ineffective since the oil-shock of 1973.

First, bureaucratic power conflicts between departments were deepening. For instance, the Ministry of Finance, which sought to correct inflationary pressures, was confronted with the planners to sustain economic growth. These conflicts had rapidly reduced the efficient coherence and coordination within the bureaucracy.

Second, the strategy of national champion firms did not necessarily guarantee the international competitiveness.[32] The economies of scale led to overcapacity and to the largest firms' heavy dependence on state-controlled financial sources. The problems of overcapacity resulted from the government's decreasing investment control over large enterprises. That is, the state managers could not prevent a determined firm from getting into an investment project that would be contrary to or beyond the scale of the original programme within the sectoral plan. Moreover, the reduced control over investment allocation led to the state's decreasing financial control over firms. In other words, the government could not avoid financing more funds to further investment projects because it had depended heavily on financial incentives in order to control the business firms. As a result, the companies became highly indebted.

The largest corporations seemed to gain the upper hand over state managers in the industrial policy-making and implementation.

The state autonomy and capacities in regard to big business had decreased while big business influence over the state had increased. In the end, the governing coalition between the state and big business reached the limits of efficiency in economic management, along with the institutional decay of bilateral relationships between the state and big business firms, and of state-led financial intervention.

The industrial adjustment in institutional disarray: the dilemma between state intervention and liberal reform

Prime Minister Barre (1976–81), of the Giscard d'Estaing government (1974–81), had pursued the market-oriented goals of economic policy: increasing free market competition, private-initiated industrial adjustment to enhance international competitiveness, reducing inflation through restrictive macroeconomic control, and stabilizing the franc.[33] Barre and Giscard fully recognized the limits of state capacities to stir up the state-led capitalist collective action of industrial promotion and adjustment, when private firms did not take the initiative; they also perceived the limits of the state-big business governing coalition that had effectively managed industrial adjustment policies.

Thus, the Giscard government tried to keep its distance from big business by encompassing more social groups. The government began to recognize the significance of small- and medium-sized firms and tried to reduce the large firms' financial dependence on state banks and to bolster the equity market. Additionally, during the 1970s, the government had received increasing political pressures from social groups that had been excluded. During the period of high economic growth, the state-led industrial strategy had overlooked and isolated such groups as shopkeepers, peasants, urban workers, and small and medium businessmen. These groups began to organize their interests and complaints. They turned to the state to protect and demand their interests.[34]

In reality, however, the liberal state managers faced the dilemma of choosing between state intervention and liberal reform. They had both liberal and interventionist strategies of industrial policy. Basically, they intended not to give up the former industrial policy tools for the purpose of economic liberalization but to streamline the role of the state and the manner of state intervention in order to overcome the side effects of state-led industrialization.

Thus, the liberal reform was a means for economic recovery rather than a goal of economic policy.

The government was changing the French financial system with a view towards recovering overall financial control over industries and firms.[35] This orientation was to strengthen direct monetary control over financial institutions and to keep indirect financial control over industries and individual firms. By failing to curb excessive investment projects, the government had been trapped by overdrawn loans from business firms during the period of high economic growth. The state managers tried to improve the financial structure of many financially depressed banks and highly indebted companies. For this purpose, the state managers created a dualistic financial system, composed both of more interventionist instruments and liberal reform measures. The government's new financial strategy was to reinforce control over banks and credit institutions by means of the '*encadrement de crédit*' (ceiling of credit amount)[36] and to increase the firms' direct external financing through the stock and bond markets by liberalizing the capital markets.

Basically, the government tried to limit state intervention to the financially depressed industries. In the late 1970s, the government intervened in the declining sectors in order to rescue hundreds of financially depressed small- and medium-sized firms, and to bail out the largest firms in the steel and textile industries.[37] The government offered massive financial supports, but hardly took measures for investment adjustment (capacity reduction), including mergers and investment designation. As a matter of fact, the weakening financial capacities for industrial adjustment could not allow the state to exercise financial control over individual firms in order to create businessmen's compliance with the investment adjustment.

In comparative perspective, France, Japan, and Korea faced the same kinds of problems during the economic recessions or crises along with a substantial decline in the institutional capacities of the state. In particular, the overgrown big business influence and the state's high dependence on big business diminished the state's abilities not only for economic management but also for political governability. The sources of potential strength in a growth-oriented industrial policy changed into causes of economic decline. The malfunctions of industrial policy pushed policy-makers to alter the policy goals of economic growth and the industrial strategy of state-led or state-controlled adjustment. They began to make greater use of market instruments to achieve economic stabilization.

During the period of institutional disorder, the Japanese government succeeded in installing the institutional design for limited state intervention, excluding mergers and excessive financial aids, in close cooperation with organized business. Thus, the Japanese state managers guided the capitalist collective action of restructuring the depressed industries by means of the government's weak financial incentives and business organizations' cooperation. The French government, in contrast, limited state intervention to providing the financially ill-managed firms with financial support. As a result, the French state managers could not stir up the capitalist collective action of investment adjustment. On the other hand, the Korean government designed institutional arrangements in order to intervene strongly in the declining industries, which led to the politicized institutions based on the collusive state-big business ruling coalition. Thus, the Korean state managers created the state-controlled capitalist collective action, including acquisitions and/or mergers, to accomplish investment adjustment by means of highly coercive enforcement and highly privileged financial benefits.

NOTES

1 The behaviour of economic agents to maximize their interests through market competition often yields desirable results to the whole economy. We call these businessmen's behaviours profit-seeking activities. The rent-seeking activities of economic agents create great costs to the whole society by gaining privileged benefits (protectionist tariffs, exclusive rights of import, etc.) through political means (Yutaka Kosai and Yutaka Harada, 'Economic Development in Japan: A Reconsideration', in Robert A. Scalapino, Seizaburo Sato, and Jusuf Wanandi, eds, *Asian Economic Development – Present and Future* [Berkeley: Institute of East Asian Studies, University of California, 1985], p. 45; and see also Anne O. Krueger, 'The Political Economy of the Rent-Seeking Society', *American Economic Review* 64 [June 1974]).

2 See Tadahiko Kawai, 'An Analysis of Business-Government Relations in Japan: The Case of the Federation of Economic Organizations', Ph.D. Diss. (University of California, Berkeley, 1986), pp. 117–19; and Chalmers Johnson, *MITI and the Japanese Miracle: The Growth of Industrial Policy* (Stanford: Stanford University Press, 1982), Chap. 6.

3 T. J. Pempel, *Policy and Politics in Japan: Creative Conservatism* (Philadelphia: Temple University Press, 1982), pp. 52–53.

4 For the organizational structure of business in Japan, see Gerald L.

Curtis, 'Big Business and Political Influence', in Ezra F. Vogel, ed., *Modern Japanese Organization and Decision-Making* (Berkeley: University of California Press, 1975); Chitoshi Yanaga, *Big Business in Japanese Politics* (New Haven and London: Yale University Press, 1968), Chaps. 2, 3; and Leonard H. Lynn, *Organizing Business: Trade Associations in America and Japan* (Washington: American Enterprise Institute for Public Policy Research, 1988), Chaps. 1, 5.

5 Hiroya Ueno, 'The Conception and Evaluation of Japanese Industrial Policy', in Kasuo Sato, ed., *Industry and Business in Japan* (White Plains, N.Y.: Sharpe, 1980): quotation in John Zysman, op. cit. [Chapter 3, note 16] (1983), p. 244. For the Japanese financial system during the period of high economic growth (the second half of the 1950s and 1960s), see John Zysman, ibid., pp. 234–51; Yoshio Suzuki, ed., *The Japanese Financial System* (Oxford: Clarendon Press, 1989), pp. 21–24; and Koichi Hamada and Akiyoshi Horiuchi, 'The Political Economy of the Financial Market', in Kozo Yamamura and Yasukichi Yasuba, eds., The Political Economy of Japan Vol.1: The Domestic Transformation (Stanford: Stanford University Press, 1987), pp. 228–45.

6 See Tadahiko Kawai, op. cit., pp. 120–22.

7 For the text of the plan, see T. J. Pempel, *op. cit.* (1982), pp. 71–78.

8 See Richard F. Kuisel, *Capitalism and the State in Modern France: Renovation and Economic Management in the Twentieth Century* (Cambridge: Cambridge University Press, 1981), Chap. 7.

9 See ibid., Chap. 8 and Stephen S. Cohen, *Modern Capitalist Planning: The French Model* (Berkeley: University of California Press, 1977), Part II. For state institutions for planning, see Pierre Bauchet (Daphne Woodward trans.), *Economic Planning: The French Experience* (New York: Praeger Publishers, 1964), Chap. I, and Pierre Bauchet, *Le Plan Dans L'Economie Française* (Paris: Economica, 1986), Part I.

10 For the French financial system, see John Zysman, *op. cit.* [Chapter 3, note 16] (1983), Chap. 3.

11 Richard F. Kuisel, *op. cit.*, pp. 246, 256; and Stephen S. Cohen, op. cit., pp. 68–76.

12 Richard F. Kuisel, ibid., pp. 236–37, 262; and Stephen S. Cohen, ibid., p. 4.

13 See Pierre Bauchet, *op. cit.* (1964), Chap. III, and Vera Lutz, *Central Planning for the Market Economy: An Analysis of the French Theory and Experience* (London and Harlow: Longmans, 1969), Chap. IV.

14 For the Japanese case of heavy and chemical industrial investment adjustment during the high growth period of the 1960s, see the Tokyo University Press Council, ed., *A Study on Japan's Industrial Policy* (Seoul: Korea Institute for Economics & Technology, 1986), Chap. III (in Korean); Korea Institute for Economics & Technology (KIET), *Industrial Policies and Practices of the United States and Japan* (Seoul: KIET, 1985) (in Korean); and the Korea Development Bank (KDB), *Japan's Industrial Adjustment Policy* (Seoul: KDB, 1981) (in Korean).

15 See Tadahiko Kawai, *op. cit.*, pp. 150–224; Chalmers Johnson, op. cit., Chap. 7; and Eugene J. Kaplan, *Japan: The Government-Business*

Relationship (U.S. Department of Commerce, 1972), Chap. VI and pp. 103–36.

16 See Subcommittee on Economic Growth and Stabilization of the Joint Economic Committee in the Congress of the United States (95th Congress 1st Session), *Recent Developments in French Planning: Some Lessons for the U.S.* (Washington: U.S. Government Printing Office, 1977), pp. 5–9.

17 Peter Hall, op. cit. [Chapter 1, note 13] (1986), p. 150.

18 Ibid., p. 174.

19 See ibid., pp. 168–70.

20 For causes and effects of the May strikes, see Stephen S. Cohen, *op. cit.* (1977), Postscript 1, and for Pompidou's policy of industrial imperative, see Lionel Stoleru, *L'Imperatif Industriel* (Paris: Seuil, 1969). After the radical and massive strikes, the government attempted to set up corporatist arrangements for incomes policy among the state, capital, and labour. However, the labour unions rejected participation in the incomes policy because 'the substantive contents of the plan's incomes policy was a squeeze on wages in favor of corporate profits' (Subcommittee on Economic Growth and Stabilization of the Joint Economic Committee in the Congress of the U.S., *op. cit.*, p. 14).

21 For the financial mechanism during the period of high economic growth, see John Zysman, 'The Interventionist Temptation: Financial Structure and Political Purpose', in William G. Andrews and Stanley Hoffmann, *The Fifth Republic at Twenty* (Albany: State University of New York Press, 1981), pp. 254–60.

22 For the creation of national champion firms, see Stephen S. Cohen, James Galbraith, and John Zysman, 'Rehabbing the Labyrinth: The Financial System and Industrial Policy in France', in Stephen S. Cohen and Peter A. Gourevitch, *France in the Troubled World Economy* (London and Boston: Butterworth Scientific, 1982), pp. 67–72; and Christian Stoffaës, 'Industrial Policy and the State: From Industry to Enterprise', in Paul Codt, ed., *Policy-Making in France: From de Gaulle to Mitterrand* (London and New York: Pinter Publishers, 1989), pp. 110–11.

23 See Suzanne Berger, 'Lame Ducks and National Champions: Industrial Policy in the Fifth Republic', in William G. Andrews and Stanley Hoffmann, *op. cit.*, pp. 295–96. For instance, exceptionally, the Kuhlmann-Ugine merger was one of the few cases in which coercive enforcement was directly or indirectly involved: 'The directors of the two companies feared that the government would force them into alliances with public enterprises for this or that of their activities. They would then have lost control of them . . .' (Maurice Ray, 'Un Mariage pas du tout Parisien', *L'Express* [30 May 1966], p. 44: quotation in John H. McArthur and Bruce R. Scott, *Industrial Planning in France* [Boston: Harvard University Press, 1969], p. 382).

24 See George C. Eads and Kozo Yamamura, 'The Future of Industrial Policy', pp. 448–68 in Kozo Yamamura and Yasukichi Yasuba, eds., *The Political Economy of Japan: Volume 1. The Domestic Transformation* (Stanford: Stanford University Press, 1987); Doug McEachern,

'Combining Democracy with Growth', and Gavan McCormack, 'Beyond Economism: Japan in a State of Transition', in Gavan McCormack and Yoshio Sugimoto, eds., *Democracy in Contemporary Japan* (Armonk: M. E. Sharpe Inc., 1986); Ellis S. Krauss, 'Politics and the Policymaking Process', in Takeshi Ishida and Ellis S. Krauss, eds., *Democracy in Japan* (Pittsburgh: University of Pittsburgh Press, 1989); and Takashi Inoguchi, 'The Political Economy of Conservative Resurgence under Recession: Public Policies and Political Support in Japan, 1977–83', Ellis S. Krauss and Jon Pierre, 'The Decline of Dominant Parties: Parliamentary Politics in Sweden and Japan in the 1970s', and Michio Muramatsu and Ellis S. Krauss, 'The Dominant Party and Social Coalitions in Japan', all in T. J. Pempel, ed., *Uncommon Democracies: The One-Party Dominant Regimes* (Ithaca: Cornell University Press, 1990). See also Leon Hollerman, *Japan, Disincorporated: The Economic Liberalization Process* (Stanford: Hoover Institution Press, Stanford University, 1988): Hollerman focused on bureaucratic infighting, interministerial rivalry, and conflict between government and business.

25 Tadahiko Kawai, *op. cit.*, pp. 323–24.

26 For the process of financial liberalization, see Koichi Hamada and Aklyoshi Horiuchi, *op. cit.*, pp. 246–56; Leon Hollerman, *op. cit.*, Chaps. 1, 3; Thomas F. Cargill and Shoichi Royama, *The Transition of Finance in Japan and the United States: A Comparative Perspective* (Stanford: Hoover Institution, Stanford University, 1988); Edward J. Lincoln, *Japan: Facing Economic Maturity* (Washington: The Brookings Institution, 1988), Chap. 4; and Yoshio Suzuki, ed., *op. cit.*, pp. 25–57.

27 For the politics of financial liberalization, see James Horne, 'Politics and the Japanese Financial System', in J. A. A. Stockwin, *et al.*, *Dynamic and Immobilist Politics in Japan* (Honolulu: University of Hawaii Press, 1988); Louis W. Pauly, *Opening Financial Markets: Banking Politics on the Pacific Rim* (Ithaca: Cornell University Press, 1988), Chaps. 2, 4; and Frances McCall Rosenbluth, *Financial Politics in Contemporary Japan* (Ithaca: Cornell University Press, 1989).

28 See Leon Hollerman, *op. cit.*, pp. 52–53.

29 For the policy-making process of the Special Measures for the Stabilization of Designated Depressed Industries, see Tadahiko Kawai, *op. cit.*, pp. 416–61.

30 Masu Uekusa, 'Industrial Organization: The 1970s to the Present', in Kozo Yamamura and Yasukichi Yasuba, eds, *op. cit.*, [Chapter 1, note 1] p. 492. For the process of industrial adjustment in the designated industries, see ibid., pp. 494–99; and the Tokyo University Press Council, ed., *op. cit.*, pp. 101–4.

31 See Peter Hall, *op. cit.* [Chapter 1, note 13] (1986), Chap. 7. For analyses of the growing inefficiency of French industrial policy, see also Helen V. Milner, *Resisting Protectionism: Global Industries and the Politics of International Trade* (Princeton: Princeton University Press, 1988), Chap. 8; and Stephen S. Cohen, 'Informed Bewilderment:

French Economic Strategy and the Crisis', in Stephen S. Cohen and Peter Gourvitch, eds., *op. cit.*

32 See Charles-Albert Michalet, 'France', in Raymond Vernon, ed., *Big Business and the State: Changing Relations in Western Europe* (Cambridge, MA: Harvard University Press, 1974). In the early 1970s, the movement of national champions to international sectors was not successful due to the state managers' inefficient intervention and big businessmen's inactive entrepreneurship: 'As a general rule, the state seemed to intervene only when firms in the private sector slipped into a situation of nearly insurmountable difficulties.... the Treasury,... saw the development of French investments abroad first of all as a drain on the reserves of the central bank.... The approach of French businessmen was still essentially commercial. When plants were built abroad, they constituted a defensive move to preserve part of a threatened market that had originally been acquired by exporting. The step was rarely taken in order to exploit the advantages offered by the conditions of production outside the national frontiers' (ibid., pp. 113, 122).

33 See W. Allen Spivey, *Economic Policies in France 1976–1981: The Barre Program in a West European Perspective* (Ann Arbor: Division of Research Graduate School of Business Administration, University of Michigan, 1982), Michigan International Business Studies No. 18; Volkmar Lauber, *The Politics of Economic Policy: France 1974–82* (New York: Praeger, 1983), Part I; and Volkmar Lauber, *The Political Economy of France: From Pompidou to Mitterand* (New York: Praeger, 1983), Part II.

34 See Suzanne Berger, *op. cit.* (1981), pp. 300–2; and Peter Hall, *op. cit.*, Chapter 1, note 13 pp. 174–75.

35 For the changing financial system, see John Zysman, *op. cit.* (1981), pp. 260–64; Philip G. Cerney, 'From Dirigism to Deregulation? The Case of Financial Markets', in Paul Codat, ed., *Policy-Making in France: From de Gaulle to Mitterand* (London and New York: Pinter Publishers, 1989); and Michael Loriaux, 'States and Markets: French Financial Interventionism in the Seventies', *Comparative Politics* (January 1988).

36 'The encadrement works by stipulating a target rate of increase in net assets for each financial institution. The penalty for exceeding the encadrement target is the imposition of a reserve requirement which rises geometrically with the extent of the transgression, and which is prohibitive at very slight levels of excess lending. There is also an implicit penalty for falling short of the encadrement, since any shortfall is built into a bank's base for the calculation of future credit ceilings, and therefore produces a permanent and cumulative loss of market share' (Stephen S. Cohen, James Galbraith, and John Zysman, *op. cit.*, pp. 58–59).

37 See Christian Stoffaës, *op. cit.*, pp. 112–14; Suzanne Berger, *op. cit.* (1981), pp. 302–6; and the KIET, *France's Industrial Policy and Prospects: Focus on Industrial Adjustment Policies during the 1970s and 1980s* (Seoul: 1985) (in Korean).

Chapter 3

The limits of state-led heavy and chemical industrialization

This chapter will first analyse how the government was able to stir up big business participation in the heavy and chemical industrial promotion, and, second, why and how efficient institutions for heavy and chemical industrialization led to the problem of over-capacity in the HCIs in the process of institutional decay.

THE STATE-LED HEAVY AND CHEMICAL INDUSTRIAL PROMOTION: INSTITUTIONAL CAPACITIES OF THE STATE

Authoritarian state institutions, state-big business governing coalition, and the state-controlled financial system had enhanced state managers' capacities in making and implementing the heavy and chemical industrial strategy. The state managers' bargaining power over big business firms relied on instruments of coercive enforcement and inducement, which led to business groups' collective action of heavy and chemical industrial investment.

The State institutions for heavy and chemical industrial promotion

During the period of the *Yushin* (Revitalizing) system (Park's authoritarian regime, 1973–79), President Park had maintained repressive state institutions in the name of high economic growth and the nation's security against North Korea's potential threat. A state of martial law was promulgated on 17 October 1972, to prepare for President Park's palace coup. The martial law's decrees suspended the existing constitution, dissolved the National Assembly, withdrew the freedoms of speech and assembly, and banned activities of political parties. On 23 December 1972, Park proclaimed the Yushin Constitution, which enabled him to become president with unlimited consecutive terms. The new constitution also greatly enhanced Park's authority and led to executive dominance over the legislative and the judiciary. The president had the rights to dissolve the National Assembly and to exercise emergency powers in all affairs.[1]

The emergence of the bureaucratic authoritarian regime enabled state managers to politically demobilize and economically mobilize social groups. In cases of economic mobilization, the government offered financial inducements to the big business sector, but imposed wage constraints on the labour sector. Shortly after the proclamation of the Yushin Constitution, President Park announced the 'Heavy and Chemical Industrialization Declaration' of 1973, reasoning that the export-oriented heavy and chemical industrialization would improve national security and economic development to realize the Yushin reforms.[2]

The Yushin reforms changed not only political institutions but those of economic policy formation and implementation. In general, the traditional bureaucratic structure of economic policy had been established since Park's military government of 1961.[3] The Economic Planning Board (EPB) is responsible for short-term management policy as well as for long-term planning management policy. The organization has played a role in granting coherence and coordination to the bureaucracy.

However, during 1973–79, industrial policies for the HCIs had not been formulated and implemented through the aforementioned normal channels of economic policy. A dualistic institutional structure of policy-making and implementation had operated during the period of heavy and chemical industrial promotion.[4] In the decision-making process, one of the most decisive motives of Park's heavy and chemical industrial promotion was derived from the need to strengthen national security against North Korea's increasing threat.[5] Park's strong commitment to the HCIs was based on the political logic that military-industrial complexes should be constructed to promote military capacities for self-defence and that, for this purpose, the heavy and chemical industrial development was necessary for building military defence industries.[6] Park organized the Second Economic Secretariat, headed by Won-Chul Oh, within the Presidential Secretariat under his direct leadership. The organization would plan and implement policies for both the defence and the heavy and chemical industries during the 1970s. Even though Park and Oh emphasized the necessity of heavy and chemical industrialization in light of both self-defence and continuous export-oriented economic growth, the political logic superseded the economic logic in the decision-making process for heavy and chemical industrial promotion.

The political rationale greatly affected the ways in which the government would achieve heavy and chemical industrialization. Originally, in the Third Five-Year Economic Development Plan (1972–76), the EPB planned to achieve an advanced and balanced industrial structure with gradual heavy and chemical industrial promotion for import substitution. Only such labour-intensive heavy industries as electronics and shipbuilding were considered in due time as export-oriented industries. Conversely, Park and Oh ambitiously chose a rapid, export-oriented heavy and chemical industrialization.[7]

After the policy choice of heavy and chemical industrial promotion, state institutions for economic decision-making and policy implementation changed from the unified structure under the EPB's leadership to a dualistic structure that would be led by both the First Economic Secretary of the Presidential Second Economic Secretariat and the EPB. The EPB continued to centralize and coordinate short-term management policies except for heavy and chemical industrial policy, as well as the Five-Year Plans' formulation and implementation.

On the other hand, the Planning Office of the Heavy and Chemical Industry Promotion Committee (HCIPC), headed by Presidential First Economic Secretary Won-Chul Oh, took the initiative in maintaining coherence and cooperation among the economic ministries, including the EPB, for effective heavy and chemical industrial policy. As the Planning Office's superior organization, the HCIPC was responsible for all plans of heavy and chemical industrial promotion. The committee was chaired by the Prime Minister and composed of the Presidential First Economic Secretary and the economic ministers. It had eighteen conferences during 1973–74 and later became a formal institution. In 1974, the Heavy and Chemical Industry Promotion Assistant Minister Level Practical Meeting (HCIPAMLPM) was established and continued to hold conferences in place of the HCIPC. The subordinate meeting was chaired by the Head of the Planning Office of the HCIPC. The Planning Office was substantially

Table 2 The distribution of administrative tasks

1. Basic plans:
The EPB: Economic prospects for the 1980s' economy
The MCI: Investment plans for policy sectors
The MC: Construction plans for industrial complexes

2. Plans for support:
The MST, the ME, and the MHSA: plans for manpower development
The EPB and the MST: plans for technology and research development
The EPB and the MF: plans for financial mobilization

3. Survey and research for support:
The planning office of the HCIPC: current situations of and prospects for world resources, prospects for the 1980s' world economy, and processes and types of industrialization in advanced countries

EPB: Economic Planning Board
MC: Ministry of Construction
MCI: Ministry of Commerce and Industry
ME: Ministry of Education
MHSA: Ministry of Health and Social Affairs
MF: Ministry of Finance
MST: Ministry of Science and Technology
HCIPC: Heavy and Chemical Industrial Promotion Committee

Source: The Changwon Machinery Industry Corporation, *The Five-Year History of the Changwon Complex* (1979), p. 54 (in Korean)

responsible for practical affairs that were involved in the heavy and chemical industrial promotion.[8]

The leading organization was composed of veteran chiefs of sections and directors-general of bureaus from the EPB, the MCI (the Ministry of Commerce and Industry), the MF (the Ministry of Finance), the Ministry of Construction, and the Ministry of Science and Technology. By 1973, the Planning Office had made a detailed plan for heavy and chemical industrial promotion.[9] Afterwards, its major functions were to coordinate and control the economic ministries' measures for policy sectors. The general strategy of heavy and chemical industrial management was to distribute specific tasks for policy sectors to the bureaucratic organizations, under the jurisdiction of the Planning Office (see Table 2). Then, the Planning Office (formally, the HCIPC) was to synthesize the practical ministries' policy planning and implementation.

In 1973, the organizations of the economic ministries, including the EPB, the MCI, and the MF, had changed into an institutional structure, to implement effective heavy and chemical industrial

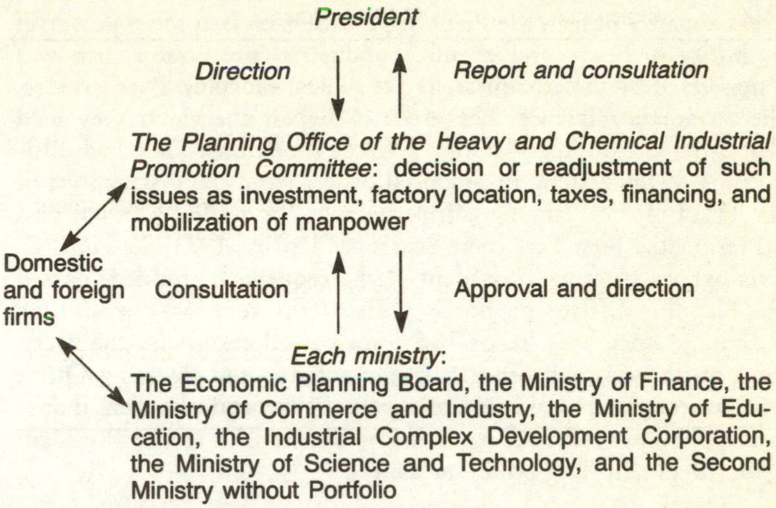

President

Direction   ↓ ↑   Report and consultation

The Planning Office of the Heavy and Chemical Industrial Promotion Committee: decision or readjustment of such issues as investment, factory location, taxes, financing, and mobilization of manpower

Domestic and foreign firms   Consultation   ↑ ↓   Approval and direction

Each ministry:
The Economic Planning Board, the Ministry of Finance, the Ministry of Commerce and Industry, the Ministry of Education, the Industrial Complex Development Corporation, the Ministry of Science and Technology, and the Second Ministry without Portfolio

Figure 5 The administrative system of heavy and chemical industrial management

Source: The Hyundai Sahoe Research Institute, The Korean Social Change and a Study on the Role of the State, Research Report '85–12 (1985), p. 60 (in Korean).

promotion by reshuffling existing organizations and establishing new subordinate organizations. In particular, the MCI's organization underwent a drastic change: it created new bureaus of Industrial Planning, Heavy Industries, and Machinery Industry, which were under the authority of the Assistant Minister of Heavy Industries.[10]

As shown above, Park's authoritarian government centralized the administrative system of heavy and chemical industrial policymaking and implementation in order to enhance institutional efficiency for prompt and ambitious heavy and chemical industrial promotion (see Figure 5). Later, bureaucrats who were concerned with the Planning Office found the successful heavy and chemical industrial construction in capacities of the state institutions. They argued that the heavy and chemical industrial promotion would have been delayed if the EPB or the MCI, instead of the Planning Office, had taken charge of the central planning and coordination; they also asserted that President Park's strong commitment to heavy and chemical industrialization minimized bureaucratic conflicts within the Planning Office.[11]

As a matter of fact, the Planning Office exercised more powerful authority in heavy and chemical industrial promotion than was empowered by the administrative organization rules. Furthermore, the economic ministries hesitated to suggest the views they held that differed from the Planning Office's directions. They had difficulty in distinguishing Presidential orders from the instructions of the Head of the Planning Office because Won-Chul Oh was also a Presidential First Economic Secretary. During 1973, the HCIPC, over whose meetings President Park frequently presided, passed the Planning Office's proposals without any revisions because the Planning Office had already had prior consultation with the President on those issues. Since 1974, as a result, the Planning Office had concentrated on investigating the heavy and chemical industrial policy process and reporting policy results to the President rather than adjusting policy measures.[12]

The institutional linkage of state-big business relationships

During the 1970s, Park's authoritarian regime had controlled social groups' interest representation with both inducements and constraints, even though the business sector enjoyed high favours and the labour sector suffered from high levels of coercion. In general, the government mobilized support from each group and, at the same time, prevented realization of its unacceptable demands by means of a corporatist structure of centralized and concentrated organizations. In the labour sector, the Federation of Korean Trade Unions (FKTU), the sole legalized national organization, was composed of seventeen constituent industrial labour federations. In the business sector, the Korean Chamber of Commerce and Industry (KCCI) encompassed all merchants and companies; the Federation of Korean Industries (FKI) represented big business interests; the Korean Foreign Traders' Association (KFTA) comprised export companies; the Korean Federation of Small-Medium Business (KFSMB) represented small and medium companies' interests; and the Korean Employers' Association (KEA) was composed of big companies for the purpose of labor-management cooperation.

Interestingly, however, the government had also used extra-mechanism to manage the labour and the big business sectors. In the labour sector, the Labour-Management Council and the Factory Saemaul (New Community) Movement as an enterprise ideology were to 'encapsulate each labor union in each enterprise unit' and 'promote conflict-free interest accommodation.'[13] More apparently, in the big business sector, the dualistic institutional structure of corporatist and non-corporatist management had been consolidated during the period of heavy and chemical industrial promotion. As a whole, the FKI supported economic policy proposals of state managers in a reactive way. It also recommended big business ideas to the government with regard to policy issues. The FKI's support for government policies resulted basically from the government's economic strategies that had promoted big business confidence in an excessive manner and had maintained small and medium business confidence at a minimum level, sacrificing labour interests and welfare to economic growth.[14]

On the other hand, for the most part, Park's government skilfully took advantage of direct interactions. These channels bypassed the big business organization and industrial associations between big businessmen and state managers in order to mobilize and control big business firms, especially during the period of heavy and chemical industrialization. The government provided business groups (*Jaebols*) with such privileges as investment licensing and financial incentives of policy loans with low interest rates through direct state-big business relationships. In general, meanwhile, in cases of big business non-compliance with government policies, the government could also threaten and impose such economic penalties as suspending loans to lead to bankruptcy and rejecting investment licensing at the enterprise level. Furthermore, the government focused on the largest business groups, even within big business, in order to easily manage the state-big business governing coalition. Therefore, most influential big businessmen frequently met the top executives, including the President and ministers, either as a small group or on an individual basis through regular or irregular channels – the monthly export promotion meeting, extraordinary conferences to adjust heavy and chemical industrial projects and big business competition, and informal meetings.

As direct means of business influence, they used not only the formal and informal meetings but also intermarriages between big businessmen and state managers, employment of ex-government officials, and political contributions to the ruling party. According to a survey research concerning channels of business influence, they preferred direct over indirect contacts through associations. Even among indirect channels, they used associations in industrial sectors rather than the peak national business associations.[15] In general, big businessmen represented their collective interests throughout the FKI with respect to macroeconomic policy decisions that were mainly made by state managers. On the other hand, most of the direct interactions dealt with financial and industrial issues in the process of policy implementation. Large entrepreneurs tried to maximize their collective or individual interests by bargaining with government officials, which had been limited by the government's inducements and constraints on big business.

The state-controlled financial system[16]

During the 1970s, the government-controlled financial system (which was mainly composed of commercial banks as well as specialized banks under government ownership and management control) had been reinforced to promote the state-led heavy and chemical industrialization.[17] The credit-based financial system was characterized by state interventions in credit allocation and government-manipulated low real interest rates. The financial policy instruments the government had used most frequently and widely were preferential bank loans and differential access to domestic and foreign credit in favour of large firms.

Under this financial system, the government had greatly enhanced the firms' business confidence in heavy and chemical industrial investment by intervening in their investment decision-making. First, the government could reduce the cost of investment and increase the expected rate of return in the HCIs by lowering interest rates and by controlling credit allocation. Between 1971 and 1982, the government adjusted official interest rates, downward in most cases (see Table 3).[18] Therefore, real deposit and loan rates turned negative because of higher inflation rates. Policy loans of lower interest rates concentrated on the HCIs and big business firms. Second, the government could reduce the perceived risk of investment by its guarantee of sufficient bank loans to the HCIs regardless of firms' business performance; thus,

> if a firm followed government policy by investing in projects which had government support, its bankruptcy risk was reduced, perhaps even eliminated.... In other words, the government, by controlling the financial sector, became a risk partner of

Table 3 Interest rates on various loans

Year	Club market[a]	Corp-orate bond	General bank loans	Export bank loans	MIPF[b]	NIF[c]	Inflation
1971	48.41	–	22.0	6.0	–	–	13.92
1972	38.97	–	19.0	6.0	–	–	16.11
1973	33.30	–	15.5	7.0	10.0	–	13.40
1974	40.56	–	15.5	9.0	12.0	12.0	29.54
1975	41.31	20.10	15.5	9.0	12.0	12.0	25.73
1976	40.47	20.40	17.0	8.0	13.0	14.0	20.73
1977	38.07	20.10	15.0	8.0	13.0	14.0	15.67
1978	41.22	21.10	18.5	9.0	15.0	16.0	21.39
1979	42.39	26.70	18.5	9.0	15.0	16.0	21.20
1980	44.94	30.10	24.5	15.0	20.0	22.0	25.60
1981	35.25	24.40	17.5–18.0	15.0	11.0	16.5–17.5	15.90
June 1982	33.12	17.29	10.0	10.0	10.0	10.0	7.60
1983	25.77	14.23	10.0	10.0	10.0	10.0	3.00
1984	24.84	14.12	10.0–11.5	10.0	10.0–11.5	10.0–11.5	3.90
1985	24.00	14.20	10.0–13.0	10.0	10.0–11.5	10.0–11.5	3.50

a: *Source*: Bank of Korea
b: Machinery Industry Promotion Fund
c: National Investment Fund

Source: The World Bank, *Korea: Managing the Industrial Transition*, Vol. II (Washington: 1987), p. 112.

firms, encouraging them to undertake projects which have been declined otherwise.'[19]

THE STATE-CONTROLLED CAPITALIST COLLECTIVE ACTION OF HEAVY AND CHEMICAL INDUSTRIAL PROMOTION

Shortly after setting up the state institutions, the authoritarian government began to change the structure of property rights in order to lower the transaction costs for promoting the heavy and chemical industrial construction. In other words, the government made every effort to induce business groups' investments in the HCIs by changing institutions between state and society, and between state and market. The state managers tried to mobilize business groups by means of coercive enforcement and privileged supports through direct interactions between the state and business groups, which would reinforce the state-big business governing coalition. Additionally, the government tightened the state-controlled financial system in order to mobilize huge capital, which would provide financial benefits for the large business firms participating in heavy and chemical industrial investment.

According to the Heavy and Chemical Industrial Promotion Plan, the government focused on the 'strategic industries' of iron and steel, machinery, non-ferrous metals, electronics, shipbuilding, and petrochemicals. Its industrial strategy would promote the HCIs as export-oriented industries in order to overcome the limits of the small domestic market and to construct large-sized facilities in terms of the economies of scale. Its economic goal was to achieve exports of $10 billion and the national income per capita of $1,000 in the early 1980s, on the basis of a self-reliant economy and balanced international payments.[20]

The government planned to mobilize domestic capital of $3.8 billion and foreign capital of $5.8 billion between 1973 and 1981. The system of domestic capital mobilization would be reinforced by deployment of a savings campaign and promotion of the capital market. Heavy and chemical industrial firms were required to finance their own funds of over 30 percent of their total amount of investment.[21] Foreign capital would be induced within 60 percent of total required funds for the purposes of the equipment import and technology transfer. In principle, the government would give priority to foreign loans; basically, it would allow direct foreign investment of less than 50 percent in joint ventures.[22]

Big business resistance and the government's coercive enforcement

After making the heavy and chemical industrial promotion plan and setting up policy measures for fiscal and financial supports in the HCIs (as I will detail in the next subsection), the government made every effort to bring about the business groups' massive investment by means of strong recommendations and financial incentives. The core of the HCIs was the defence-related machinery industry, which needed the largest amount of capital and the most advanced technology among the heavy and chemical strategic industries. Thus, the analysis that follows will focus on the machinery industry.

The government began to construct the Changwon Machinery

Industrial Complexes (Estate), where machinery industrial firms were supposed to build their factories, in order to foster cooperation among the concerned machinery fields. By 1974, it established the Changwon Machinery Industry Corporation (CMIC), whose major task was to induce domestic firms' investment in the industrial complexes.

Shortly after the declaration of heavy and chemical industrial promotion, businessmen hesitated to invest in the HCIs because their already highly indebted firms were short of internal savings and because they were faced with a long period of return on their heavy and chemical investment and opaque prospects for the markets. In April 1974, the MCI held the first investment inducement meeting, to which not only large but also small and medium firms were invited. Afterwards, the CMIC explained the heavy and chemical investment plan to domestic businessmen in the major cities. Furthermore, it invited foreign businessmen to the Changwon industrial estate to induce foreign capital; and the state-run corporation dispatched its investment inducement teams to advanced countries.[23]

However, both domestic and foreign businessmen were sceptical about the government's plan, despite the CMIC's investment inducement strategies, which were based on fiscal and financial incentives. When they made an on-site inspection of the Changwon Machinery Industrial Complexes, where, at that time, only lands for factory construction and roads were being constructed, they were further frustrated. They thought that both the investment plan of, and the financial support plan for, the machinery industry were too ambitious and not realistically feasible.

For instance, one top manager of the Daewoo Business Group explained low confidence of big business in heavy and chemical industrial investment as follows: the uncertainty of the investment plan strongly affected the big businessmen's hesitance; they had many doubts about their ability to successfully mobilize capital for investment, despite the government's guarantee of financial supports, and about their ability to manage the plants once they had built factories without high technological accumulation; and they wanted their factories to be built near large cities rather than at Changwon (a small town in the southeast province) because such locations would be more convenient for transportation.[24] In one case involving a foreign lender, for instance, the IBRD (the International Bank for Reconstruction and Development) in 1975 made an investigative tour of the Changwon Industrial Estate in order to check Hyundai International's huge machinery project (at that time, Hyundai International had applied for foreign loans from the IBRD). Like the domestic business groups, the IBRD was sceptical not only about the project but also about the whole machinery industrial plan.[25]

As a matter of fact, until the end of 1974, only twenty-seven firms, including only two business groups, had been selected and moved to the industrial estate. Until then, almost all the business groups had maintained a management strategy of wait-and-see, in the least, and resistance of foot-dragging against the government's inducement policy, at most. Basically, the business groups had advocated a gradual heavy and chemical industrialization from labour-intensive to capital-intensive industries. In contrast to the case of the machinery industry, some business groups participated actively in the export-oriented and labour-intensive automobile, shipbuilding, and electronics industries among the heavy and chemical strategic industries.[26]

In response to the oil-shock of 1973 and even during the economic recession period of 1974–75, Park's government chose the economic policy of growth rather than stability. In January 1974, there was a policy debate as to whether the government should give priority to growth (argued by the Presidential Secretariat) or stability (argued by the EPB). Finally, Park announced the growth-oriented Presidential Emergency Economic Decree, which would continue economic growth based on people's economic stability.[27] In January 1975, President Park directed the economic ministries towards intensive investment in the HCIs during his annual inspection tour, even though economic technocrats were hesitant to push heavy and chemical industrial investment projects due to the economic recession.[28]

During 1975, newspapers expected that the heavy and chemical industrial plan would be modified and argued that its projects should be delayed and adjusted.[29] But, on the contrary, President Park made an investigative tour of the machinery estate and spurred investment inducement. At the initial stage of heavy and chemical industrial transformation, big business firms hardly wanted to invest in the machinery industry despite the government's promise to guarantee direct and indirect financial support – privileged access to policy loans and state funds for plant construction and operation, and the government's infrastructure investment in building industrial complexes. They were sceptical about the feasibility of achieving state-led heavy industrial projects. More importantly, in general, their heavy and chemical industrial investment was not compatible with their investment strategy based on profit maximization. Presidential First Economic Secretary Won-Chul Oh selected appropriate large firms and strongly recommended that they invest in the machinery industry. It was alleged in the process of selection and recommendation that the Planning Office took both compulsory and conciliatory measures for enforcing big business participation by means of the so-called 'defeating one by one' strategy.[30] Its means of enforcement was state control over the financial system. That is, the strategy of political threat assumed that non-compliant business groups would suffer economic penalties of either bankruptcy or severe financial difficulties because the government would suspend or sharply reduce financing funds to them. The strategy of appeasement assumed that compliant business groups would enjoy privileged financial benefits.

The government's investment inducement policy and the financial mechanism

Shortly after Park's declaration of heavy and chemical industrial promotion, the government embarked on taking specific measures for inducing businessmen's investment in the HCIs. The state managers relied mainly on such financial supports as public financial investment and loans, bank policy loans, and foreign loans and direct foreign investment. Additionally, they took advantage of tax reduction and exemption for heavy and chemical industrial firms, infrastructure investments for industrial complexes, and quantitative import restriction and tariff protection for heavy and chemical industrial products (see Figure 6).

Domestic capital

The most important domestic financial resources for heavy and chemical industrialization had been preferential policy loans and the National Investment Fund (NIF), whose law was enacted in January 1974. The major sources of the NIF had been issues of the NIF's bonds, government expenditure, and temporary loans from the Bank of Korea. The NIF's bonds would be acquired

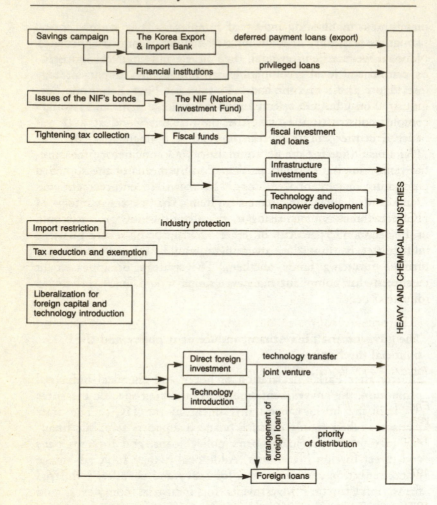

Figure 6 Support policies for heavy and chemical industries

Source: Jin-Sook Lim, 'State–Capital Relationships in Peripheral Capitalism: The Korean Policy of Heavy and Chemical Industrialization', M.A. Thesis (Seoul National University: 1985), p. 54 (in Korean).

mainly by compulsory deposits from financial institutions, national savings associations, insurance and trust companies, the planned National Welfare Pension Fund, and various public funds managed by central and local governments and other public organizations (see Figure 7).[31] The NIF had been used for heavy and chemical industrial facilities and operation funds and for funds for industrial complex construction. During the period of 1974–79, an average of 59 percent of the total NIF had been invested in the HCIs.[32]

As a result, during the period of 1975–79, the share of preferential policy loans in the total bank loans had increased from 53 percent to 63 percent (see Table 4); during 1976–78, more than 77 percent of all manufacturing facilities investment went to the HCIs; and thus, an increasing share of bank credit (54.2 percent in 1976 and 59.5 percent in 1978) had been allocated to these industries, even though the share of the HCIs in the total manufacturing output was only about 50 percent (see Table 5). The mechanism of policy loans in association with the NIF was as follows:

The primary source of the heavy industries' long-term investment capital and policy loans was the Korea Development Bank

Table 4 Policy loans: 1975–79 (unit: billion won (%))

End of year	DMB policy loans	DMB total loans	KDB	KEIB	Total policy loans	Total bank loans
1975	1,449 (38)	3,248 (85)	578 (15)	–	2,027 (53)	3,826 (100)
1976	1,861 (37)	4,071 (85)	740 (15)	–	2,601 (54)	4,811 (100)
1977	2,487 (39)	5,216 (82)	1,008 (16)	121 (2)	3,616 (57)	6,345 (100)
1978	3,970 (43)	7,708 (83)	1,443 (15)	165 (2)	5,578 (60)	9,316 (100)
1979	5,820 (46)	10,701 (82)	2,138 (16)	226 (2)	8,183 (63)	13,064 (100)

DMB: Deposit Money Bank
KDB: Korea Development Bank
KEIB: Export-Import Bank of Korea

Source: Ministry of Finance: quotation in Seok-Ki Kim, 'Business Concentration and Government Policy', D.B.A. (Harvard University: 1987), p. 181.

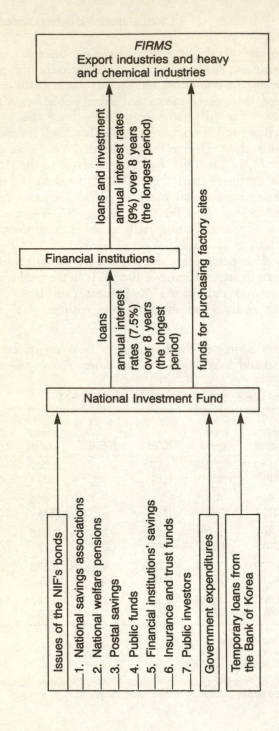

Figure 7 The mechanism of the National Investment Fund

Source: The Korean Chamber of Commerce and Industry, Heavy and Chemical Construction, and Capital Mobilization (Seoul: 1975), p. 133 (in Korean).

Table 5 Distortion in resource allocation

Share of heavy and chemical industries in total manufacturing (%)	1976	1977	1978
Value added	46.8	48.5	48.8
Output	49.5	50.4	51.4
Bank credit (DMB and KDB)	54.2	56.4	59.5
Facility investment	74.2	75.4	82.5
Share of preferential policy loans in total bank loans	56.6	55.7	68.7

Source: Sang-Woo Nam, 'Korea's Stabilization Efforts since the Late 1970s', in Joong-Woong Kim, ed., *Financial Development Policies and Issues* (Seoul: Korea Development Institute, 1986), p. 50.

[KDB]. It has provided long-term investment loans for heavy industries, underwritten corporate bonds and stocks, and guaranteed foreign loans. The KDB's share of total equipment investment lending, which had declined since the mid-1960s, rose from 40.3 percent in 1972 to 44.7 percent in 1975 and to 49.6 percent in 1979. Another development financial institution, which was involved in the heavy industrialization process, was the Export-Import Bank of Korea [EXIM]. Its main business was to provide medium- and long-term financing for domestic exporters and foreign importers of Korea's heavy industrial goods and to underwrite export insurance for domestic corporations and financial institutions. ... Compulsory deposits by the banking institutions at the NIF have put a further constraint on the asset management of the banking institutions. The NIF's share in total equipment investment loans of commercial banks soared from 4.6 percent in 1974 to 16.3 percent in 1976 and to 20.3 percent in 1978. Moreover, even when the KDB and NIF loans proved insufficient, deposit money banks [DMBs] were urged to make additional preferential policy loans available for heavy and chemical industrial projects.[33]

As shown above, a huge amount of domestic capital had been mobilized for the heavy and chemical industrial construction. The excessively skewed credit allocation had been controlled by the state not only at the industry level but also at the firm level. Most domestic financing funds had been poured into large firms of business groups that were superior to small and medium firms in terms of equity mobilization and advanced technology. In general, large firms had had better access to and less average cost of borrowings than did small and medium firms.[34] As a result, the government had distributed the middle and lower classes' (the majority) deposits as preferential loans for big businessmen's (the minority) investments.

Foreign capital

During the 1970s, a massive amount of foreign capital (of which over 90 percent was loans) had flowed into the Korean economy. During the period of 1973–79, the EPB had allocated 32 percent ($3.8 billion) of the total foreign loans to the HCIs, of which payments were guaranteed by the KDB and other banking institutions. In particular, public foreign loans had increased rapidly to finance infrastructure investments in heavy and chemical industrial estates.[35]

Foreign borrowings had been screened and approved, guaranteed, and directly or indirectly distributed by the government. The state-controlled inducement of international borrowings resulted in further state intervention in domestic credit allocation to the HCIs. The largest business groups were the largest users of foreign loans. Foreign loans had brought privileged benefits to the borrowers.[36] Interest rates of foreign loans were below 10 percent and lower than domestic bank lending interest rates (from 15.5 percent to 19.0 percent). Their real interest rates were negative due to the rate of inflation (from 13.4 percent to 29.5 percent).[37]

The government revised the Foreign Capital Inducement Law in 1973. The law prohibited 100 percent foreign capital ownership and limited the share of foreign investment in joint ventures to 50 percent in order to make it difficult to obtain approval for a majority foreign-owned venture; it also set a minimum scale of investment amount to prevent inefficient and small-sized investments. Its specific measures were taken to control direct foreign investment applications in order to exclude projects that might compete with existing domestic firms in the domestic and international markets or that would provide only capital without advanced technology. As a result, direct foreign investment played a relatively minor role in the heavy and chemical industrial construction.[38]

Policy measures of inducement for direct foreign investment had been paralleled with those of constraints. The government intended to maintain state autonomy from the foreign investors in its industrial strategy and to minimize the domestic firms' dependence on foreign partners in enterprise management. Tax exemptions for foreign-invested enterprises were to be limited to the HCIs and might be reduced and abolished in the consumer products and textile industries. The government explicitly shifted its policy of direct foreign investment by reducing government support for export-oriented light industries (which were located in the Masan Free Trade Zones) and by increasing special financial assistance for heavy and chemical industrial joint ventures (which were constructed in the heavy and chemical industrial complexes).[39]

From big business quasi-voluntary compliance to voluntary compliance: the 'Changwon Rush'

In response to the aforementioned coercive enforcement and inducement measures, at the end of 1975 business groups began to invest in the machinery industry. Additionally, the top executives's strong commitment to the machinery industrial construction and financial supports had greatly affected big business participation in the Changwon industrial complexes; in 1975, the fact that the government had speedily finished preparing one of factory estates increased big business confidence in the government's commitment.

In 1976, the so-called 'Changwon Rush' had begun; large business firms began to invest competitively in the machinery industry. Their full confidence in investment was based not on quasi-voluntary (involuntary to the coercive enforcement policy and voluntary to the inducement policy) compliance for fear of unfavourable treatment, but on voluntary compliance in expectation of favourable benefits. Furthermore, foreign lenders and investors were deeply impressed by the early construction of the industrial estate; foreign loans increasingly flowed into the industry, and direct foreign investments began to form joint ventures.

The total number of move-in firms (installed in the estate) had increased sharply from thirty-eight in 1975 to fifty-two in 1976, eighty-eight in 1977, and 122 in 1978. Until 1977, almost all concerned large firms affiliated with the business groups had moved into the industrial estate. Furthermore, by 1978, even small and medium firms participated actively in the machinery industry with the catchphrase, 'Don't miss buses to go to the Changwon'.[40]

In brief, at the initial stage, the authoritarian government had made it possible for large firms to start participating in the state-led heavy and chemical industrial promotion by means of coercive enforcement and inducement. In particular, it changed the firms' payoff structure by lowering the transaction costs of industrial adjustment (transformation) in favour of the large firms that were participating in the HCIs. The reduced transaction costs shifted big business interests from labour-intensive light industries to the HCIs in compliance with the state managers' interests in heavy and chemical industrial promotion; they also greatly increased big businessmen's investment capabilities. Thus, the state managers stirred up the collective action of big business participation in the HCIs by breaking through the deadlock game-like situation of the business groups' foot-dragging resistance with the privileged financial incentives.

THE HEAVY AND CHEMICAL INDUSTRIALIZATION IN INSTITUTIONAL DECAY

This section will show the process of institutional decay in the state-controlled financial system and within the state-big business relationships. It will focus on how the failure of investment control had decreased the government's financial control over the business sector and had created the problem of surplus capacity in the HCIs.

The weakening capabilities of the state-controlled financial system

During the 1970s, the growth rate of the financial sector had slowed down in comparison to the previous period (1965–71) of rapid financial growth:[41]

> Heavy government financial intervention interfered with the development of the financial sector not only with respect to its growth, but also with respect to quality of its services. Intervention in the banking industry [i.e., in its asset management and day-to-day operations] removed any incentive for the banks to innovate in their operations or to become more efficient in

the intermediation of financial resources. Nor did the banks have much incentive to select profitable borrowers because they were not rewarded for doing so. Rather, banks passively accommodated the credit demands of the government-favored borrowers. The repressed interest rates which fluctuated around zero or were negative in real terms made bank deposits quite unattractive financial assets and made the holders of bank deposits the ultimate bearer of the cost of financial intervention. Consequently, the financial sector's growth was more sluggish than it would otherwise have been. Furthermore, in the process of channeling government-directed loans, the commercial banks accumulated a substantial amount of nonperforming loans which reduced profitability and limited its future development.[42]

As a consequence, the financial repression, or deceleration of the 1970s resulted in a gap between the growth of the financial sector and that of the real economy. The insufficient role of the government-controlled financial system was supplemented by foreign capital, internal savings of corporations, and an informal (unregulated) financial market.[43] Under the government-controlled financial system, the economy faced unbalanced industrial structures between big business and small and medium businesses as well as between the heavy and chemical and the light industries, and it suffered from excessive investments in comparison to domestic demands in the HCIs in the late 1970s. A following subsection will analyse the weakening process of government-controlled financial institutional capabilities.

The institutional decay of state-big business relationships

In the late 1970s, however, the institutions of state-big business relationships were rapidly weakening when the government's control over labour became unstable. The corporatist control, which had been achieved through the FKI, became inefficient in the late 1970s. In 1977, the chairman of the FKI, Joo-Young Chung, announced a 'private-initiated economy' to enhance business autonomy, as opposed to state interventions in the market – excessive regulatory policies to shrink business activities and, especially, interventions in investment decision-making.[44] Since then, the FKI frequently demanded big business autonomy for their free activities. Ironically, however, its announcements neither included a reduction of existing indirect government supports, including tax exemptions and policy loans with low interest rates, nor mentioned problems of monopoly or oligopoly and business concentration as side effects of the state-led heavy and chemical industrialization. These kinds of big business demands can be interpreted as expressions of the FKI's autonomous interest representation in the long term as well as of its discontent regarding the strong state interventions in businessmen's investment decision-making in the HCIs in the short term.

In the labour sector, the corporatist control of a high degree of repressive constraints had operated through the FKTU, while the non-corporatist mechanism of the Labour-Management Council and the Factory Saemaul Movement provided a low degree of inducements. The corporatist mechanism had also been eroding rapidly during the late 1970s due to the growing activation of labour unions and the rank-and-file at the enterprise level. Increasing labour conflicts reduced business confidence in economic activities. In 1979, the limits of labour control ignited a series of political crises that led to Park's assassination and the breakdown of the authoritarian regime. The process of decreasing labour control and increasing labour disputes will be discussed in later chapters. Those portions will also mention institutional attempts by the government and the big business circle to mitigate labour demands in dealing with labour-management problems.

In addition, as I will analyse in the next subsection, the government was confronted with big business pressures and competition to such an extent that the government could not control big business demands. In the late 1970s, the government became trapped in the direct channels between the state and the business groups, which had operated for efficient government inducement of heavy and chemical industrial investment; the state managers were losing their investment control, which had greatly reduced the financial institutional capacities for efficient credit allocation.

The failure of investment control: the problem of overcapacity in the HCIs

In the 1970s, the government used not only credit allocation but also investment licensing as policy instruments for strong state intervention in industries and individual firms. The policy instrument of credit allocation was closely related to that of investment licensing for the big push of heavy and chemical industrialization. Investment allocations were given to business groups that participated in the HCIs. The government guaranteed big businessmen's profits through either monopoly or oligopoly because heavy and chemical industrial projects required scale merits in the small domestic market and in the competitive international market. Licensed or even designated investments made big businessmen mono-oligopolize large heavy and chemical industrial sectors. Besides, selective credit allocations offered financial incentives to business groups that had been initially reluctant to invest in the HCIs due to a lack of financial resources. Except for the steel industry, where the government had ownership and management control, a small group of the largest business firms were given licences in such strategically selected HCIs as non-ferrous metals, petrochemicals, machinery, shipbuilding, and electronics.

During the 1975–79 period, approximately 70 percent of the policy loans went to the HCI sectors.[45] At the end of 1979, the so-called heavy and chemical industrial rush among business groups surpassed a government-scheduled target of investments for heavy and chemical industrial projects in the Fourth Five-Year Economic Plan (1977–81).[46] The problem of overcapacity stemmed from the overly ambitious and inconsistent government policy and from power struggles among business groups for hegemonic positions in the heavy and chemical industrial sectors. The excessive big business competition was accompanied by big business pressures and lobbying on the government, which had sharply decreased state autonomy of investment allocation from the business groups.

Six sectors in the HCIs faced a serious problem of surplus capacity: the power-generating equipment, automobile, heavy electrical equipment, electronic switching system, diesel engine, and copper smelting industries. The overall operation ratio in the machinery industry (the process of the government's failure in controlling investment allocation will be analysed in the next subsections) was 53.6 percent in 1977, 62.2 percent in 1978, 61.2 percent in 1979, and 54.4 percent in 1980.[47]

The power-generating equipment field

Government control over investment allocations had decreased in the field of power-generating equipment.[48] The Ministry of Commerce and Industry (MCI) announced that the government would give high priority to the field of power-generating equipment for the promotion of machinery industries by 1976. Shortly after the statement, the public enterprise of the Korean Electric Power Corporation (KEPC) announced that the company would leave construction of two power plants to domestic companies. Along with the KEPC's announcement, the Hyundai Business Group, with the joint technology of Westinghouse (of the United States) and the Daewoo Business Group, with Brown Boveri (of Switzerland), won bids of the Asan and the Ulsan power plant construction projects, respectively. The Samsung Business Group, which had been one of the three largest conglomerates, together with the Hyundai and Daewoo groups, failed to participate in the above projects. Nevertheless, it established a joint company with Ishigawajima Harima (of Japan) for subsequent power plant construction projects and invested in a boiler plant at the Changwon Machinery Industrial Complex.

However, Samsung's case provoked opposition from Hyundai International and the IBRD.[49] In 1976, Hyundai International had already started to construct a huge factory of general machinery plants, including power-generating equipment. Actually, Hyundai International had a privileged claim for production of power plant facilities because the IBRD, as its lender, had required the Korean government to guarantee the monopolized production right of the company for the first five years of its operation. After all, in May 1977, the Economic Ministers Meeting allowed Hyundai International to monopolize the production of such power-generating equipment as boilers, turbines, and generators. According to this policy decision, Hyundai and Daewoo would have to specialize only in construction works of power plants to accumulate engineering technologies instead of production of equipment. The meeting also decided that the Samsung Group would have to concentrate on boilers, not for power plants but for general industrial plants.

Surprisingly enough, however, in March 1978 the government chose the Hyundai Heavy Industries (a subsidiary of the Hyundai Group) instead of Hyundai International to manufacture the Kori nuclear power plant equipment. After this policy change, other conglomerates put pressure on the government so that they could produce power plant facilities. Finally, the Economic Ministers Informal (Consultation) Meeting allowed two groups, Hyundai and Daewoo, to produce power-generating equipment in April

1978. The excluded Samsung Group protested against this policy and lobbied the MCI, arguing that its factory at the Changwon Industrial Complex was initially built to produce boilers used for power plants. In the end, the government permitted the Samsung Group to join the power plant sector.

As a consequence, the business competition and frequent policy changes of the government led to overcapacity: the annual total production capacity of the four companies was 8 million kilowatts in 1978 over an expected domestic demand for power plants of about 2 million kilowatts. Later, the overinvestment brought in the state-controlled investment adjustments in the field of power-generating equipment.

The automobile field

Overcapacity in the automobile industry also had been created by the government's excessive investment inducement and inconsistent policy, and the business groups' competitive pressures on investment licensing (see Table 6).[50] In 1963, the government announced the 'Automobile Industry Promotion Law'; it also announced plans to allow only one firm to manufacture automobiles for the economies of scale in the small domestic market. In the late 1960s, however, three firms (the Shinjin Motor Company, the Asia Motor

Table 6 Indicators of major automobile companies (at the end of 1979)

	Hyundai Motor Company	Saehan Motor Company	KIA Motor Company
Capital (million won)	38,250	18,500 (GM 50%)	15,000
Investment (billion won)	Prior to 1979: 131.6 1980–86 plan: 334.6	Prior to 1979: 87.2 1980–86 plan: 920.2	Prior to 1979: 66.1 1980–86 plan: 292.0
Production capacity (unit/ year) of passenger cars	114,000	71,000	50,000
1979 production (units)	71,744	18,430	22,140

Source: The Korea Exchange Bank, 'Adjustment of Korea's Heavy and Chemical Industry Investment', Monthly Review (December 1980), p. 12.

Company, and the Hyundai Motor Company) became engaged in passenger car manufacturing as a result of big business pressures on government investment approval.

In May 1974, the MCI announced a plan for long-term development of the automobile industry: its major goals were to manufacture a Korean-made car by 1975 and to export 75,000 cars by 1981. The ministry requested that the automobile firms submit their own proposals for developing a Korean original model. Not only the Hyundai Motor Company and General Motors Korea (the joint venture of the Shinjin Motor Company and General Motors: it was established in 1972, renamed the Saehan Motor Company in 1976, and taken over by the Daewoo Business Group in 1978) but also the Kia Motor Company (which had produced only three-wheel cars) made proposals; the Asia Motor Company failed to submit its plan. As a result, the Kia Motor Company was allowed to produce passenger cars.

Faced with the increasing investment competition of business groups in the machinery industry, the MCI by 1978 attempted to adjust the business groups' planned investments according to machinery fields. Nevertheless, it failed to adjust investment plans because of big business competition. The ministry asked the business groups concerned to report their investment plans. At that time, the owners of the business groups came up with overly ambitious investment plans to obtain investment licensing of larger allocated amounts. Ironically, the attempt of investment guidance boosted investment in the machinery industry, including the automobile sector.[51]

Furthermore, by 1979, the MCI announced a plan for promoting ten strategic industries (including the automobile industry) of the 1980s. The government promised financial support for the automobile industry and asked the motor companies to increase their production capacity up to 2 million cars by 1986. Shortly after the policy announcement, the automobile firms devised production schemes that were more ambitious than the government's plan.[52] As a result, in August 1980 the operation ratios for passenger car, truck, and bus manufacturing were 34.5 percent, 45.7 percent, and 82.4 percent, respectively.[53]

As shown above, the failures of the government's investment controls in the strategically-targeted sectors of the HCIs raised the problem of surplus capacity without international comparative advantage in the small domestic market. Under the government-controlled financial system, the financial policy of selective and privileged credit allocation to big businesses joining the HCI sectors created both serious power struggles among, and hasty and short-sighted rushes of, big business firms. Thus, such financial incentives as preferential loans for plant construction and operation, tax exemption, and privileged access to domestic and foreign loans brought about inefficient investment allocations and serious problems of overcapacity, low operation, and delayed plant construction in the late 1970s.

By 1979, the phenomenon of financial shortage resulted not only from the limits of capital mobilization from the overall financial repression but also from excessive capital demands from the heavy and chemical industrial companies in operation and under construction.[54] Many heavy and chemical industrial projects under construction were suspended and new ones were postponed due to financial shortages. Finally, the institutional capacities of the existing financial system had deteriorated in the face of the weakening of the state managers' investment control.

Chapters 4, 5, and 6 will deal with attempts at state-controlled investment adjustment in response to the serious problem of overcapacity in the HCIs. Chapter 4 will focus on inefficient state institutions following the institutional decay of both financial control and investment control over big business.

NOTES

1 There have been several kinds of arguments about why the authoritarian regime emerged. See Wan-kyu Choi, 'A Politico-Economic Analysis of the Emergence of an Authoritarian Regime: The Case of the Yushin System', *Korea and World Politics* 3 (Summer 1987) (in Korean); and Hyug Baeg Im, 'The Rise of Bureaucratic Authoritarianism in South Korea', *World Politics* (January 1987).

2 See the Office of the Presidential Secretariat, *A Collection of Park's Speeches*, Vol. 10 (in Korean).

3 'The EPB was created in July 1961, immediately after the military coup led by President Park Chung Hee. The establishment of the EPB symbolized the military government's resolve to give top priority to economic development and its commitment to a systematic and sustained pursuit of long-term economic development plans. It took over comprehensive development planning functions and foreign cooperation activities from the Ministry of Construction, which was established only one month earlier by the military junta. . . . the EPB also

absorbed the Bureau of Budget from the Ministry of Finance and the Bureau of Statistics from the Ministry of Home Affairs to facilitate comprehensive planning and to insure effective execution of development programs. . . . To signify the seriousness of the regime's planning efforts, the military government elevated elevated the head of the EPB to a rank of the Deputy Prime Minister [DPM] in December 1963.

'The change did not go far as to elevate the hierarchical order of the EPB Minister among economic ministers, but it endowed the DPM with a formal authority to coordinate a wide range of economic policies for effective execution of economic development plans'. Byung-Sun Choi, 'Institutionalizing a Liberal Economic Order in Korea: The Strategic Management of Economic Change', Ph.D. Diss. (Harvard University, 1987), pp. 23–25.

4 The concept of dualistic policy-making is indebted to Callaghy's argument that there has been a mixed decision-making system of both the political logic of the executive and the economic logic of technocrats in African states. Thomas M. Callaghy, 'Lost between State and Market', in Joan M. Nelson, ed., *Economic Crisis and Policy Choice: The Politics of Adjustment in The Third World* (Princeton: Princeton University Press, 1990), pp. 263–64.

5 Basically, motives for the state-led heavy and chemical industrial promotion are explained by the following factors: the necessity of self-defence in response to the change of the East Asian security environment during the early 1970s; the limits of labour-intensive and export-oriented light industrialization during the slow-down of economic growth; and the legitimacy of political power for the establishment of authoritarian government (for these arguments, see Inwon Choue, *op. cit.* [Introduction, note 2], Chap. 5; Dae-Whan Kim, 'The Change of International Economic Environment and Heavy and Chemical Industrialization', in Hyun-Chae Park, *et al.*, eds., *A Study on the Korean Economy* [Seoul: Kachi Press, 1987] [in Korean]; and Kwan-Yong Jung, 'The Characteristics of the Korean State in the Heavy and Chemical Industrial Policy', in the Korean Industrial Society Council, *Today's Korean Capitalism and the State* [Seoul: Hangil Press, 1988] [in Korean]).

6 For a detailed description of Park's strong will and the decision-making process for heavy and chemical industrial promotion, see Jung-Ryum Kim (the Chief of the Presidential Secretariat during 1969–78), 'Memoir: Nos. 58, 59, 71–76', in *The Joong-Ang Daily News*, 1989. In accordance with the Nixon Doctrine of 1969, the U.S. Seventh Division (some 20,000 military personnel) withdrew from South Korea in March 1970 in spite of Park's strong opposition to the U.S. troop withdrawal plan. In response, Park tried to build factories for military weapons with every effort. But he received the EPB's report that the United States, the European countries, and, especially, Japan had rejected an offer of loans to Korea to help build heavy industrial factories that would produce the special steel and the heavy machinery that could have given the basic facilities to produce arms. Park was deeply disappointed and frustrated, but Won-Chul Oh, an Assistant

Minister of the Ministry of Commerce and Industry presented Park with his interesting ideas of military-industrial promotion through heavy and chemical industrialization. Park accepted his proposals and appointed him First Economic Secretary of the Presidential Second Economic Secretariat in November 1971; he would take charge of both the defence and the heavy and chemical industries.

7 See the Korean Chamber of Commerce and Industry (KCCI), *Reflections and Lessons of the Korean Twenty Years' Economy* (Seoul: KCCI, 1982), pp. 180–211 (in Korean); and Inwon Choue, *op. cit.*, p. 330.

8 See Inwon Choue, ibid., pp. 326–36; [Introduction, note 2] the Planning Office of the HCIPC, *The Conference Records of the Heavy and Chemical Industry Promotion Committee* (1980) (in Korean).

9 In 1972, before the Declaration of Heavy and Chemical Industrialization, the government made a general draft of heavy and chemical industrial plans with the assistance of domestic and foreign research institutes (Changwon Machinery Industry Corporation, *The Five-Year History of the Changwon Complex* [1979], p. 53 [in Korean]).

10 The Hyundai Sahoe Research Institute, *The Korean Social Change and a Study on the Role of the State*, Research Report 85–12 (1985), 52–55 (in Korean).

11 The Planning Office of the Heavy and Chemical Industry Promotion Committee, *An Investigation Study on the Development of Korean Industrialization: The Behind-the-Scenes History of the Policy-Making Process* (Seoul, 1979c), p. 325 (in Korean).

12 The Hyundai Sahoe Research Institute, *op. cit.*, pp. 57–58.

13 Jang-Jip Choi, 'Interest Conflict and Political Control' in South Korea: Ph.D. Diss., (University of Chicago: 1983), p. 305.

14 For the history and activities of the FKI, see the FKI, *The FKI's Twenty Years: Retrospect and Prospect* (Seoul: 1982) (in Korean); Myo-Min Lim, '*Jaebols* and Power', *Sin Dong-A* (April 1983) (in Korean); and Myo-Min Lim, 'Conflicts of *Jaebols*', *Sin Dong-A* (March 1983) (in Korean).

15 See Leory Jones and Il Sakong, *op. cit.* [Chpter 1, note 8], p. 72.

16 Zysman classified types (institutional arrangements) of economic adjustment as 'company-led', 'negotiated', and 'state-led' in terms of characteristics of financial system – 'capital market with competitive prices', 'credit-based with price formation dominated by banks', and 'credit-based with administered prices'. See John Zysman, *Governments, Markets and Growth: Financial Systems and the Politics of Industrial Change* (Ithaca: Cornell University Press, 1983). In the Korean case, a general type of state-controlled financial system under an authoritarian regime can be added to Zysman's three types. Like the state-led financial system, the state-controlled financial system is characterized by 'overloans' and 'overborrowings' for financial incentives to targeted industries and firms (discretionary field manipulation). Unlike the Japanese and French financial system, this financial system has the policy instrument of coercive enforcement for economic penalties – financial control through withdrawing or suspending loans (discretionary command).

17 For the Korean financial institutional structure, see David C. Cole and Yung Chul Park, *Financial Development in Korea* (Cambridge, MA: Harvard University Press, 1983), Chap. 3.
18 For the interest rate policy, see ibid., Chap. 5.
19 The World Bank, *Korea: Managing the Industrial Transition: Volume II. Selected Topics and Case Studies* (Washington: 1987), p. 99.
20 The Planning Office of the Heavy and Chemical Industry Promotion Committee, *The Heavy and Chemical Industry Promotion Plan* (Seoul, June 1973), pp. 7–9, 94 (in Korean), and see also the Planning Office of the Heavy and Chemical Industry Promotion Committee, *An Investigative Study on the Development of Korean Industrialization: The Heavy and Chemical Industrial Policy History* (Seoul, 1979b), pp. 241–94 (in Korean).
21 However, large heavy and chemical industrial firms had relied heavily on debts by failing to meet the required 30 percent because of their weak financial structure. For instance, the top ten business groups' average increase ratio of liabilities to the increase of their total assets was 78.8 percent during the period of 1972–79 (Seok-Ki Kim, 'Business Concentration and Government Policy: A Study of the Phenomenon of Business Groups in Korea, 1945–85', DBA [Harvard University, 1987], p. 170).
22 The Planning Office of the Heavy and Chemical Industry Promotion Committee, *op. cit.* (June 1973), p. 14.
23 For the activities of the CMIC's investment inducement, see the Changwon Machinery Industrial Corporation, *op. cit.*, pp. 125–48.
24 Dongkwang Press, *Wind and Clouds: Economic Inside Stories about High Growth* (Seoul: 1986) (in Korean), p. 292.
25 See ibid., p. 288.
26 For these industries, see the Planning Office of the Heavy and Chemical Industry Promotion Committee, *An Investigative Study on the Development of Korean Industrialization: The Heavy and Chemical Industrial Development History* (Seoul, 1979a), Chaps. 4, 5, and 6 (in Korean).
27 For the decision-making process, see the Planning Office of the Heavy and Chemical Industry Promotion Committee, *op. cit.* (1979c), pp. 394–99.
28 *The Kyunghyang Daily News*, 1 February 1975.
29 *The Seoul Daily News*, 20 March 1975; and *The Chosun Daily News*, 30 September 1975.
30 Dongkwang Press, *Wind and Clouds: Economic Inside Stories about High Growth* (Seoul: 1986) (in Korean), p. 285.
31 For the sources and management of the NIF, see the Korean Chamber of Commerce and Industry (the Korean Economic Research Centre), *Heavy and Chemical Industrial Construction, and Capital Mobilization* (Seoul, 1975), pp. 131–34 (in Korean) and for the detailed amounts of sources of the NIF, the World Bank, *Korea: Managing the Industrial Transition*, Vol. II (Washington, 1987), p. 110. 'The banking institutions have been required to contribute about 13 percent of the increase in their time and savings deposits to the NIF. The insurance

companies and the national savings associations were required to contribute 50 percent of their insurance premiums and 100 percent of their saving funds, respectively. The sale of the NFI bonds to the public constituted only a small proportion' (Byung-Sun Choi, *op. cit.*, p. 118).

32 For the detailed amounts of uses of the NIF, The World Bank, *op. cit.* (198), p. 111.

33 Byung-Sun Choi, *op. cit.*, pp. 117–19.

34 For the detailed statistical analysis of average cost of borrowing and access to borrowings by each sector, The World Bank, *op. cit.* (1987), Vol. I, p. 43, Vol. II, pp. 116, 118.

35 Byung-Sun Choi, *op. cit.*, pp. 120–21 and for the detailed inflow of foreign capital during 1972–79, see Seok-Ki Kim, *op. cit.*, p. 183.

36 See Byung-Yun Park, *Jaebols and Politics* (Seoul: Hankook Yangsu Press, 1982), pp. 209–13 (in Korean).

37 For interest rates of domestic and foreign loans during the 1970s, see Seok-Ki Kim, *op. cit.*, p. 184.

38 During the 1970s, direct foreign investment in Korea typically amounted to less than 5 percent of gross foreign capital inflows, compared to 85 percent in Singapore, 50 percent in Hong Kong, 25 percent in Brazil, and between 12 percent and 18 percent in Mexico, Argentina, the Philippines, and Indonesia. The World Bank, *Korea: The Management of External Liabilities*, A World Bank Country Study (Washington, 1988), p. 72.

39 See Ryuji Yasuda, 'Politics of Industrial Financing Policy: Korea and Japan', Ph.D. Diss. (University of California, Berkeley, 1979), pp. 200–10.

40 For the detailed process of the firms' move-in, see the Changwon Machinery Industry Corporation, *op. cit.*, pp. 148–76.

41 The ratio of domestic financial assets to GNP had increased from 0.81 in 1965 to 1.49 in 1970, but had increased more slowly to 1.86 in 1978. In September 1965, a monetary reform raised the ceiling on interest rates on bank time deposits from 15.0 percent to 26.4 percent in order to realize a positive interest rate. The government channelled higher domestic savings and inflows of foreign capital into exporters (see Dukhoon Lee, 'The Role of Financial Markets in Korea's Economic Development', *KDI Working Paper* 8801 [January 1988], pp. 27–34).

42 The World Bank, *op. cit.*, Vol. II (1987), pp. 106–7.

43 The Korean financial system has formed a dualistic structure that consists of a highly regulated formal sector, composed of deposit money banks, specialized banks, and non-bank financial institutions, and another, unregulated (informal) sector (the curb market). See Joong-Woong Kim, 'Economic Development and Financial Liberalization in Korea: Policy Reforms and Future Prospects', *KDI Working Paper* 8514 (December 1985), pp. 50–52, and see also David C. Cole and Yung Chul Park, *op. cit.*, Chaps. 4, 5.

44 Bum-Sung Chun, *Chung Joo-Young (Biography)* (Seoul: Su Moon Dang Press, 1984), pp. 353–54 (in Korean); the FKI, *op. cit.* (1982),

pp. 299–301, 314–17; and Joo-Young Chung, 'FKI Chairman Chung's Special Speech', *The Korean Business Review* 53 (November 1979).
45 See Seok-Ki Kim, *op. cit.*, p. 186.
46 While the original plan of the Fourth Five-Year Economic Plan was to invest 2,892.5 billion won by the end of 1981, the total amount of heavy and chemical industrial investments was 2,868 billion won by the end of 1979. Of the total investment, 75.5 percent was spent on heavy and chemical industrial projects over the planned proportion of 60 percent in the HCI sectors. Myoung Soo Ki, 'The Making of Korean Society: The Role of the State in the Republic of Korea [1948–79]', Ph.D. Diss. (Brown University, 1987), p. 123.
47 Korea Exchange Bank, 'Adjustment of Korea's Heavy and Chemical Industry Investment', *Monthly Review* (December 1980), p. 6.
48 For the field of power-generating equipment, see Byoung Yun Park, 'Wild Currents in the Business Circle in 1978', *Sin Dong-A* (December 1978) (in Korean); Byoung Yun Park, 'The Inside Story of the Heavy and Chemical Industrial Industries', *Sin Dong-A* (May 1980) (in Korean); Nak-Dong Choi, 'The Inside Story of the Machinery Industrial Circle', *Sin Dong-A* (April 1980) (in Korean); and KIET (Korea Institute for Economics & Technology), *Problems of the Korean Heavy Machinery Industries and Policy Orientation*, Research Report, pp. 19–170 (in Korean).
49 Originally, Hyundai International was a subsidiary of the Hyundai Business Group at the time when the IBRD made a contract of loan with the Hyundai Group. An owner (In-Young Chung) of Hyundai International was a younger brother of the owner (Joo-Young Chung) of the Hyundai Group. But, after conflicts arose between them, Hyundai International was separated from the Hyundai Group.
50 For the automobile industry, see Byoung Yun Park, 'The Inside Story of the Automobile Industry', *Sin Dong-A* (December 1979) (in Korean); Nak-Dong Choi, *op. cit.*; KDI, *Development Orientation of the Automobile Industry and Policy*, Research Report 81–03 (1981) (in Korean); and KIET, *Problems of the Automobile Industry and Promotion Orientation*, Special Analysis 23 (1982) (in Korean).
51 Byoung Yun Park, *op. cit.* (December 1978), p. 118.
52 'Hyundai announced plans for investing 720 billion won by 1986 with foreign and domestic loans, to increase the production capacity to 1 million cars. [Saehan], after Hyundai's announcement, revised its original plan for producing 700,000 cars to 1 million cars ... [Kia] announced plans for producing 700,000 cars by 1985, ...' (Eun Mee Kim, 'From Dominance to Symbiosis: State and Chaebol in the Korean Economy, 1960–1985', Ph.D. Diss. [Brown University, 1987], p. 202).
53 Korea Exchange Bank, *op. cit.*, p. 9, and for the units of production capacity and real production, see p. 12.
54 The total capital demand of major heavy and chemical industrial firms in operation and under construction was 1,907 billion won in 1979. Only 30 percent (562 billion won) was supposed to be covered by self-financing. The government made every effort to cover the lack of

capital with the National Investment Fund, the Industrial Rationalization Fund, and the Special Support Fund. However, the expected shortage of domestic external financing funds was 483 billion won (see Byoung Yun Park, *op. cit.* [May 1980], pp. 206–7). For financial difficulties in the HCIs, see also Suk-Woong Yun, 'Large Firms' Fund War', *Sin Dong-A* (December 1978) (in Korean).

Chapter 4

The policy formation of investment adjustment for economic stabilization

Chapters 4 and 5 will show two things: first, how serious bureaucratic conflicts under presidential influence had occurred in dealing with the problem of overcapacity in the HCI sectors, in response to the government's rapidly weakening credit and investment control; and second, why and how the weak institutional capacities of the state had affected the policy formation and implementation of economic stabilization and the policy failure of the first heavy and chemical investment adjustment.

THE POLICY MAKING OF THE COMPREHENSIVE MEASURES FOR ECONOMIC STABILIZATION (CMES) AND THE FIRST INVESTMENT ADJUSTMENT

During 1975–78, after the first oil-shock, the new institutions ambitiously pushed the HCIs in an efficient manner. With the overboomed period of 1976–78, however, serious side effects became apparent, not only in the heavy and chemical industrial sectors but also in the whole economy, due to the ultimately overambitious and untimely industrial strategy. After 1978, the economy faced high inflation, accumulated foreign debt, and an unbalanced industrial structure which resulted mainly from overinvestment in the HCIs. Extreme competition among big business firms in heavy and chemical industrial projects led to increasing demands for external financing (see Table 7), which was required to finish ongoing construction and operate factories. The general fiscal policy for retrenchment made the corporations' financial difficulties worse.

By 1978, the dualistic policy structure, which existed between the Planning Office of the HCIPC and the EPB, began to break

Table 7 External fund of corporate business sector
(unit: million won (%))

	1965–69	1970–74	1975–79	1980–84
Indirect financing	87.8 (47.4)	391.2 (55.9)	1,885.7 (56.5)	5,284.4 (53.0)
Borrowing from financial institutions	87.8 (47.4)	387.9 (55.4)	1,883.7 (56.5)	5,001.8 (50.2)
Banks	69.5 (37.5)	282.8 (40.4)	1,197.9 (35.9)	2,372.9 (23.8)
Non-banks	18.3 (9.9)	105.1 (15.0)	685.8 (20.6)	2,628.9 (26.4)
Government loans	–	3.3 (0.5)	2.0 (0.1)	282.6 (2.8)
Direct financing	27.1 (14.6)	145.3 (20.8)	767.9 (23.0)	4,083.7 (41.0)
Stock	26.4 (14.3)	124.6 (17.8)	458.0 (13.7)	2,059.3 (20.7)
Bonds	0.7 (0.4)	12.0 (1.7)	216.5 (6.5)	1,441.9 (14.5)
Commercial paper	–	8.7 (1.2)	93.4 (2.8)	582.5 (5.8)
Foreign debts	70.2 (37.9)	163.3 (23.3)	681.1 (20.4)	601.6 (6.0)
Total	185.2 (100.0)	699.8 (100.0)	3,334.7 (100.0)	9,969.7 (100.0)

Source: Financial System in Korea, September 1985: quotation in Yoon Je Cho and David C. Cole, 'The Role of the Financial Sector in Korea's Structural Adjustment', KDI Working Paper (December 1986), p. 23.

down in the process of economic adjustment. This section will deal with the following: how an economic stability-oriented reform group emerged along with the institutional decay of the state institutions for heavy and chemical industrial promotion, and how the policy measures for economic stabilization were made in the middle of bureaucratic politics including presidential influence.

The emergence of an economic stability-oriented reform

By 1978, a small group within the EPB started to evaluate problems of existing economic policies, including heavy and chemical industrial policy. At that time, however, the dominant strategy of economic policy was to continue the export-oriented growth that was based on heavy and chemical industrialization. In December 1977, the Korea Development Institute (KDI: a state-run economic policy institute that helped EPB's policy-making) compiled a report entitled, 'Long Term Economic and Social Development: 1977–1991' at the request of the EPB. In January 1978, Assistant Minister of Planning Kyung-Sik Kang, as the leader of the reform-oriented group, could not avoid briefing to President Park KDI's future plans that reflected the growth-oriented position of the majority of economic technocrats.[1]

After the report, during the presidential annual visit of inspection, the small group embarked on an investigation of structural problems in the economy. The group was mainly composed of young bureaucrats of the Planning Bureau within the EPB and was led by the Assistant Minister of Planning. During 1978, they conducted a series of studies for a fundamental change of policy goals and instruments. Their works resulted in two internal circular reports entitled, 'Current Problems of the Korean Economy' in March and August 1978. The reports' major proposals for economic stabilization included a change of the financial system towards financial liberalization, measures to counter inflation, and import liberalization. With these studies, the group made an effort to persuade high government officials to realize the need for economic stabilization.

However, they failed to convince high-level decision-makers to adopt their ideas as an official economic policy of the EPB. In 1978, almost all high government officials were obsessed with the rapid heavy and chemical industrial promotion for export-oriented economic growth. These economic technocrats were greatly influenced by President Park's strong commitment to the HCIs. The economic policy-makers, including Park, worried about the high inflation that had resulted from overinvestment, increased issue of currency, and rapid wage increases. Nevertheless, this dominant group regarded these phenomena as the temporary side effects of an economic stage, which could be overcome by a continuous export strategy.

In particular, Park still had a strong will to achieve export-oriented heavy and chemical industrialization. That is, he was determined to pay any price for export-oriented economic growth based on the HCIs. In August 1978, he announced that the country should keep its export promotion policy through heavy and chemical industrial products in spite of its detrimental impact on prices.[2] In December 1978, at a ceremony marking the completion of a plant extension of the Pohang Iron and Steel Company (POSCO), Park declared that the expected output in the cement, iron and steel, shipbuilding, petrochemical, and automobile industries would be ranked within the top ten in the world by 1986.[3]

His economic strategy was further strongly influenced by his national security concerns about the U.S. troop withdrawal.[4] The Carter administration had announced a plan to withdraw U.S. ground troops from Korea in 1977; a portion of the U.S. troops began to leave Korea by 1978.[5] With these security concerns in mind, Park pushed defence industrial promotion towards self-defence that was based on heavy and chemical industrial capacities. He thus continued to rapidly carry out heavy and chemical projects with both the economic and the political rationale.

In addition, the Planning Office of the HCIPC (Planning Office) and the Ministry of Commerce and Industry (MCI) continued to spur heavy and chemical industrial projects for export-oriented economic growth. In December 1978, the Heavy and Chemical Industrial Promotion Assistant Minister Level Practical Committee (HCIPAMLPC), chaired by the Head of the Planning Office, made a decision on the plan of 1979 to manage the National Investment Fund in the HCIs. The committee increased the amount of the fund from 256 billion won in 1978 to 263 billion won in the 1979 plan with the following objective: the entire necessary expenses for supporting the HCIs should be supplied because they would finish preparing heavy and chemical industrial complexes in 1979.[6] The Planning Office continued to plan funds for construction of heavy and chemical industrial complexes and to select firms that would be engaged in such projects.

Likewise, in December 1978, the MCI was determined to expedite exports of such strategic items as heavy construction equipment, machine tools, textile machinery, auto components, and shipbuilding components in the machinery industry by strengthening supportive measures. Moreover, it planned to reinvigorate the local shipbuilding industry, which had suffered from a worldwide depression of the industry, by releasing a total of 121,200 million won in support funds including domestic and foreign capital. At the same time, the ministry planned to release some $1,800 million in foreign loans and 450,000 million won from the national treasury and the state-run Korea Development Bank in 1979 to finance facilities expansions of such strategic export items as machinery, electronics, ships, ¬d automobiles. Thus, the MCI stirred up not only the emerging industries but also the declining industries for the exports of heavy and chemical industrial products. In addition, it decided to increase even the annual production capacity of its already projected third petro-chemical industrial complexes and to shorten the construction period by one year.[7]

Basically, the Ministry of Finance (MF) was in the position to follow the policy of continuous heavy and chemical industrial promotion led by the dominant group that was composed of the MCI and the Planning Office under Park's leadership. Even though it recognized that the tight monetary policy should curb the high inflationary trend of the year, the ministry planned to operate a flexible credit supply scheme. Its credit supply concentrated on export and heavy and chemical industrial financing funds. More long-term bank credit was given to exporters in order to urge overseas sales of heavy and chemical industrial goods on a deferred payment basis. Commercial banks were also instructed to suspend loans to firms with a poor financial status and little retained earnings, and to supply loans to those with a healthy financial structure.[8] Thus, the MF did not consider a fundamental change of the financial policy for economic growth in order to prevent over-boomed heavy and chemical industrial investment.

Policy conflicts among state managers and the policy-making of the CMES

In December 1978, Duck-Woo Nam, a growth-oriented Deputy Prime Minister (the head of the EPB), was replaced by Hyun-Hwak Shin, who was stability-oriented. The reform group success-fully convinced the new EPB head of their economic stabilization programmes. In contrast, they had barely persuaded the former head of the EPB and President Park to implement even anti-inflation policies as temporary measures. The new Deputy Prime Minister firmly supported the reform group and made an effort to receive Park's approval. Thus, the reformers' stabilization pro-grammes became a dominant strategy of economic management within the EPB.

In the end, on 11 January 1979, the EPB reported to the President the 'Current Issues and Policy Measures for Our Economy', which would recommend a drastic change of economic management. Its policy orientation was to consider economic stability along with lower growth, which meant consolidating the base for stability and adjusting the contents for economic growth, including heavy and chemical industrial promotion; financial liberalization, including a raise of interest rates; import liberalization to expand domestic supply; and heavy and chemical industrial adjustment.[9]

The report could not, however, easily change Park's strong commitment to export-oriented economic growth. On 19 January 1979, he confirmed his position on economic strategy during his annual press interview. He objected to the idea that Korean economic management should emphasize economic stabilization by reducing economic growth rate and amount of exports, and then justified a continuous push for heavy and chemical industrial promotion.[10] On 29 January, the Deputy Prime Minister of the EPB briefed President Park during the presidential annual investigation tour. There, Park said that the basic policy direction of the economy was to pursue 'harmony in growth and stability' in such a way that the economic policy would stabilize prices and maintain the continued economic growth.[11] Thus, he allowed for only price stabilization as a measure to prevent high inflation, but still had not accepted the EPB's long-term policy change in economic management.

In addition, the EPB met with resistance not only from the President but also from the MCI. Bureaucratic conflicts occurred mainly between the stability-oriented EPB and the growth-oriented MCI in the process of policy-making for economic stabilization. In January 1979, the EPB was confronted by the MCI as the economic ministries attempted to decide on targets for export and the economic growth rate for 1979: the MCI argued for higher rates of export and economic growth than the EPB. Finally, surprisingly, the government announced the planned export amount of $15.5 billion, which was more than the $15.3 billion planned by the MCI and the $15.0 billion targeted by the EPB.[12]

Furthermore, the MCI presented a report entitled 'Ten Strategic Industries Promotion' in its briefing for Park's annual investigation tour; the Minister of the MCI said that the ministry would put emphasis on the ten strategic industries, including machinery, shipbuilding, electronics, and petrochemicals, in order to reach the whole export target of $50,000 million in the mid-1980s.

Specifically, according to the minister, 'the government plans to expand the facilities of the ten strategic industries by three times and to develop the machine industry as a major export industry'.[13] After hearing his briefing, Park was very satisfied with the ambitious plan. He also expressed the uncomfortable feeling he had had during his investigation tour, thereby indirectly criticizing the EPB's economic stabilization plan. He said, 'recently, there are some absent-minded persons who see export in a negative regard'.[14] The MCI, furthermore, urged big business firms to expand facilities of heavy and chemical industrial production during early 1979.[15]

Nevertheless, the EPB tenaciously continued to ask Park for a shift of economic management towards economic stabilization. Finally, Park made an on-site inspection of the Changwon Machinery Industrial Complex in order to check on heavy industrial overinvestment. After that inspection tour, the President instructed Won-Chul Oh (the Head of the Planning Office of the HCIPC) to examine overlapped investment in the HCIs.[16] In March 1979, he ordered the EPB to investigate heavy and chemical industrial overinvestment and ordered three other agencies to report their independent studies on current economic problems and policy directions of economic management. The three studies were reported to the President for a comparison of ideas.[17] Contents of the reports suggested policy recommendations giving priority to economic stabilization in line with EPB's policy report.

In the end, President Park accepted the EPB's original policy programmes with the following instructions:

> All three reports unanimously indicate that the Korean economy currently faces serious problems. Our economy is suffering from an excessive burden beyond its capacity which hinders sound economic development. Therefore, I may ask the EPB to make a proposal for comprehensive measures to adjust ongoing policies where necessary. The new proposals may have to include such policies as the export drive, the heavy and chemical industry policy, and the rural housing project, although I have endorsed and strongly emphasized their current policies so far. In pursuit of this task, let me suggest that the Vice Minister of the EPB be in charge as the team leader.[18]

President Park requested that the EPB prepare a policy package by synthesizing the three studies.

On 17 April 1979, Deputy Prime Minister Hyun-Hwak Shin announced the Comprehensive Measures for Economic Stabiliz-ation (CMES) that would construct a base of long-term economic stability for the purpose of ending the '30-year-old inflationary trend': a smooth supply-and-demand relationship for daily necessi-ties and stabilization of their prices; tight fiscal policy to generate a fiscal surplus; improvement of the export financing system for selective support; adjustment of heavy and chemical industrial projects; and improvement of the overall banking system. The minister devised these economic guidelines to the effect that under the present economic circumstances, the country was given no choice but to slow down the export drive and scale down heavy and chemical industrial investment in order to cool down the high growth economy.[19]

As shown above, the CMES was formulated without a consensus not only among the economic ministries, including the Planning Office of the HCIPC and the Presidential Secretariat, but also even within the EPB at the initial stage. The coherent and well-coordinated dualistic institutional structure, which by 1973 emerged between the Planning Office of the HCIPC and the EPB, had begun to crumble in the process of heavy and chemical industrial promotion. To make matters worse, by 1979, President Park's ambivalent position had aggravated the institutional disorder of economic policy-making in sharp contrast to his strong leader-ship of the previous years. Therefore, bitter bureaucratic conflicts were expected in the process of implementation even after the announcement of the CMES.

Clearly, then, the long-term and short-term management policies of the EPB, including the tight monetary and fiscal policy, were no longer compatible with the existing heavy and chemical indus-trial policy. The high level of cooperation between the EPB and the Planning Office of the HCIPC had rapidly decreased. Institutional malfunctions in regard to continuous heavy and chemical industrial promotion occurred in the organizational structure led by the Planning Office of the HCIPC. Serious bureaucratic conflicts appeared between the Planning Office of the HCIPC and the MCI, on the one side, and the EPB on the other side: the former's position was to continue and finish planned heavy and chemical industrial projects, whereas the EPB wanted to suspend or delay new projects and adjust overlapping investments.

By 1978, the MCI and the Economic Ministers Roundtable

(Consultation Meeting) guided the licensing and allocation adjustment of heavy and chemical industrial investments, which was independent of the Planning Office and the Heavy and Chemical Industry Promotion Assistant Minister Level Practical Meeting (HCIPAMLPM). The Economic Ministers Roundtable, headed by the Deputy Prime Minister, was established in 1977 to discuss policy proposals or issues for intra-government coordination due to the increase in the number of controversial policy issues.[20] The Planning Office, therefore, had much difficulty in centralizing and coordinating its practically subordinate economic ministries, including the EPB and the MCI, for heavy and chemical industrial promotion.

The next subsection will analyse how this ineffective structure of state institutions had affected the implementation of economic stabilization and the policy-making of the first comprehensive and compulsory adjustment of heavy and chemical industrial investments. It will also show how bureaucratic conflicts occurred; how the institutional decay affected the interests and capacities of state managers, business interest groups, and big business firms; and how they chose their own positions based on their costs and benefits.

The ineffective implementation of economic stabilization: organizational interests and conflicts

The lack of consensus among the economic technocrats (including the President) in the process of policy-making resulted in an incoherent and inconsistent policy operation in the process of policy implementation. The implementation of the CMES occurred in the same kind of institutional disorder as the policy-making, as explained by the following.

The economic stabilization programmes had not been realized in a consistent way because of a lack of strong presidential leadership, organizational conflicts among the economic ministries, and state-big business conflicts up until the time when the military coup-leaders took over political power on 31 May 1980.

Presidential influence

Shortly after the announcement of the CMES on 27 April, President Park explicitly expressed his understanding of the CMES:

In spite of the economic stabilization policy, there is no change of the basic orientation in government economic policy. The CMES was just to slightly reduce economic growth speed as a partial policy adjustment in order to subdue the overheated economy and to stabilize people's daily life.[21]

Park regarded the CMES not as a long-term economic strategy for fundamental policy change but as a short-term management policy. Thus, the EPB could not convince the President of its original purpose to change the existing economic management strategy, even though it succeeded in gaining his approval of the CMES.

Additionally, in 1979, Park was still obsessed with promoting the defence industries for self-defence in the wake of the Carter administration's pending decision on continuing the U.S. troop withdrawal. Later, the Carter administration decided to suspend the plan of ground troop evacuation, but the President continued to make a strong commitment towards further defence industrial promotion and complete security self-reliance.

Furthermore, Park was not satisfied with self-sufficiency in conventional weapons production. By 1979, the government began to push for a transition from military import substitution to export promotion of conventional weapons.[22] Therefore, he did not want to scale down defence-related heavy and chemical industries. Rather, he seemed to think of the defence industries as a sector of sanctuary which could be exempted from the planned adjustment of heavy and chemical industrial investment.

The highly centralized and closed decision-making structure of defence industrialization had been insulated not only from the private sectors but also from bureaucratic conflicts. Policies related to the defence industries were decided by three people: President Park, Won-Chul Oh (the Head of the Planning Office of the HCIPC), and the Director of the Agency for Defence Development (ADD). Moreover, the government 'prohibited any public debate on the validity of the rate and direction of defense industrialization for national-security reasons.'[23] The highly autonomous group, immune to outside pressures, did not take any responsibility for its decisions. As a result, Park was able to easily extricate the defence industries as part of the HCIs from the policy measures for economic stabilization, particularly heavy and chemical industrial adjustment.

Bureaucratic conflicts

The MCI, the Planning Office of the HCIPC (headed by the First Secretary of the Second Presidential Economic Secretariat) and the Presidential Economic Special Aide still supported the priorities of economic growth and unbalanced heavy and chemical industrial promotion, whereas the EPB put a strong emphasis on economic stability and a balanced industrial structure.

The Planning Office objected to any attempts of heavy and chemical industrial investment adjustment and regarded investment adjustment as useless.[24] The MCI mapped out a set of special measures for ailing export firms for fear of a setback of the export drive; it also planned to legislate a Heavy and Chemical Industrial Promotion Law and special laws for key industries to support ongoing heavy and chemical industrial projects more efficiently.[25] Thus, the MCI continued to maintain the existing industrial strategy of the drive for export and HCIs which had been pushed since 1973. The ministry hardly changed its organizational interests and policy instruments even though it had agreed reluctantly to several heavy and chemical industrial adjustments at the minimum level.

The Ministry of Finance (MF) was in a position of ambivalence. In general, the ministry supported the tight fiscal and monetary policy of the EPB during the first half of 1979. In February 1979, the Minister of the MF called on entrepreneurs to refrain from expanding their facilities in line with the ongoing anti-inflationary efforts while the MCI planned to promote the ten planned strategic industries.[26] In April, after the bankruptcy of the Yulsan Business Group (one of the largest conglomerates), the MF was determined to strictly control concessional export financing loans and to suspend loans to financially ill-managed firms. It decided to establish a new export financing system because exporters, who possessed export letters of credit, were almost automatically given concessional export financing loans in spite of the ongoing tight monetary policy.[27]

However, the MF was in a position opposite the EPB in dealing with a reform of the financial system as a policy guideline of the CMES. Nevertheless, the Bank of Korea, which had been controlled by the MF and followed its policy instructions, supported the EPB's financial policy. The EPB and the Bank of Korea argued for a hike, or realization of bank interest rates and a privatization of commercial banks for financial liberalization. The MF, however, had no intention of raising bank interest rates for fear of creating a cost-push factor for business enterprises; instead, it tried to raise exchange rates for export promotion. The MF was also reluctant to allow the existing commercial banks under its control to go public at that time, despite persistent demands for immediate privatization from the banking community.[28] Furthermore, after the decline in business activities during the latter half of 1979, the ministry provided heavy and chemical industrial projects and export firms with additional policy loans against the policy orientation of financial liberalization.

Conflicts between bureaucrats and big businessmen

Big businessmen were also in an ambiguous and self-contradictory position. On 4 January 1979, the chairmen's group of the FKI (the Federation of Korean Industries: the big business interest group) boldly criticized the economic management of the government in its annual press conference. The group strongly demanded businessmen's participation in an economic policy-making process in opposition to the top-down economic policy-making and implementation by the government; moreover, they argued for a change of economic management from the 'government-led' to a 'private-initiated' economy. As a practical plan for this diversion of economic administration, the big businessmen called for the establishment of a permanent organization where the business circle would discuss, in a sufficient manner, policy alternatives with government officials before adopting an economic policy; and they also asked for a price increase for their mono-oligopolized products, financial liberalization including privatization of commercial banks, and state non-intervention in their investment activities and in the selection of chairmen for business interest organizations.[29]

In response to these demands, the EPB harshly attacked these requests, saying that the big businessmen were obsessed with their selfish interests under the pretence of a 'private-initiated' economy. Basically, the ministry agreed to the change of economic management towards a private-led economy through such long-term policy goals as reduced state intervention in firms' activities, increased market function, and financial liberalization. However, the EPB's views were different from those of big business regarding ways to promote a business and market autonomy. The EPB emphasized that big business firms had benefited from their privileged access to supports and protections from the government in the state-led economy, and, worried about the likelihood that without government regulations, big businesses would dominate the economy in the situations of incomplete market competition and high business concentration. The EPB's bureaucrats said, 'the big businessmen seem to misunderstand "private-initiated" as "*Jaebols* [conglomerates]-led" economy', and 'a raise in prices of their product will maximize their profits'.[30]

Shortly after the announcement of the CMES, the peak business organizations (the FKI, the KCCI, the KFSMB, and the KFTA) demanded a mitigation of the tight fiscal and monetary policy in order to reduce current financial difficulties.[31] Thereafter, they continued to call for lower interest rates as a measure for loosening the policy of retrenchment. The business circle cared little about price stabilization. However, the Deputy Prime Minister of the EPB and the Minister of the MF rejected these demands in several meetings with the chairmen of the peak business organizations.[32]

Ironically, big businessmen wanted continuous government support for their heavy and chemical industrial projects with privileged access to policy loans and low interest rates. In this respect, their position was similar to the MCI. They believed that big business interests could be continuously maximized by adhering to the policy goal of export-oriented economic growth and the economic strategy of heavy and chemical industrial promotion based on business concentration.

As a result, this mechanism of economic adjustment, which was characterized by unstable institutions, inconsistent and conflicting organizational interests, and fluctuating organizational capacities, also operated in the policy-making and implementation of heavy and chemical industrial investment adjustment (HCIIA).

The policy-making of the first comprehensive HCIIA

Just as the tight monetary policy for price stabilization was the essence of the long-term measures of the CMES, so the HCIIA policy was the core of the short-term measures. In the Korean history of state-business relations, the investment realignment was one of the strongest state interventions in individual firms. The investment adjustment was an authoritarian intervention in businessmen's investment decision-making that was in line with the disposals of financially ill-managed firms, among highly foreign-debted firms in the late 1960s and as part of the so-called industrial rationalization in the mid-1980s.[33]

The former case in 1979 was attempted through mergers and investment reallocations among the largest business groups, whereas the latter cases in the late 1960s and the mid-1980s were mainly achieved by large conglomerates which acquired financially depressed individual companies. The disposals of poorly managed business firms heightened business concentration in the name of scale merits for economic efficiency, which resulted in business groups' rapid growth based on financial privileges. In contrast to these policy measures, the HCIIAs were to constrain big business competitive expansion without sufficient financial incentives and thus were unsuccessful in the wake of conflicts both between the state and big business, and among big business firms.

This subsection will explain in what ways and to what extent the declining institutional capacities of the state had affected interests and capabilities of state managers and big businessmen in the cases of HCIIAs, and subsequently led to conflicts within the state-big business governing coalition.

Shortly after the announcement of the CMES, the Investment Industry Adjustment Committee (IIAC) was established according to one of the policy measures of the CMES; it was composed of the Deputy Prime Minister of the EPB (the chairman) and economic ministers, including the Head of the Planning Office and the presidential first economic secretaries.[34]

The meeting of the committee was held on 30 April. There, serious bureaucratic conflicts appeared between the EPB on the one side, and the MCI and the Planning Office on the other side. That is, the EPB argued for a substantial adjustment in overall heavy and chemical industrial sectors while the MCI asserted a minimum adjustment which would exclude projects already under construction. The MCI's views were similar to those of the business circle, which worried about the expected heavy burdens of interest rates from high external financing, if suspension of ongoing construction works were to occur.[35]

In this meeting, the committee could not make a decision on specific ways and objects of investment adjustment. The committee members came to an agreement in principle only about orientation of adjustment and criteria for selecting concerned firms. The prin-

ciples of investment adjustment were as follows in line with the
concerned contents of the CMES:[36]

Direction of support
   (i) Improve the underlying environment for heavy industrial-
       ization through manpower development, liberalization of
       foreign technology inducement, and the establishment of an
       efficient financial supporting system.
  (ii) Build up the centralized support systems until sufficient
       technological expertise has been accumulated.
 (iii) Strengthen competitiveness through selective specialization.

Projects Subject to Investment Adjustment
   (i) Projects which lack long-term competitiveness, e.g., goods
       which are much cheaper to import than to produce dom-
       estically.
  (ii) Projects liable to insolvency due to overcapacity or dupli-
       cated investment.
 (iii) Projects in which the sponsors have invested a very low
       proportion of their own capital and have relied heavily on
       borrowings.

Implementation of Adjustments
   (i) New Projects: complete evaluation of the feasibility of those
       projects which involve investments of more than five
       million dollars in foreign loans or loans in foreign currency.
  (ii) Projects yet to be started: assessment of the possibility of
       postponement or cancellation.
 (iii) Projects under construction: examination of measures for
       suspending construction where possible and for raising
       additional funds.
 (iv) The execution of postponed projects to be considered
       during the 5th Five-Year Economic Development Plan.

Finally, on 8 May 1979, the EPB made a compromise with the
MCI, agreeing that the scope of adjustment would be limited
to the shipbuilding and machinery industries. In particular, the
agreement was supposed to focus on both the Okpo shipbuilding
and the Hyundai International machinery manufacturing construc-
tions.[37] Therefore, the EPB yielded to challenges from the MCI
and the Planning Office in regard to the scope of investment
adjustment.[38]
Until then, they could not reach an agreement regarding a

specific scheme for, and ways of, adjustment. For this task, the committee established the Working Level Adjustment Committee as its subordinate organization. This working committee consisted of working-level bureaucrats from the Bureau of Machinery Industry in the MCI, the Section of Investment Investigation in the EPB, and the concerned bureau in the MF; it was led by their section chiefs.

First, the EPB's bureaucrats evaluated the concerned projects in terms of demand prospects, amounts of investment, and degrees of profitability. The MCI's team investigated the technological aspects and financial situations of the firms. In an initial stage of the policy-making process, they asked concerned big businessmen for their views on the objects and ways of investment adjustment.[39]

Here, the big businessmen made every effort to persuade the bureaucrats to accept their own ideas so that they could maximize their firms' profits or monopolize their product markets. Hyundai International asserted that it had to monopolize domestic supply until the end of 1985 because the domestic markets of power-generating and heavy construction equipments were too small. It also justified its monopoly of production on the basis that the industrial plants could not be exported without an adequate experience of technological accumulation based on domestic supply. On the other hand, other concerned companies' views were as follows: basically, the heavy industries should be oriented to exports because of the small domestic market; the government should not grant monopoly rights of production and sales to Hyundai International, which had suffered from financial difficulties due to its high debt-equity ratio; an excessive protection of the financially ill-managed company would deprive firms of business confidence in investment; and thus, concerned firms should compete with one another in the free market for the purposes of keeping costs down and developing high technology.[40]

After listening to big businessmen's ideas, the working committee completely closed its policy-making process in order to insulate it from business influence. The contradictory positions of the concerned economic ministries existed in the process of policy-making for the first HCIIA on 25 May 1979. The MCI and the EPB agreed to the scope and object of HCIIA with the minimum consensus that heavy and chemical industrial projects under construction should be completed except for those of the excessively overinvested power-generating equipment sector. For the most part, their conclusions were not to curtail the already overheated actual investments but to scale down future investment plans.

The essential policy measure was to reduce the four companies, which belonged to the largest business groups in the field of power-generating equipment, to two companies: merging the Hyundai Heavy Industries Co. and the Hyundai International Inc. through a capital increase of the former, on the one hand, and merging the Samsung Heavy Industries Co. with the Daewoo Heavy Industries Co., or interlocking their investments, on the other hand.[41] This compulsory measure imposed the strict principle of adjustment – the so-called 'first merging, later settling accounts' between the business groups. Only merged business entities were supposed to be eligible for taking part in biddings to be hosted by the Korea Electric Power Corporation (KEPC) from that time. However, it was said that international biddings for power plant construction would not be affected by the guideline. The reason was that the Ministry of Power and Resources (MPR) objected to making the domestic firms monopolize the production of power plant facilities. The ministry and the KEPC wanted to open biddings for planned nuclear or thermoelectric power plant construction to both domestic and foreign companies. The organizational interests of the MPR were concerned with cost-down and high technology.[42]

The remaining measures were to suspend, postpone, or reserve only planned projects in such fields as tyres, zinc smelters, industrial machines, and diesel engines: the introduction of technological know-how from the Caterpillar Co. of the United States for manufacturing heavy construction equipment, requested by the Daewoo Heavy Industries Co., would be considered after completion of the proposed two-tier industrial structure of power-generating equipment production; the Okpo Shipbuilding Yard constructed by the Daewoo Heavy Industries Co. would be continued; the Hyundai International Business Group (Hanla Business Group) should dispose of its key subsidiaries that were not directly linked with the Changwon industrial plant construction project; the planned construction of the third petrochemical industrial complex would be considered later after taking into account the international oil supply-and-demand situation; zinc smelter construction would be postponed for another year; two tyre manufacturing plant construction projects planned by the Hyundai Business Group and the Daewoo Business Group would not be considered for the time being; and construction of a diesel engine manufacturing plant for heavy construction equipment would be suspended. As a result, according to the policy announcement, the whole scheme of investment adjustment was said to save 372,721 million won, which would otherwise have been invested in the aforementioned projects.

As shown above, the scope and degree of adjustment were insufficient in terms of the original purpose of HCIIA in line with the CMES. As a matter of fact, as a whole, the scheme of adjustment was little more than a form of traffic control that dealt with overcompetition among business groups in the HCI sectors. The contents of the adjustment on 25 May reflected the conflict between the EPB and the MCI, and the position of the EPB constrained by Park's firm adherence to the HCIs that included and were closely related to the defence industries.

Big business responses to the investment adjustment

Shortly after the announcement of the adjustment on 28 May the business circle criticized the adjustment of investment: the investment realignment was not based on a long-term policy of heavy and chemical industrial development, but was instead a myopic and temporary policy to avoid investment pressures that had resulted from the government-led heavy and chemical industrial promotion. The group also denounced the compulsory government measure to suspend financial supports and ignore interest conflicts between business groups. The concerned business groups made complaints about the merger plan in the field of power-generating equipment. Hyundai International said that the company had been technically tied up with foreign companies after its approved right of monopolizing power plant facilities construction in May 1977, and that it was thus unreasonable to merge with the Hyundai Heavy Industries. The Daewoo Business Group said that it was an ambiguous traffic control to merge the Daewoo Heavy Industries, including a joint venture with West Germany, with the Samsung Heavy Industries with Japan, for boiler production.[43] The business groups resisted the compulsory investment adjustment, as it did not reflect their individual interests. They emphasized that state managers would have much difficulty in realizing the merging plan because of the tie-ups of joint ventures and technology.

Ironically, before the announcement of the adjustment policy, the bureaucrats received notes of mutual agreement from the concerned big businessmen on the scheme of power plant facilities adjustment. At that time, the owners of the business groups had no choice but to agree to the compulsory merger or interlocking plan that the state managers had imposed. The four business groups were compelled to accept the adjustment way of consolidation suggested by the authoritarian government because their high debt-equity firms still depended heavily on domestic and foreign loans that had a government guarantee. The government still controlled credit allocation through policy loans and investment licensing to a large extent, even though the state's control over the financial system had rapidly decreased. Thus, the government could always let a big business firm go bankrupt by suspending loans as a penalty for its non-compliance with government policy.

Even after their reluctant consent to the investment realignment, however, the business groups expressed their complaints about the policy measure, as outlined above. Subsequently, they skilfully opposed implementation of the mergers in a passive and indirect way. The next section will show two things: first, how the policy implementation of the first HCIIA was delayed in light of conflicts within the bureaucracy, between bureaucrats and big businessmen, and among the business groups; and second, how the process had occurred within the context of inconsistent and crumbling implementation of economic stabilization along with the political crisis of the authoritarian regime's breakdown.

THE CRUMBLING STATE-BIG BUSINESS GOVERNING COALITION

During the first half of 1979, the authoritarian government created tensions within the symbiotic state-big business relationships, which had formed its supporting coalition, by imposing the tight money policy and the compulsory investment adjustment. In the economic crisis management, the government took the policy measures of the CMES and the first HCIIA against even big business interests. These policies had rapidly decreased the confidence of big as well as small and medium businesses in government economic policy. In particular, the big business confidence, which had been enormously enhanced through heavy and chemical industrial promotion, plummeted due to the state intervention in investment decision-making.

To make matters worse, growing labour activation led to wage increases, thereby aggravating the financial structure of the already financially troubled companies during the second half of 1979. Furthermore, a vehement labour strike gave rise to a political crisis that resulted in the expulsion of an opposition party leader from the National Assembly membership and, finally, the assassination of Park. Thus, in this atmosphere of political instability, big businessmen, who benefited more than any other group from the authoritarian regime, felt insecure in their business activities.

Ironically, the business groups could not stop financing more funds for ongoing heavy and chemical industrial projects. In spite of the sharp decline of big business confidence in investment, they were trapped in continuous investments for ongoing construction and operation of facilities.

Faced with the economic and political crisis, during the latter half of 1979, the government attempted to find a breakthrough to ease big business concerns about the financial difficulties of the depressed and overinvested HCIs, rather than to help a number of ailing small and medium-sized firms and soothe the ever-mounting popular discontent caused by the ensuing economic recession. That is, within the limit of tight money policy, state managers intended to finish ongoing massive projects except for the objects of investment adjustment in the HCIs that business groups had dominated. They also attempted to enhance low operation of already constructed factories in the HCIs through an effective and selective financing support system.

Financial difficulties in the HCIs

The economic situation worsened during 1979. The rate of unemployment became 4 percent in the first quarter of 1979; and the current wholesale and consumer prices at the end of July 1979 were 19.9 percent and 14.3 percent, respectively, which already surpassed the planned guidelines of constraint (10.5 percent and 12.5 percent, respectively). In the business sector, 3,244 (22.3 percent) companies reduced and 624 (4.3 percent) suspended or closed down operation among the 14,640 small and medium-sized firms; the Yulsan Business Group, one of largest business groups, went bankrupt in April; several large business groups dishonoured a bill and the government saved the conglomerates that faced bankruptcy by means of special rescue funds and by disposing of their affiliated companies.[44] In addition, the operation ratios of HCI sectors in August 1979 were as follows: general machinery (64.4 percent), electrical machinery (72.5 percent), transport machinery (43.8 percent), iron and steel (73.9 percent), and non-ferrous metal (54.8 percent).[45]

The government faced the dilemma of whether or not it would continually support ongoing construction and operation of heavy and chemical industrial projects. A huge amount of financing funds was required to finish construction of projects and to normalize the operation of already built facilities. The financial demands of the major heavy and chemical enterprises amounted to 1,907 billion won, mainly for equipment investment (1,358 billion won) and loan repayment (225 billion won) during 1979. The funds were supposed to be provided by self-financing of 562 billion won, foreign capital financing of 554 billion won, and domestic capital financing of 791 billion won. However, the domestic loans available amounted to only 308 billion won; thus, the predicted shortfall of domestic capital was 483 billion won.[46] In addition, in 1979, 99 percent of the investments in heavy and chemical facilities depended on external financing funds. To make matters worse, some companies under construction began to repay their loans even before they began operation of their factories. These firms were thus compelled to borrow additional loans for redemption.

The average operation ratio of sixty firms in the Changwon Machinery Industrial Complex, the essential estate of the HCIs, was below 30 percent in September 1979. The heavy industrial companies suffered seriously from a financial shortage because half of their turnover went to pay for the principals and interests on their loans. The MCI planned to offer the support funds of 360 billion won to this sector until the end of 1979.[47] However, the government could not provide an adequate amount of rescue funds for the financially depressed factories within the limits of tight money policy. In particular, Hyundai International, which was supposed to be taken over by the Hyundai Business Group according to the first HCIIA, lacked funds to finish its construction works: its shortage of domestic loans was 53,000 million won in 1979. The heavy equipment and general machinery facilities, which had been already built by Hyundai International, were in very low operation ratios due to a lack of orders from the small domestic market. At that time, some commentators pointed out cynically that the entire amount planned for investment in the Hyundai International facilities (the original amount: 350 billion won, the adjusted amount: 290 billion won) could rescue all the financially troubled small and medium firms.[48]

The activation of labour unions: the limits of state corporatist control

In 1979, rapidly growing labour demands and political crises also contributed indirectly to the sharp decline of business confidence in economic activities. State corporatist control over labour unions through the FKTU (Federation of Korean Trade Unions) and industrial federations had been eroding in the late 1970s. The sources of the institutional decay were not only growing activation of labour unions in opposition to the leadership of union leaders in the national and industrial peak organizations, but also increasing rank-and-file demands and protests at the enterprise level.[49]

Industrial workers' consciousness grew as a result of the side effects of growth-oriented industrialization through labour repression: increasingly unequal income distribution, unjust rewards for hard and long work, and a sense of relative deprivation in a rapidly growing economy. The unequal income distribution had worsened on a national scale. The income share of the lowest 40 percent of urban households decreased from 18.9 percent in 1970 to 15.3 percent in 1980, while that of the highest 20 percent increased from 43.0 percent to 46.9 percent in that period.[50] In the mid-1970s, a split at the enterprise level occurred between state-controlled unions and the activated autonomous labour unions from the FKTU. The number of labour unions from the latter group was small. But they were supported by students, intellectuals, and religious organizations – mainly the Urban Industrial Mission and the JOC (Jeunesse Ouvrière Chretienne: the Young Men's Catholic Labour Association). The labour union movement became a driving force of labour activation.

Another source of labour activation came from national labour union leaders.[51] This trend moved in opposition to the businessmen's position on labour control mechanisms; employers and their associations wanted to achieve wage settlements and keep wage bargaining processes restricted in a single company. In 1979, the FKTU and the national industrial federations of labour unions

intervened in some cases of wage settling even though wage bargaining generally took place at the enterprise level.[52] In January,
the FKTU argued for an average wage rise ratio of 48 percent,
whereas the KEA (Korean Employers' Association) insisted on
that of 19.2 percent. In response to this conflict, the government
instructed the two parties to restrict wage increases within 20
percent. National industrial federations of labour unions in such
industries as textiles and chemicals suggested a wage increase ratio
that conflicted with industrial business associations. Later, the
government determined their wage increases with adjustment
authority. Despite the state-controlled wage settling, the increasing
labour pressures and disputes, which generally occurred in small
and medium firms, led to rapid wage rises aggravating the high
inflation. As a result, the government's tight monetary policy could
not satisfy financing demands (for operation and ongoing
construction) of financially depressed firms and also reduced business confidence in new investments. Finally, the limit of labour
control, as I will discuss later, ignited a series of political crises
that led to Park's assassination and to the breakdown of the authoritarian regime.

Policy changes in economic crisis and bureaucratic conflicts

Among the different organizational interests, the groups' capacities
of policy-making depended on presidential influence. In other
words, an ultimate policy decision-making was determined by
which group or actor was able to convince the President of the
merits of its policy alternative. A typical case of such a power
struggle took place among the economic ministries and big businessmen in the process of implementing economic stabilization
policy. This was the so-called 'economic *coup d'état*' on 25 June
1979.[53]

The government suddenly neglected the overall orientation of
anti-high-inflationary policy and expanded preferential financing
to support export firms. It revised export financing loan guidelines
in order to reinvigorate the sluggish export industries. The
maximum amount of concessional loans, which local exporters
could use on the basis of export letters of credit, was increased by
30 won per one U.S. dollar across the board.[54]

The process of policy-making occurred in the absence of Deputy
Prime Minister Hyun-Hawk Shin and Assistant Minister Kyung-

Sik Kang of the EPB, the core reformers for economic stabilization, who were participating in an international conference. Ironically, the decision of the CMES was made while Minister of the
MCI Kak-Kyu Choi was also abroad. These abnormal and
untimely policy decision-makings showed how serious bureaucratic conflicts had been in the process of economic policy formulation and implementation.

When influential big businessmen (owners of the largest business
groups) took part in the Expanded Meeting for Trade Promotion,
presided over by President Park, they demanded an increase of
export financing funds to break through export stagnation. The
MCI also reported to Park, in collaboration with Presidential Economic Special Aide Duk-Woo Nam, the financial difficulties of
export companies; their demands were approved by the President.

When the two EPB members returned from abroad, they were
very embarrassed by this sudden policy change. Their views ran
counter to the policy change, but they could not go against the
President. The Deputy Prime Minister visited Park and persuaded
him to implement the policy measure of export financing in a
cautious manner so that the revised export financing system should
not impede the overall tight money policy.

On the day after the announcement of the new export financing
rules, Hyun-Hwak Shin, at a meeting with reporters, said that the
policy measure was mapped out within the scope of the ongoing
policy of tight money control; that is, as of June, the increase of
the total money supply by 25.5 percent and that of money supply
by 11 percent would be manageable within the planned increase
of money supply (25 percent) of 1979 and left some room for
loosening the ongoing tight money control. He also said that the
government would still continue to pursue a fiscal and monetary
policy of retrenchment despite its measures of financial support.[55]
The head of the EPB tried to solve the policy conflicts in this
way.

However, the policy measures of EPB-initiated economic stabilization became ineffective after the measure of expanding export
funds as a turning point. In spite of the advice of the Deputy
Prime Minister, the President was already prepared to prevent a
further decline of business activities and pull up, to some degree,
big business confidence, even at the sacrifice of anti-inflation policies. On 12 July President Park declared, at the Expanded Meeting
for Trade Promotion where the owners of the largest business

groups had gathered, that there would be no more investment adjustment in the HCIs. On the same day, the government announced the upward readjustment of the predicted ratios of increase in wholesale and consumer prices for the end of 1979 from 14 percent and 16 percent to 24–25 percent and 21–22 percent, respectively.[56]

In the aggravated economic situation during the latter half of 1979, the MCI's technocrats began to reinvigorate export and heavy and chemical industries and to mitigate the tight money policy of the EPB as their general policy guideline. As a result, the MCI seemed to take the initiative in industrial policy management. The ministry tried to find a breakthrough in these industries in order to get out of the worsening economy. In August, it decided to take public measures to support heavy and chemical industrial development. It regarded as undesirable that big industrial plants almost near completion should be idled simply to observe the tight money policy guidelines; thus, it planned to extend operating funds to those big business firms for their normal operation.[57]

The MF followed the MCI's position; in August, it planned to expand the domestic credit supply, which would increase by 95,600 million won in the government sector and 1,216,500 million won in the private sector during the July to December period.[58] As a matter of fact, at the end of July, before the public announcements of its forthcoming support of the industries, the government already supplied, in absolute secrecy, nine big business firms in the HCIs with 83,000 million won as part of an emergency policy for heavy and chemical industrial rescue funds. Shortly after the ministries' policy statements on 30 August, the Economic Ministers Meeting, which was also held under tight secrecy, decided to provide 200,000 million won for thirty-eight firms in the defence and heavy and chemical industries.[59]

Interestingly, these two supportive measures occurred in secret; furthermore, the former took place even before the public announcements and the subsequent official agreement of the concerned ministries. There was a high possibility that the first case was implemented by the MCI and MF, under Park's approval and without a consensus with the EPB, by bypassing the Economic Ministers Meeting or the Economic Ministers Roundtable. The second case seemed to have the secret meeting in order to avoid showing the inconsistent policy change to the public. In addition, the policy-makers carried out both these supports confidentially, for they chose the financially troubled firms in a discretionary manner and had to head off complaints from other firms. Later, the government decided to aid fourteen heavy and chemical industrial firms in September and thirty-four firms in October with 97,300 million won and 125,000 million won, respectively.[60] Therefore, the accumulated amount of the special rescue funds for heavy and chemical industrial firms (505,300 million won) surpassed that of the expected cut from the first HCIIA (372,700 million won) by 132,600 million won.

Park agreed to the partial pump-priming measures to cope with the deepening economic crisis. The economic decline had been aggravated not only by the second international oil-shock but also by the socio-political crisis, triggered by a violent labour dispute, which I will detail later. Thus, given challenges to his authority, Park seemed to be making serious efforts to prevent a breakdown of the state-big business governing coalition that had maintained his own legitimacy, under the authoritarian regime, based on export- and growth-oriented heavy and chemical promotion.

State managers' and big businessmen's reactions to labour pressures

In August 1979, the Y.H. labour incident[61] broke out as a result of the growing grassroot labour movement and the strong protests of leaders who opposed Park's authoritarian regime during the late 1970s.[62] The labour strike was instigated by the Urban Industrial Mission and encouraged by the major opposition party. Government officials regarded the anti-government coalition between labour and the opposition party to be a serious threat to the regime's security. In response to the labour dispute, the government repressed the opposition party on the one side and took new policy measures for labour control on the other side.

Shortly after the incident, President Park emphasized labour-management cooperation to overcome the situation of economic emergency; he ordered the agencies concerned to investigate actual incidents of outside forces' intervention in labour disputes and to take proper steps to solve labour-management problems.[63] According to Park's instructions, the state managers' countermeasures were to reorganize existing state corporatist control over labour unions on the one hand and to reinforce non-corporatist control over labour-management relations on the other hand.

First, the Workers' Welfare Policy Deliberation Committee (WWPDC) was held for the first time since its establishment. It was set up under the jurisdiction of the EPB in July 1978 according to a special presidential decree. Major decisions of the meeting were to offer financial support to solve labour-management problems within the restrictions of the government's tight money policy, to cut off labour disputes from the interventions of external groups, and to establish a dismissal investigation system.[64] The meeting of the committee was quickly arranged after the Y.H. incident. The government attempted to solve labour disputes by imitating corporatist arrangements of Western European countries that deal with labour-management problems among the state, capital, and labour. In reality, the committee did not implement collective wage bargaining and dealt with labour-management issues within the limit of labour union autonomy, although its institutional structure resembled the liberal corporatist mechanism.[65]

Second, the MCI attributed the Y.H. case to an unsuccessful implementation of the Factory Saemaul (new community) Movement through cooperation between the labour and the management. Thus, the ministry came up with a set of comprehensive measures to revitalize the factory movement drive.[66] The selective incentives to business firms were planned to prevent a recurrence of the Y.H. incident: special funds of some 1,000 million won would be given to the industrial firms that were successful in implementing the movement by increasing productivity and labour-management cooperation; and the government would seriously consider extending tax favours and bank loan privileges to the business firms that would greatly improve working conditions and welfare facilities for their workers. In addition, the Labour-Management Councils within companies, then held once a month, would be increased to twice a month to promote more frequent exchanges between workers and managers.

Finally, the government and the ruling party agreed to a revision of labour relation laws, especially in order to prevent external intervention in labour disputes.[67] The FKTU and the KEA expressed their suggestions for the planned revision.[68] The FKTU argued for labour contracts between industrial federations of labour unions and employers' organizations instead of the existing labour-management negotiations at the enterprise level. Its purpose was to enhance workers' bargaining power. On the other hand, the KEA asserted that the functions of existent Labour-Management Councils within individual firms should be reinforced. Their reasoning was that labour-management inter-actions at the industrial level would lead to a spread of firm level labour disputes to each industrial sphere. Supporting the big businessmen's position, the government excluded a change of the collective bargaining system from the agenda of planned revision. The state managers objected to the industrial collective bargaining system, citing the fact that 95 percent of all labour disputes had been solved at the enterprise level.

Therefore, the authoritarian government reacted to the volatile labour unrest by attempting to increase businessmen's rapidly fall-ing confidence in their investment decisions. That is, the state managers imposed tighter control over labour unions, including the FKTU by the labour policy-making mechanism: they tried to minimize the collective bargaining power of the peak labour organizations with a view to solving labour disputes within indi-vidual firms. They also emphasized labour-management cooper-ation through direct negotiation in order to deprive the workers' collective bargaining power in advance by bypassing unit labour unions. Moreover, the incentives for improving labour-manage-ment harmony were directly oriented towards employers rather than employees.

As shown above, the government's crisis management demon-strated its efforts to overcome the economic crisis through the economic adjustment between the state and business, excluding labour.[69] A typical policy measure towards this end was introduced on 13 August 1979, when the Administration of Labour Affairs and the Ministry of Health and Social Affairs asked for 100 billion won in special funds to be used for preventing further unemploy-ment. The EPB rejected this bid for financial support because it would not be compatible with the general strict monetary policy.[70] Ironically, however, as I mentioned previously, the government supplied in strict secrecy huge special funds for the financially depressed big business firms in the HCIs.

In addition, the government did not pay adequate attention to permanent or temporary shutdowns and short-time operations of small and medium firms, whereas it was very sensitive to those of big business firms and, thus, supported emergent and special funds. The number of those cases among small and medium companies had been rapidly increasing during the first and second quarters of 1979. In August, during the emergency Economic Ministers Meeting in the presidential house (the Blue House), the Deputy Prime Minister of the EPB reported to the President on the 'Recent Economic Situation and Present Countermeasures', saying that it was inevitable that financially troubled firms would close down or reduce their operation in the process of economic stabilization in a retrenchment economy.[71] Therefore, unlike the advanced democratic countries' reform response during economic crisis, the authoritarian regime forced labour and small and medium businesses to bear the costs of economic crisis adjustment. On the other hand, it made every effort to minimize big business costs to such an extent that the sharp decline of big business confidence would not threaten the legitimacy of political power, which state managers in power seats had justified in the name of rapid economic growth during the 1970s.

Under this basic governing orientation of economic crisis management, President Park was not prepared to adopt the new long-term policy goals and reforms proposed by the EPB. The EPB's policy-makers regarded the CMES as an epoch-making policy change for short- and long-term management. However, Park wanted to accept the measures for economic stabilization as short-term management policies, including the investment adjustment during the period of economic crisis. Moreover, he thought that the measures should not be strictly applied to the export and heavy and chemical industries for short-term management but should maintain flexibility.

President Park was very reluctant to slacken the rapid promotion of the HCIs, related to the defence industries, under the condition of overcapacity because of the U.S. troop withdrawal planned by the Carter administration. Even after the cancellation of the troop evacuation, he continued to promote the defence industries towards the goal of complete self-defence and the industrial transition from military import substitution to export orientation. Just as the political rationale of national security had affected the economic rationale of hasty and ambitious heavy and chemical industrial motives in the early 1970s, so did the political logic of self-defence expedite the same economic logic of rapid and massive heavy and chemical industrial promotion in the latter half of the 1970s.

Ironically, however, in the early 1970s, Park's strong commitment to the HCIs to improve military capacities built the highly centralized and coordinated state institutions for heavy and chemical industrialization, whereas, in the late 1970s, his firm will for self-defence facilitated the inconsistent economic stabilization policies, including the heavy and chemical industrial investment adjustment, which resulted from the sharp bureaucratic conflicts.

In the end, until the regime breakdown of Park's assassination on 26 October 1979, the government had not effectively implemented the policies of the CMES. The worsened economic depression during the second half of 1979, which was accompanied by the socio-political crisis, resulted in the slight policy change of loosening the tight money policy. In brief, the policy measures for economic stabilization had drastically decreased big business confidence and had led to conflicts within the state-big business governing coalition. Nevertheless, the authoritarian government did not want a collapse of the ruling coalition between the state and big business (its supporting partner) at the risk of suffering political costs of ungovernability or regime breakdown.

NOTES

1 For the policy-making process of the Comprehensive Measures for Economic Stabilization (CMES) of 17 April 1979, see Kyung-Sik Kang, *Beyond Economic Stability* (Seoul: Korean Economic Daily News Press, 1988), pp. 28–36 (in Korean); KDI, *Collection of Government Documents and Study Reports Related to Economic Stabilization Policies*, Vol. I, pp. 17–24; EPB, *Economic Policy of Development Period: Twenty Years' History of the EPB* (Seoul: 1982), pp. 200–1; and In-Jong Whang, 'Korea's Economic Management for Structural Adjustment in the 1980s', *KDI Working Paper* 8606 (December 1986), pp. 10–20.

2 *70s' Korean Chronology* (Seoul: Chungsa Press, 1984), p. 371 (in Korean).

3 *The Chosun Daily News*, 9 December 1978.

4 See 'Annual Press Interview on January 18, 1978' in the Office of the Presidential Secretariat, *Collection of President Park's Speeches*, Vol. 15, pp. 10–22 (in Korean).

5 For Park's reaction to the plan of troop withdrawal and his big push for defence industrial promotion see Jung-Ryum Kim, *op. cit.* [Chapter 3, note 6], Nos. 61, 62, 63, 93, and 94.

6 Planning Office of the HCIPC, *op. cit.*, (1980) [Chapter 3, note 8], p. 141.

7 See *The Korea Herald*, 5, 13, and 14 December 1978.

8 See *The Korea Herald*, 28 and 31 October, 4 and 10 November 1978.

9 See KDI, *Collection of Documents and Study Reports Related to Economic Stabilization Policies*, Vol. 1, pp. 221–56.

10 See the Office of the Presidential Secretariat, *Collection of President Park's Speeches*, Vol. 16, pp. 63–65.

11 *The Korea Herald*, 30 January and *The Chosun Daily News*, 30 January.

12 *The Chosun Daily News*, 7 and 9 January 1979.

13 *70s' Chronology*, p. 393; and *The Korea Herald*, 9 February 1979.

14 An interview; and Kyung-Sik Kang, *op. cit.*, p. 35.

15 Minister of the MCI Kak-Kyu Choi was opposed to a drastic change of economic strategy in a National Assembly conference, saying that the existing export-led economic policy should be continued for the Korean economic development even in the process of economic stabilization (see the National Assembly Records, *The 4th Session of the Commerce and Industry Committee in the 101st National Assembly Meeting* [Seoul: 1979], pp. 26–33 [in Korean].

16 An interview.

17 The reports were 'Current Issues and Policy Directions for Our Economy' by the Bank of Korea, 'Direction for the Economic Stabilization Policies' by the KDI, and 'Current Issues and Policy Measures for Our Economy' by the National Council on Economy and Science. See the KDI, *Collection of Government Documents and Study Reports Related to Economic Stabilization Policies*, Vol. 1, pp. 297–344.

18 Quoted from In-Jong Whang's interview (In-Jong Whang, *op. cit.*, p. 13).

19 For the background, contents, and purpose of the CMES, see the KDI, *Collection of Government Documents and Study Reports*, Vol. 1, pp. 345–87; *The Chosun Daily News*, 18 April 1979; the National Assembly Records, *The 5th Session of the Economic and Science Committee on April 20, in the 101st National Assembly Meeting* (Seoul: 1979) (in Korean); the EPB, *Economic Policy of Development Period*, pp. 201–3; and the EPB, *White Paper on the Economy* (Seoul: 1980), Chap. 2 (in Korean).

20 The Economic Ministers Roundtable has the same membership as the Economic Ministers Meeting. The consultation meeting plays an important role in coordinating major economic issues through an informal and free discussion, whereas the Economic Ministers Meeting is 'a formal institution to satisfy legal requirements for final approval of the economic proposals that have already been agreed upon by the concerned ministries'. '. . . the Economic Ministers' Consultation Meeting has been held more often (usually twice a week) than the formal Economic Ministers Meeting (usually once a week). Most short-term economic management policies have to be submitted to the Economic Ministers Consultation Meeting since they usually require considerable intra-government coordination. The proposals submitted to the consultation meeting do not require prior approval by the Economic Vice-Ministers Meeting.' Miyohei Shinohara, Toru Yanagihara,

and Kwang Suk Kim, 'The Japanese and Korean Experiences in Managing Development', *World Bank Staff Working Paper* 574 (1983), pp. 66–67.

21 *70s' Korean Chronology*, p. 403.

22 Just as the overall HCIs suffered from small market size and diseconomies of scale in the late 1970s, so the defence industry began to face the same dilemmas from military industrialization. The domestic market saturation made the Korean government and defence contractors seek and expand export markets. The amount of military exports, which were mainly composed of uniforms and other non-lethal equipment, was minimal until 1978. Since 1979, however, the Korean government had changed 'export items from software to conventional weapon systems'. Korea is now 'one of the most competitive exporters of infantry munitions and weapons as well as of light naval vessels'. By 1982, the country became the fifth largest military exporter in the Third World (Chung-in Moon, 'U.S. Third Country Arms Sales Regulation and the South Korean Defense Industry: Supplier Control and Recipient Dilemma', in Manwoo Lee et. al., *Alliance Under Tension: The Evolution of South Korean-U.S. Relations* [Boulder: Westview Press, 1988], pp. 84–90).

23 Chung-in Moon, 'South Korea: Between Security and Vulnerability', in James Everett Katz, *The Implication of Third World Military Industrialization: Sowing the Serpents' Teeth* (Lexington: Lexington Books, 1986), pp. 250–51.

24 Interviews.

25 *The Korea Herald*, 19 May, and 9 and 11 August. The planned Promotion Law, which would integrate such existing laws as the machinery, electronics and aviation industrial development laws, would include 'special tax breaks and administrative incentive measures designed to inject fresh vigor into the heavy and chemical industrial sectors'. One of the planned special laws was intended to promote industrial estate construction.

26 *The Korea Herald*, 17 February 1979.

27 *The Korea Herald*, 7 and 15 April 1979. At that time, export financing loans were used with an annual interest rate of 9 percent, which was only half the rates for other banking loans for non-export business firms. The new export financing system was supposed to make a rule that concessional export banking loans should be provided for business firms on the basis of export performance by setting an annual ceiling for each firm.

28 *The Korea Herald*, 15 June and 23 September 1979; and Kyung-Sik Kang, *op. cit.*, pp. 40–41. For views of the Bank of Korea, see 'The Backwardness of the Financial Industry', on 7 February 1979, pp. 559–71; for views of the EPB, 'Policy Measures for a Reform of Financial Institutions: Internal Circular', on 27 August 1979, pp. 639–59; and for the views of the MF, 'Views and Policy Measures on a Reform of Financial Institutions: Internal Circular', in September 1979, pp. 661–78, in the KDI, *Collection of Government Documents and Study Reports Related to Economic Stabilization Policies*.

29 *The Chosun Daily News*, 6 January 1979.
30 Ibid.
31 *70s' Korean Chronology* (Seoul: Chungsa Press, 1984), pp. 403, 413 (in Korean).
32 Ibid., pp. 409, 413.
33 For the disposals of financially depressed foreign-debted firms, see Jung-Ryum Kim, Memoir, No. 21; and for the policy measures of industrial rationalization, see Chapter 8.
34 The EPB, 'Comprehensive Economic Stabilization Measures', on 17 April 1979, in the KDI, *op. cit.*, p. 365.
35 *The Chosun Daily News*, 1 May 1979; and *The Maeil Kyungje Daily News*, 1 May 1979.
36 Korea Exchange Bank, 'Adjustments of Korea's Heavy and Chemical Industry Investment', *Monthly Review* (December 1980), p. 16; and also, the EPB, 'Comprehensive Measures for Economic Stabilization', p. 365.
37 *The Maeil Kyungje Daily News*, 8 May 1979.
38 For instance, the EPB insisted that the petrochemical industrial projects be largely scaled down in consideration of uncertain market prospects. But the MCI opposed the idea (see *The Korea Herald*, 21 April 1979).
39 An interview.
40 The EPB, 'Policy Measures on the Changwon Factory of the Hyundai International Inc. and the Okpo Shipbuilding Yard', on 25 May 1979, in KDI, *op. cit.*, Vol. 2, pp. 1164–65.
41 For the contents of the HCIIA see the EPB, 'Policy Measures on the Changwon Factory of the Hyundai International Inc. and the Okpo Shipbuilding Yard', in KDI, *op. cit.*, pp. 1149–73; Korea Exchange Bank, *op. cit.*, pp. 15–16; *The Maeil Kyungje Daily News* 25 May 1979; and *The Korea Herald*, 26 May 1979.
42 An interview.
43 *The Maeil Kyungje Daily News*, 28 May 1979.
44 The Korean Council of Christian Churches, *Labour Site and Testimony: 1970s* (Seoul: Pul Bit Press, 1984), pp. 434–35 (in Korean).
45 Korea Exchange Bank, *op. cit.*, p. 6.
46 The EPB, 'Current Problems of Heavy and Chemical Industrial Promotion and Policy Measures: Internal Circular', August 1979, in KDI, *op. cit.*, p. 1185.
47 *The Dong-A Daily News*, 7 September 1979.
48 For the problems of the Hyundai International Inc., Byung-Yun Park, *op. cit.* [Chapter 3, note 48], (May 1980), pp. 208–9 and the EPB, 'Current Problems of Heavy and Chemical Industrial Promotion and Policy Measures', in KDI, *op. cit.*, pp. 1181, 1188.
49 For the following explanation, see Jang-Jip Choi, 'Interest Conflict and Political Control in South Korea', Ph.D. Diss., University of Chicago, p. 505; and Alexander Irwin, *op. cit.* [Chapter 7, note 26], pp. 392–402.
50 Sang-Mok Suh, 'Economic Growth and Change in Income Distribution: The Korean Case,' *KDI Working Paper* 8508 (1985), p. 9.

51 Jang-Jip Choi, *op. cit.*, pp. 503–8.
52 See the Korean Christian Council of Churches, *op. cit.*, pp. 699–702.
53 For the detailed policy-making process, Interviews. For the contents of the policy measure, see *The Dong-A Daily News* and *The Korea Herald*, 26 June 1979. Also, see Kyung-Sik Kang, *op. cit.*, pp. 39–40; and Jai-Myung Kim, 'The Godfather of the TK (Taegu City and Kyung Sang North Province) Corps: Shin Hyun-Hwak', *Monthly Chosun* (November 1988), pp. 381–82 (in Korean).
54 In addition, as other measures, the amount of export financing loans for import of raw materials and collection of goods at local markets for export purposes would increase from 420 to 450 won per one U.S. dollar; the ceiling of the concessional loans would also be expanded, on the basis of export performance, from 1.2 months to 1.5 months in terms of export results.
55 *The Chosun Daily News*, 27 June 1979; and *The Korea Herald*, 27 June 1979.
56 *70s' Korean Chronology*, p. 412.
57 *The Korea Herald*, 25 August 1979.
58 *The Korea Herald*, 16 and 19 August 1979.
59 *70s' Korean Chronology*, p. 419.
60 *70s' Korean Chronology*, pp. 422, 424.
61 Dismissed workers of the Y.H. company had been staging a protest demonstration over the shutdown of their factory. Early in August 1979, the firm went bankrupt and closed down its factory. This closure infuriated the factory workers because the president of the company had pocketed company bills collected on its sales in the United States. The labour union of the company launched a sit-in overnight demonstration, asking the government to take an appropriate step for normalization of the company. But managers of the company expelled them with the help of policemen. Thus, the workers went to the headquarters of the New Democratic Party (NDP: the major opposition party) in order to gain its assistance. There, they staged a sit-in hunger strike. President of the NDP Young-Sam Kim welcomed and encouraged them and requested the government to solve the labour dispute. Instead, riot policemen stormed the NDP headquarters, dragged out the young female workers, and injured some NDP National Assemblymen and reporters in dismissing the strike. See Koon Woo Nam, *South Korean Politics: The Search for Political Consensus and Stability* (Washington: University Press of America, 1989), pp. 159–62; the Former Y.H. Labour Union and the Korean Workers' Welfare Council, *The History of Y.H. Labour Union* (Seoul: Hyungsung Press, 1984) (in Korean); and *The Dong-A Daily News*, 9–14 August 1979.
62 The public opinion against Park's regime was manifested in the National Assembly election held on 12 December 1978. The election was to choose two-thirds of the assemblymen. In spite of the usual advantages of the ruling party (Democratic Republic Party: DRP) in the authoritarian regime, the DRP lost a significant portion of its former poll. It gained sixty-eight seats with 30.9 percent of the popular vote, whereas the New Democratic Party (the major opposition party)

won sixty-one seats with 34.7 percent of the whole poll. The DRP got seven more seats than the NDP because of the medium electoral district system (two in a district) although the former gained less votes than the latter. In addition, the ruling party could still retain its dominant position in the National Assembly due to the presidential prerogative to appoint one-third of the assemblymen. The election gave a significant meaning to the Korean political history in that an opposition party outpolled a governing party at the first time. (See C. I. Eugene Kim, 'Significance of Korea's 10th National Assembly Elections', *Asian Survey* [May 1979]; and *The New York Times*, 14 December 1978.) Following up the electoral victory, the NDP launched an offensive attack against Park's dictatorship for the purpose of political liberalization. Along with this political trend, a series of serious labour disputes, increasing anti-government student demonstrations, and other acts by influential dissidents had threatened Park's political governability. Importantly, on 1 March 1979, the three prominent opposition leaders, Bo-Sun Yun (a former President), Sok-Hon Ham, and Dae-Jung Kim (a former presidential candidate) formed the National Coalition for Democracy and Unification; they declared that 'the national unification was to be achieved by a democratic government relying on the people' (Koon Woo Nam, *op. cit.*, p. 146).

63 *70s' Korean Chronology*, pp. 417–18.

64 *The Chosun Daily News*, 5 September 1979; and *The Korea Herald*, 4 September 1979. The committee under the chairmanship of the EPB was attended by the Ministers of Finance, Agriculture and Fisheries, Commerce and Industry, Construction, and Government Administration, the First Minister without Portfolio and the Second Minister without Portfolio, the First Presidential Economic Secretary, the Director-General of Administrative Coordination at the Premier's Office, the Chairman of the Korean Employers' Association (KEA), and the Chairman of the Federation of Korean Trade Unions.

65 Before the establishment of the WWPDC, some institutional arrangements had been formed to allow labour union leaders' participation in labour-management and economic planning at the national level under the state corporatist mechanism. Although their function was minimal in solving issues of industrial relations, labour union leaders were given opportunities to express their demands. First, labour representatives were invited to join the planning process for the Fourth Economic Development Plan (1977–81) through the Economic Plan Coordination and the Economic Plan Deliberation Committees. Second, the Central Labour Management Friendly Meeting (CLMFM) was established to exchange information and avoid labour disputes through consultation among the government, the FKTU, and the KEA. Finally, the WWPDC was in part an outcome of 'the FKTU leaders' unremitting demand for greater participation in such an economic policy-making structure as the EPB', Jang-Jip Choi, *op. cit.*, pp. 395–96, and for the detailed explanation of participatory arrangements for labour in government consultative organizations from 1967 to 1980; see ibid., pp. 374–403.

66 *The Korea Herald*, 18 and 24 August 1979.
67 For the planned revision of labour laws, see *The Chosun Daily News*, 14 August and 27 September 1979; and *The Dong-A Daily News*, 22 August 1979.
68 *The Dong-A Daily News*, 31 August 1979.
69 In particular, 2,000 workers lost their jobs in the attempted process of merging Hyundai International with the Hyundai Heavy Industries according to the principle of 'first merging, later settling accounts' of the first HCIIA (Sung-Joon Cho, 'Scenes of Labour Disputes', *Sin Dong-A* [June 1980], p. 180 [in Korean]). They were not able to organize their interests and protest against their abrupt dismissal because a labour union was not established within the firms. As a matter of fact, at that time, there were no labour unions in almost all largest business groups, including the two conglomerates.
70 *70s' Korean Chronology*, p. 417.
71 *The Chosun Daily News*, 25 August 1979. As of July 1979, the number of the small and medium firms permanently shut down was 179, 1,623 were in closedown, and 8,198 had curtailed working operation. (As of July 1978, the numbers were 128, 1,097, and 3,667, respectively.)

Chapter 5

The policy failure of the first investment adjustment

The aforementioned policy change wi'' 'n the economic framework of stabilization could not implement, in an effective manner through active state intervention, the planned mergers of the heavy and chemical industrial firms. The institutional decay of implementation, which had been characterized by the bureaucratic conflicts under presidential influence, could not efficiently enforce the policy of HCIIA. The government could not strongly push an implementation of merger or interlocking investment between the concerned big business firms.

It was not until September 1979 that the President of Hyundai International, In-Young Chung, and the Chairman of the Hyundai Business Group, Joo-Young Chung (his elder brother), agreed to the planned merger: the Hyundai Heavy Industries would acquire and merge Hyundai International by investing in Hyundai International through an increase of equity capital. However, the brothers made the agreement with different hidden interests. In-Young Chung assumed that his brother would rescue the company with his investment and leave its management to him. On the other hand, Joo-Young Chung later insisted on his brother's complete withdrawal from the management of Hyundai International.[1] Actually, their merger agreement was non-voluntary, as their compliance was based on government coercion. If they did not choose the way of investment adjustment, they would suffer penalties for their non-compliance. But they faced serious conflicts of interest in the practical process of merging. The business firms concerned calculated their costs and benefits in order to maximize their own interests. First of all, they did not reach an agreement on their asset estimates of the company to be merged. Later, this kind of big business conflict became one of the passive and indirect ways that big businessmen used to resist the compulsory merger. In addition, the other scheme of either interlocking investment or merger between the Samsung Heavy Industries and the Daewoo Heavy Industries had been in a stalemate without any progress. Until Park's regime breakdown, the two companies could not agree to a compromise on a way and object of investment adjustment between themselves.

POLITICAL CRISIS AND THE BREAKDOWN OF PARK'S REGIME

After the Y.H. incident, the opposition party (New Democratic Party [NDP]) was sharply confronted with the ruling party (Democratic Republic Party) without any attempted negotiations for political compromises. The government and several disgruntled NDP members formed a conspiracy to deprive Young-Sam Kim (the President of the NDP) of his position. In August, the NDP members filed a lawsuit for the nullification of his recent election as party president. As a result, the government-controlled court prohibited him from acting as NDP head.[2] Furthermore, in September, Young-Sam Kim made harsh anti-government remarks in an interview with the *New York Times*.[3] The authoritarian government took advantage of the anti-government interview in order to banish the intransigent opposition leader from the political scene. The authorities expelled Kim from the National Assembly, but shortly after his dismissal, all of the opposition assemblymen tendered their resignations to protest against his expulsion. Park's regime had underestimated and miscalculated the extent of the opposition's protest.[4]

As a result, in October, massive and violent anti-government demonstrations took place in the cities of Pusan (the home of Young-Sam Kim) and Masan.[5] A number of students and citizens called for the overthrow of President Park and protested Kim's expulsion from the National Assembly in the wake of economic hardship and political repression. The government declared the martial law in Pusan (the second largest city) and imposed the 'garrison decree' (a form of military control second to martial law, which allows the authority of the civil courts) in Masan and Changwon (a city that contained a heavy industrial complex).

In response to anti-government pressures, political institutions, which operated for Park's authoritarian regime security, increasingly had difficulties in controlling opposition parties, leaders, social groups, and student demonstrations. They reacted by means of tight coercive repression and political conspiracy. However, the more the government took repressive measures, the more vehement and stronger were the protests.

In the meantime, just as conflicts had arisen among state managers over how to manage the economic crisis (as I mentioned previously), so too did discord develop within the power bloc that sought to cope with the political crisis. Even though Park stuck to and took hard-line countermeasures against the anti-government protests, some political leaders within the inner ruling circle as well as a group of leaders within the military, supported soft-line measures that would be accompanied by political liberalization. Ruling party leaders wished to achieve political solutions through threats and inducements. But, under the security agencies' dominance, they were compelled to follow the decisions of the core group that held political control. This power bloc was composed of the Head of the Korean Central Intelligence Agency (KCIA), the Chief of the Presidential Security Office (PSO), and the President. At that time, President Park and the hard-liners around the Chief of the PSO took the initiative in propelling harsh and repressive measures. However, a division between hard-liners and soft-liners both within the security community and within the military led to intense power struggles through political crisis management. The authoritarian regime broke down in the process of the power struggles within the security institution, which was connected with the military division. The transition from authoritarian rule occurred abruptly without an opening (political liberalization) of Park's regime in response to pressures from opposition forces.

However, on 12 December 1979, the military hard-liners' coup within the military was led by the security force of the Defence Security Command. The coup aborted an opportunity for a transition towards a democratic regime even though Park's death could have played a major role in facilitating the authoritarian regime's transformation. On 17 May 1980, the coup leaders established the military-controlled government through another coup under the interim government in order to complete their control over political power.

THE INSTITUTION DISORDER IN CRISIS MANAGEMENT

The institutional disorder of state institutions in political crisis management

The interim government had been led by Kyu-Ha Choy, who had served as Prime Minister under Park's regime and became President on 6 December 1979, according to the Yushin constitutional rule of presidential election through the National Council for Unification (electoral college). However, Choy had been a long-standing bureaucrat and thus did not have an independent power base either in the ruling party or in the military; he possessed only administrative authority rather than political power. Furthermore, President Choy and new Prime Minister Hyun-Hwak Shin (the former Deputy Prime Minister and Head of the EPB), the top executives of the interim government, tended to maintain the former authoritarian political order for the time being and to delay the adoption of a democratic constitution, citing the importance of political stability. They did not want to totally deny Park's dictatorship. In March 1980, Prime Minister Shin explicitly declared, 'the Yushin system [Park's regime] was a necessary regime for adequate national defence and economic development'. He also said that priorities of government policy would be given to national security, economic development, and political development, in that order.[6]

In addition, Choy's government had been heavily influenced by the military during the period of martial law. In particular, after the coup on 12 December, coup leaders, led by General Doo-Hwan Chun, the Head of the Defence Security Command, began to take control of the interim government in terms of political crisis management.[7] As a result, a political transition towards democracy had been delayed and disturbed by the military; ultimately, the coup leaders interrupted the political process towards a possible democratization and established another authoritarian regime.

The institutional disorder of state-society struggles in economic crisis management

In contrast to political crisis management, the interim government attempted to realize reforms in economic crisis management.

Choy's government and the new military leaders had common interests in dissolving the collusive government-big business coalition that had existed under Park's regime. In the December manifesto, the coup leaders criticized the practices of rich big businessmen who damaged the public interest by violating business ethics.[8]

However, the government neither wanted to push big business confidence to the bottom nor intended to overcome the economic crisis at the expense of big business interests. Shortly after the emergence of Choy's regime, there were rumours that several entrepreneurs would be punished because of their profiteering at the public's expense. The rumours were based on the following logic: the punishment would 'find a support among the majority of South Koreans who were struggling with high inflation and were angry at the sight of those individuals who were getting rich quickly because of their government connections'.[9] The rumours seemed to originate from the new military leaders, for they emphasized 'business ethics' in their manifesto. It was highly possible that high government officials may have persuaded them to regard big business punishment as an untimely and inadequate measure in the economic crisis situation. In response to these rumours, the state managers issued denials through a series of statements. Basically, they objected to punishing big businessmen, who had illicitly accumulated their wealth, for the purposes of economic stability and a guarantee of foreign credits.[10]

Unlike Park's regime, Choy's government could not enact economic penalties for big business non-compliance with state interventions in investment decision-making. The state's control over big business faced limits because its administrative order was not sustained by political power. Furthermore, pressures against big businessmen from the state and other social groups provoked opposition and challenges from the big businessmen.

In January, in response to the aforementioned pressures, the FKI (the association representing big business interests) argued that the firms' growth had nothing to do with illicit wealth accumulation and should not be an object of suspicion and criticism during every transitional period.[11] In April, the big business association established 'the Special Countermeasure Committee for Political-Economic-Social Problems' within its organization in order to cope with the social criticisms of big business firms. Big businessmen regarded excessive denunciations of their business activities as a challenge to the liberal economic system. They decided to make every effort to step up their public activities on merits of the liberal firms' system and to increase their interactions with the political circle through frequent politics-business roundtables.[12] Furthermore, it was alleged that the owners of several of the largest business groups attempted to form a new political party as part of a long-term strategy to protect their business interests. This party would be based on political connections with some of the former high government officials and influential ruling national assemblymen under Park's regime.[13] The concerned former state managers and rich entrepreneurs tried to resurrect the state-big business ruling coalition of Park's regime with a view towards regaining their political power through a new political party in the next election.

Likewise, the institutional disorder of state-labour relations led not only to an increase in labour disputes but also to a breakdown of the state-corporatist control system that had operated under Park's regime. The hierarchical structure of the FKTU began to collapse in two ways after Park's assassination. First of all, power struggles within the upper union hierarchy took place as the legitimacy of its authoritarian leadership was called into question. In February 1980, the chairmen of the eight national industrial federations of labour unions called for the immediate resignation of the Chairman of the FKTU Young-Tai Kim, who was also Chairman of the National Textile Federation of Labour Unions. Textile union leaders also adopted a resolution demanding his expulsion. In both cases, the leaders accused Kim of abusing his power during his service under Park's regime by repressing legitimate labour disputes and activities through corrupt connections with the state managers.[14]

In addition to the voluntary move by the union leadership against the existing labour control policy of the state, rank-and-file discontent and criticism regarding the corrupt and government-patronized (so-called *Yeoyoung*) union leadership under the former regime motivated the labour union leaders to take steps to protect and improve workers' rights and interests. As a result, the FKTU in April declared that labour unions would participate in political activities in an indirect manner, by supporting political parties and leaders who would represent workers' interests.[15] This decision violated the existing Labour Union Law which had prevented labour unions from supporting a specific political party or politician in elections. As a matter of fact, the National Security Law as its higher law, which had restricted labour rights of collective bargaining and action, was no longer effective under the interim government.[16]

The emergence of EPB leadership and bureaucratic consensus

As a result of the oil-shock and political instability, the government predicted 1980's economic growth of zero percent or a negative percent by 1980. In January 1980, in his New Year's address, President Choy slightly changed the government orientation of economic management from the loose to a tight stabilization policy in this deteriorating economic situation. His government would concentrate on solving the side effects of heavy and chemical industrial promotion and of the government-controlled financial system, which had been driven from the process of high economic growth; he also paid attention to the development of small and medium firms.[17]

By 1980, the emergence of EPB leadership, supported by the Prime Minister (the former Deputy Minister and Head of the EPB), considerably increased the degree of coherence and coordination among the economic ministries in economic stabilization policy-making and implementation. The new Minister of the MCI, Jai-Suk Jung, was a former Deputy Minister of the EPB, one of the reform-minded group leaders for economic stability within the EPB under Park's regime. Unlike the sharp bureaucratic conflicts under the former authoritarian regime, a relatively high consensus of bureaucratic interests in economic crisis management enabled Choy's government to pursue a strict stabilization policy. In general, the technocrats' relative autonomy from the military in economic management made it possible to support economic reforms. Furthermore, the interim government, based on administrative power without political power, could afford to be less concerned than the former government about the level of business confidence in investment. In other words, the state managers under Choy's regime had little interest in staying in their power seats because the government was compelled to give priority to a political transition.

In January 1980, during the President's annual inspection tour of the EPB, the EPB outlined a strict stabilization policy for economic crisis management and came up with a long-term strategy of economic liberalization for continued growth within stability. The economic management plan for the 1980s highlighted a clear-cut change from the previous heavily government-led economy to a private-initiated economy. Originally, the reform group, who made the CMES in early 1979, had in mind a civil-led economy as a long-term strategy for economic management. However, they could not explicitly express and push the long-term policy change in the face of opposition from the conservative techno-bureaucrats of the MCI and the MF under Park's strong influence.

Deputy Prime Minister and Head of the EPB Hahn-Been Lee said the following: while acknowledging the necessity of a protectionist industrial policy at the early time and phase of development, the economic management plan notably would overhaul the existing economic system that had accumulated its inherent inefficiency and problems; the state interventionist policy during the past years had been the very cause of the chronic high inflation; the efficiency of the economy would depend entirely on how much emphasis would be put on the free competition market that would be able to bring a stabilized economic growth through the improved quality of commodities priced at a reasonable level; for financial liberalization, bank interest rates would be permitted to float in relation to an uncontrolled demand-and-supply mechanism in the long run, and the government-owned and controlled commercial banks would be gradually transferred to private hands so as to liberalize domestic banking activities; and thus, it was imperative that the nation should dissociate itself from the state-intervened economic system in order to enhance the efficiency of its economy and thus reach its ultimate goal of a highly sophisticated industrialized country.[18]

As a whole, in their briefings during the annual inspection tour, the MF and the MCI followed and supported the EPB's short-term stabilization policy measures within the tight money policy. Minister of the MF Woun-Gie Kim reported the basic financial policy: the year's monetary policy priority would be given to curbing the inflationary trend to the maximum extent through a strict credit supply restraint; unlike the previous rule concentrating on facilities loans, the bank lending priority would focus on the operational funds of business firms producing the daily necessities along with a gradual financial liberalization; bank loans would also be extended to small and medium industrial firms, which would help them survive serious financial difficulties; and the supporting funds would be scaled up to 669,000 million won from the previous year's 516,000 million won.[19]

Minister of the MCI Jai-Suk Jung reported to President Choy that investment realignments would be finished not only in the power-generating equipment field but also in such other heavy and chemical industrial fields as engines and heavy electric equipment. Following the conclusions of the MCI's intensive survey on the nation's heavy and chemical industries, he also prepared for integrated support measures to help operational funds of already constructed heavy and chemical industrial plants. There, the President instructed the ministry to take measures for active support for small and medium business firms.[20] Therefore, the MF and the MCI cooperated on the short-term macroeconomic management of tight money policy. Nevertheless, it was doubtful that the MF and the MCI would agree fully to the EPB's idealistic long-term economic liberalization policy to exclude industrial and policy loans.

The MCI's policy for the financially depressed heavy and chemical industries was not completely compatible with the EPB's and MF's restricted monetary policy. During early 1980, its stance already tilted towards heavy and chemical industrial stabilization instead of towards heavy and chemical industrial promotion, and it planned to strongly push investment adjustments in the HCIs. Moreover, it planned to implement substantial supports for financially troubled small and medium firms.

However, Minister of the MCI, Jai-Suk Jung, a former leader of the reform group within the EPB, seemed to be subject to the MCI's organizational interests in industrial policy. The MCI still intended to deal with the HCIs as an exceptional case, to some extent, from the framework of economic stabilization. The MCI's goal for the year was to establish a firm heavy and chemical industrial base (internal stabilization) for another leap in export-oriented growth in the 1980s. In particular, the ministry adopted the ear of 1980 as the turning point for machinery industrial development; thus, it argued for the funds necessary for completing construction of plants near the finishing stage and for operating already completed factories even at the risk of sacrificing the policy of tight money supply.[21] In the end, the bureaucratic conflict between the MCI, on the one side, and the EPB and the MF, on the other side, regarding this relief measure was settled on the condition that the MCI would induce foreign loans of $800 million that would not be counted as a factor in tallying domestic money supply figures.[22]

Big business responses to economic crisis management: state-big business struggles

Since the late 1970s, big businessmen had demanded a 'private-initiated' economy based on investment decisions independent of state intervention. In a speech in September 1979, the Chairman of the FKI, Joo-Young Chung, represented big business interests regarding decision-making in management, price mechanisms, financial liberalization, labour-management relations, and economic policy formation. Additionally, he indirectly criticized the government's economic management for stabilization.[23]

Ironically, big business firms, which had enjoyed privileged benefits from strong state interventionist industrialization during the 1970s, called for economic liberalization to alleviate the economic crisis. Later, the basic ideas of the aforementioned big business demands were reflected in the EPB's long-term strategy of January 1980 for economic crisis management. The long-term interests of state managers, however, were incompatible with those of big businessmen in terms of their purposes and understandings of economic liberalization. In general, the FKI emphasized business autonomy in investment, financing, and marketing decision-making in order to maximize big businessmen's growth-oriented interests against the economic stabilization policy, whereas the EPB focused on government guarantees of fair opportunities and conditions in market competition between large, and small and medium-sized firms so as to realize economic stability in the long run through liberalization.

More specifically, by 1980, relatively high interest rates and a lower ratio of policy loans in domestic credits were maintained under state control within the framework of economic stabilization, which was no longer substantially supportive for big business activities. Therefore, the big businessmen expected to be more effectively supported by uncontrolled bank interest rates and credit allocation under a liberalized financial system. Meanwhile, on the government side, government officials were prepared to intervene strongly in the market, especially mono-oligopolistic price and industrial structures, in order to set up a sound base for long-term economic liberalization. They planned to enact a new law for fair trade and price mechanisms. In February 1980, they also made strict rules to protect small and medium business firms from big business dominance in the market. That is, the designation of twenty-three business lines currently dominated by small and medium industrial firms would prevent such companies with financially poor structures from being taken over by big business firms; if a big business firm acquired small-medium firms within the specified categories, the businessmen implicated would be punished by up to three years' imprisonment or a fine of 30 million won.[24]

Big business responses to labour disputes

In addition to the strict stabilization policy for economic stability, the rapidly increasing and violent labour disputes under Choy's regime pushed business confidence still lower. During the first half of 1980, under the interim government, the vacuum of political power resulted in an unprecedented rise in labour disputes. From January to April 1980, 809 disputes took place. In particular, labour disputes began to occur in big business firms affiliated with business groups; male workers of heavy industrial companies participated actively in violent strikes. The major demands of the disputes during the period were settlement of delayed payments, higher wages, and a democratization of labour unions, in that order.[25]

Big businessmen reacted to the explosive labour disputes in two contradictory ways. One way was to prevent labour's industrial collective actions for wage bargaining in advance through an institutional change of labour-management relations. Like the state managers' and big businessmen's responses under the Park regime in late 1979, the interim government and the KEA (the business association composed of big business firms for labour-management relations) planned to solve labour-management conflicts within the enterprise. As a result, they intended to minimize workers' collective bargaining power by enacting a new labour law to invigorate existing Labour-Management Councils at the enterprise level and by blocking the FKTU's demands for an industrial bargaining system through an industrial labour coalition.[26] The alternative method was to induce big businessmen's collective action to increase their wage bargaining power. Actually, some large enterprises that were members of the KEA formed a cartel for a wage freeze while they objected to industrial collective bargaining.[27]

The institutional disorder of both state-big business and state-labour relations within the context of the economic and political crisis nullified, to a large extent, the state managers' strong will for economic stabilization. In the wake of its plummeting control over the big business and labour sectors, the government could not effectively implement such policy measures as import liberalization, reform of the financial system, readjustment of bank interest rates and prices to realistic levels, and the first adjustment of heavy and chemical industrial investments. In particular, the explosive eruption of labour demands, which had been suppressed for a long time under the Park regime, demolished the government and the business circle's defensive guidelines for the purpose of wage restraints. As I will detail in the next section, big business opposition led to the policy-makers' failure to implement the first HCIIA.

In brief, the state managers' policy-making, which was not sustained by political power, had not been successful because of their lack of enforcing power to realize economic stability. Furthermore, faced with the crisis situation of the minus economic growth within political instability, the government had no choice but to take short-term measures for necessary economic activation within the tight money policy.[28]

THE POLICY FAILURE OF THE FIRST HCIIA: THE UNSUCCESSFUL STATE-CONTROLLED CAPITALIST COLLECTIVE ACTION

This section will focus on state-big business conflicts in the implementation of the first HCIIA after the breakdown of Park's authoritarian regime and will focus on the following questions. Why did state managers fail to implement the first HCIIA? How had institutional disorders of state institutions, state-society, and state-market relationships affected state-big business conflicts in association with a foreign creditor – more specifically, big businessmen's and state managers' interests, and their relative bargaining power? And how had these variables at the micro- (actors' interactions) and macro- (institutional constraints) levels been interconnected with one another within the context of economic and political crisis management after the fall of the authoritarian regime?

During the transitional period between Park's assassination (26 October 1979) and Chun's takeover of political power (31 May

1980), the disorder of state institutions for political power in the process of political crisis management led to big business non-compliance with the implementation of investment adjustment. As a consequence, the state managers' weak enforcing power for discretionary command, which was only based on the administrative order, led to the big businessmen's negative response to the collective action of investment adjustment. The institutional chaos of state-big business relations, along with the discontinued government-big business ruling coalition, resulted in the businessmen's direct demands for huge privileged supports and indirect opposition to the investment realignment of merging, which was manifest in their interest conflicts. It also enhanced the individual bargaining power of the concerned big business firms over the government. Here, their demands were aimed at minimizing their costs and maximizing their benefits in the process of merging. Moreover, they did not regard the expected outcomes (a settlement of their overlapped investments to mitigate their financial difficulties) of merging as their collective good.

Finally, the institutional confusion of state-market relations, especially the financial system, in the process of economic liberalization could not satisfy the big businessmen's demands for financial support during the merging process. In other words, they could not have their privileged access to such policy instruments as low bank interest rates and unlimited policy loans in the liberalizing financial system within the tight money supply. The limits of the state managers' financial control decisively reduced their bargaining power over the big business firms. Therefore, the interim government was able to provide them with neither sufficient financial support nor coercive enforcement measures, including economic penalties for business non-compliance; otherwise, both of these positive incentives and coercive threats might have brought about a successful implementation of the compulsory investment adjustment policy without big business agreement on 25 May 1979. In addition, the IBRD, a foreign public lender, and the involved joint ventures had a significant influence on delaying the investment adjustment. The foreign actors weakened the state managers' enforcement power for and strengthened the big businessmen's resistance to the scheme of consolidation.

Business groups' demands

Since the policy-making of the first HCIIA on 25 May 1979, interest conflicts among the big business firms and their own requests for preferential prerequisites in the process of implementation had brought the scheme of merging to a standstill. After the sudden collapse of Park's regime, the Hyundai Business Group and the Daewoo Business Group actively and boldly asked the interim government for its guarantee of privileged conditions before they would merge their counterparts. The Hyundai Group requested that the government guarantee its exclusive sales of power-generating equipment, monopoly of power plant construction, and financial supports for facilities and operation funds: the Hyundai Heavy Industries should receive the planned orders of the seventh and eighth nuclear power plants on a turn-key base; the government should guarantee an adequate operation ratio of Hyundai International's merged factories for five years; it should support funds for additional facilities and operation investment from the Korea Development Bank and the National Investment Fund and offer tax privileges; it should delay the date of maturity in repaying the export financing funds on a deferred payment basis for Hyundai International's heavy equipment; and it should prohibit further overlapped investments of other companies in this field.[29]

In the meantime, the Daewoo Business Group and the Samsung Business Group agreed to merge the Daewoo Heavy Industries with the Samsung Heavy Industries in the boiler field, but had not decided on a way of merging. Furthermore, before merging, the Daewoo Group called for a government guarantee of financial support for completing and operating at an adequate level the Okpo Shipbuilding Yard as its subsidiary. At that time, the Daewoo Group was under financial pressures from the construction of shipbuilding yards. Under Park's regime, in 1978, it was compelled to absorb the financially troubled state-run factory because of the almost compulsory recommendation of President Park and the Deputy Prime Minister of the EPB. Therefore, the group insisted that the government should keep its promise of sufficient financial supports and a guarantee of sales at the time of acquisition. After settling the remaining problems from the former merger case, the conglomerate planned to join the unwilling merger with the Samsung Heavy Industries.[30]

On 29 November 1979, the Economic Ministers Roundtable seriously considered the Hyundai Group's demands and urged the concerned companies to complete the delayed mergers as soon as possible. However, the ministers' decisions did not promise any substantial financial aid and still persisted in the principle of first merging and later settling financial and marketing supports.[31] In fact, the government could not afford to provide a huge amount of funds for investment adjustment within the framework of economic stabilization towards liberalization. The government faced a serious lack of heavy and chemical industrial financing funds for 1980.

Big business resistance

On 11 January 1980, the government decided to allow the Hyundai Heavy Industries to monopolize the turn-key base order of auxiliary equipment and construction for the planned seventh and eighth nuclear power plants. In response to Hyundai's monopoly right on power plant construction works, several large construction companies strongly objected to this policy decision, saying that the designated order would be an unfair contract against free competition. The Daewoo Group, whose power-generating equipment section was supposed to be merged with that of the Samsung Group, also protested against the measure by notifying the government that it would give up constructing the Okpo Shipbuilding Yard. At the same time, the government imposed the principle of 'first merging, later supports', which meant that it would not offer financial supports unless the firms concerned completed their mergers.[32]

In spite of this strong government position to enforce merging, Hyundai International, which was to be absorbed by the Hyundai Group, harshly criticized the policy of investment adjustment under the interim government that lacked a political power basis. The President of Hyundai International, In-Young Chung, protested that the problem of overlapped investment in the power-generating equipment field was caused by the inconsistent policies of the government; the government had allowed other business firms to participate in producing power plant facilities and thus violated the original agreement to grant his company the monopoly right of production.[33]

Foreign actors' opposition

Moreover, the resistance of Hyundai International and the Daewoo Group to the planned consolidation was encouraged by foreign actors' opposition to the scheme of investment adjustment. In 1977, the IBRD completed an agreement to lend the huge amount of $80 million for the construction of Hyundai International factories. In November 1979, the foreign lender decided to suspend its remaining loans of $24 million as a means of protesting against the government's merger decision. The IBRD's rationale was that the Korean government had already violated the contract with the IBRD. According to the contract, the government was supposed to monopolize the production of power plant equipment and to guarantee an adequate operation ratio to Hyundai International for five years after the completion of construction.[34] The cutoff of foreign loans brought about serious financial difficulties for Hyundai International because of its debt service of accumulating interests before finishing the construction. In fact, the suspension of further loans continued until November 1980 because the government had not settled the conflicts both between state managers and big businessmen and between the concerned business groups.

Additionally, foreign companies, which were technologically tied up or formed a joint-venture company with either the Daewoo Heavy Industries or the Samsung Heavy Industries, had different views from these two business groups in regard to dealing with the problem of merging. The two business groups' economic dependence on foreign investment and technology made it more difficult to adjust their interests.

The limits of the state's financing capabilities

In the wake of the aforementioned state-big business struggles, the government announced in February 1980 financial support for heavy and chemical industrial firms and a revision of the original scheme of the first HCIIA.[35] According to the revised plan, the Hyundai Heavy Industries would merge Hyundai International by establishing a new company until the end of March, instead of pursuing a capital increase of the former in the latter; the Samsung Heavy Industries would concentrate on producing boilers by acquiring the counterpart of the Daewoo Heavy Industries; and the Daewoo Heavy Industries would take exclusive charge of the production of turbine generators through interlocking investment with the Samsung company.

At the same time, the government decided to provide 30 billion won and 20 billion won to Hyundai International and the Okpo Shipbuilding construction, respectively, along with the special supply of 200 billion won to heavy and chemical industrial plants that were either almost complete or at an initial operating stage. However, the financial supports to these companies were far below the original demands of the Hyundai Group and the Daewoo Group (some 100 billion won to Hyundai International and about 40 billion won to the Okpo Shipbuilding Yard). The planned amount of 200 billion won as a general support for the HCIs was only half of 400 billion won the firms had requested as a rescue fund for overcoming their financial difficulties.

Furthermore, the interim government could not afford to mobilize the planned heavy and chemical industrial fund. The financing scale of the National Investment Fund was too small to cover the amount. Thus, the financing capacity of policy loans was able to supply only 100 billion won.[36] As a result, under the interim government, the capabilities of the financial system had been, to a large extent, constrained both by the situation of indispensable monetary retrenchment and by the process of financial liberalization.

Interest conflicts between business groups

To make matters worse, the Hyundai Group and Hyundai International still could not complete their merger because of their different asset estimates of the Changwon factory of Hyundai International, even after they had agreed to the revised scheme of incorporation. Hyundai International insisted on receiving 39 billion won from the Hyundai Heavy Industries because the assets and liabilities of the former were 249 billion won and 210 billion won, respectively. On the other hand, the latter argued for only 400 million won to settle accounts.[37]

They were not prepared to implement the involuntary investment adjustment at the sacrifice of their cost-and-benefit calculation by compromising their highly different estimates. They protested indirectly against the compulsory merger scheme by taking advantage of the asset estimate conflict. Still, the state failed to adjust their sums by issuing a compulsory command in order to solve the conflict between the two companies. Unlike Park's authoritarian government, Choy's government did not have the coercive enforcement power without legal bases, which would impose economic penalties (suspending or withdrawing loans to create a possible bankruptcy and tax investigation) for the businessmen's non-compliance. Thus, the state managers' lack of capacities for providing sufficient financial incentives and solving the conflict of interests among the big businessmen largely reduced the state's bargaining power over the big businessmen's foot-dragging resistance through interest conflicts and demands; consequently, the government failed to generate a capitalist collective action of merger.

The failure of state capital participation

Finally, after the failure in implementing the first HCIIA, the Economic Ministers Roundtable in May 1980 decided to establish a government-invested corporation that would merge both the Hyundai Heavy Industries and Hyundai International and be managed by one of the former high government officials. Its authorized capital of 128,500 million won would be collected from the state-owned specialized banks, such as the Korea Development Bank (45,000 million won) and Korea Exchange Bank (10,000 million won), the Hyundai Heavy Industries (45,000 million won), and Hyundai International (28,500 million won).[38] The government-run banks would transform large portions of their loans already given to Hyundai International into their investments.

After facing the policy failure of the first HCIIA, the interim government, as a last resort, chose its capital participation in the big businessmen's power-generating equipment production. Originally, the government was reluctant to invest state capital against its long-term policy goal of market-oriented management. However, the state managers had no choice but to adopt the policy measure for the purpose of the industrial adjustment. It was expected that the new scheme of merging, which would be joined by state capital, would resolve, to some degree, the big businessmen's financial demands, opposition, and interest conflicts. Later, however, the President of Hyundai International, In-Young Chung, ignored the planned establishment of the government-invested enterprise, even after he had agreed to the method of merger. Furthermore, he recommended the withdrawal of the first HCIIA to the MCI and the EPB.[39] In the end, the new merger scheme was no longer effective after the emergence of the completely military-controlled government at the end of May 1980.

In brief, the weak institutional capacities of the state during the period of economic and political crisis had affected the policy formation and implementation of economic stabilization, particularly those of investment adjustment in the HCIs as the short-term core policy measure for stabilization. The disorder of political institutions, of policy networks between the state and social groups, and of the financial system led to the ineffective implementation of economic stabilization policy measures. The institutional disorder could not offer sufficient coercive enforcement and financial incentives to the concerned business groups. Finally, the government failed to create the state-controlled capitalist collective action for investment adjustment. The next chapter will analyse how and why changes of state institutions for political transition and economic policy, of institutions between state and big business, and of the financial system resulted in the policy failure of the second investment adjustment.

NOTES

1 Eui-Kyun Kim, *op. cit.* [Chapter 6, note 52], p. 258.
2 See the *New York Times*, 20 August 1979; and *Far Eastern Economic Review*, 21 September 1979.
3 For the content of the interview, see the *New York Times*, 16 September 1979 and *The Chosun Daily News*, 16 September 1979. He said, '... the time has come for the United States to make a clear choice between a basically dictatorial regime and majority who aspire to democracy ...'.
4 For the incident of Kim's expulsion, see *The Chosun Daily News*, 20, 22, 23, 27, and 30 September, 3, 5, 13, and 14 October 1979, and *The Dong-A Daily News*, 21 September, 16 October 1979.
5 For the Pusan and Masan uprisings, see Koon Woo Nam, *op. cit.* [Chapter 4, note 61], pp. 167–69; *New York Times*, 17, 18, 19, 20, and 21 October 1979; and Gap-Je Cho, *Yugo (Accident)*, Vols. 1 and 2 (Seoul: Hangil Press, 1987), Chaps. 5–10 (in Korean).
6 *The Chosun Daily News*, 13 March, 1980; and *The Dong-A Daily News*, 13 March 1980.
7 See Koon Woo Nam, *op. cit.* [Chapter 4, note 61], pp. 185–86: for original sources, see the *New York Times*, 29 and 31 October, 2 and 4 November 1979; and *Newsweek*, 2 November 1979. After the

December coup, the newly emerged military leaders issued a manifesto that alluded to the military's intention to play a crucial role through political, social, and economic purification in political crisis management. See *The Dong-A Daily News*, 18 December 1979.

8 *The Dong-A Daily News*, 18 December 1979. 'The new military chiefs were relatively free of business connections which were prevalent at high levels in the armed forces, and they resented the corruption and softness of senior generals' (Koon Woo Nam, *op. cit.* [Chapter 4, note 61], p. 201, note 56: original source, *Washington Post*, 19 December 1979).

9 Koon Woo Nam, *op. cit.* [Chapter 4, note 61], p. 206: original sources, *New York Times*, 25 November 1979; and *Washington Post*, 19 December 1979.

10 Koon Woo Nam, *op. cit.* [Chapter 4, note 61], p. 206: original source, *The Dong-A Daily News*, 1 January 1980.

11 *The Korean Society of Turmoil Before and After 1980: A Selected Collection of the Contemporary History*, Vol. 1 (Seoul: Sageijul Press, 1984), p. 169 (in Korean).

12 *The Dong-A Daily News*, 15 April 1980. The press also drove business groups into a corner and boosted public opinion against immoral big business activities. For instance, in April, an article entitled, '*Jaebols* and Cornering of Real Estate', blamed business groups for their non-productive interest maximization. That is, it maintained that big business firms had a corner on non-business real estate even during the economic depression period despite their financial difficulties within the tight money policy; thus, they took advantage of their privileged access to domestic loans for non-business investment and, subsequently, their financial status worsened (*The Chosun Daily News*, 17 April 1980).

13 *The Dong-A Daily News*, 24 January and 22 February 1980.

14 *The Chosun Daily News*, 15 February. Also, on 9 May 1980, the representative conference of the National Industrial Federation of Metal Labour Unions was broken into and occupied by metal workers who demanded that existing authoritarian labour leaders be expelled and replaced by new ones in order to achieve democratic leadership (*The Chosun Daily News*, 10 May 1980).

15 *The Chosun Daily News*, 30 April 1980.

16 For labour-related laws under Park's regime, see Ryung-In Shin, *Labour Laws and Labour Movement* (Seoul: Ilwulsugak Press, 1987), pp. 97–110 (in Korean). On 13 May 1980, a rally for securing labour's three primary rights and political activities was held by the FKTU (*The Chosun Daily News*, 13 May 1980).

17 *The Chosun Daily News*, 19 January 1980.

18 *The Korea Herald*, 23 January 1980.

19 *The Korea Herald*, 24 January 1980.

20 *The Korea Herald*, 24 January 1980.

21 'This Year's Biggest Task of Our Economy', *Monthly Joongang* (March 1980), pp. 211–20 (in Korean).

22 *The Korea Herald*, 6 February 1980.

23 See FKI Chairman Chung's Special Speech, 'How Far Does the Prosperity of Korea Depend on Greater Independences by Business?', *The Korean Business Review* (published by the FKI) (November 1979). In December 1979, the FKI also expressed its policy suggestions for a civil-led economic management as a means for overcoming economic crisis. See the FKI, *Twenty Years' History of the FKI* (Seoul: 1983), pp. 574–76 (in Korean).

24 *The Korea Herald*, 8 February 1980.

25 June-Sik Park, 'Labour Movement Before and After 1980 and State Intervention', in the Korean Industrial Society Research Council, ed., *Today's Korean Capitalism and the State* (Seoul: Hangil Press, 1988), pp. 329–33 (in Korean); Sun-June Cho, op. cit.; *The Dong-A Daily News*, 30 April and 2 May 1980; and *The Chosun Daily News*, 27 April 1980.

26 *The Chosun Daily News*, 3 May 1980.

27 *The Chosun Daily News*, 1 February 1980.

28 For information regarding increases in export financing and domestic credit supply credits, see *The Korea Herald*, 6 December 1979 and 8 May 1980.

29 *The Maeil Kyungje Daily News*, 29 November 1979 and 8 January 1980. The National Assembly Records, *The 9th Session of the Commerce and Industry Committee in the 103rd National Assembly Meeting* (Seoul: February 1980), p. 49 (in Korean).

30 *The Maeil Kyungje Daily News*, 29 November 1979 and 8 January 1980. For the detailed process of Daewoo's absorbing and merging the Okpo Shipbuilding Yard in 1978, Bum-Sung Chun, *Kim Woo Joong* (the Chairman of the Daewoo Business Group) (Seoul: Su Moon Dang Press, 1987), pp. 364–78 (in Korean).

31 See KDI, *Collection of Government Documents and Study Reports Related to Economic Stabilization Policies*, Vol. 1, pp. 84–86.

32 *The Maeil Kyungje Daily News*, 11 January 1980.

33 *The Maeil Kyungje Daily News*, 24 January 1980.

34 Eui-Kyun Kim, *op. cit.* [Chapter 6, note 52], pp. 258–59; and *The Maeil Kyungje Daily News*, 23 January 1980. The following generalized argument of Stallings fits in this Korean case: '. . . a distinction must be drawn between public and private lenders since public lenders are more likely to maintain control over their funds. For example, just as much as direct investors, although in different ways, bilateral and multilateral agency officials want to determine how their money will be spent. Project loans are carefully monitored, and deviations from agreed plans lead to a cut-off of disbursement'. Barbara Stallings, 'International Lending and the Relative Autonomy of the State: A Case Study of Twentieth-Century Peru', *Politics & Society* 14 (No. 3, 1985), pp. 260–61.

35 *The Maeil Kyungje Daily News*, 14 February 1980.

36 *The Maeil Kyungje Daily News*, 3 April 1980.

37 *The Maeil Kyungje Daily News*, 24 April 1980.
38 *The Maeil Kyungje Daily News*, 14 May 1980.
39 Eui-Kyun Kim, *op. cit.* [Chapter 6, note 52], p. 258.

Chapter 6

The policy failure of the second investment adjustment

This chapter will focus on why and how the new repressive military regime failed to achieve the second heavy and chemical investment adjustment within the framework of institutional change.

THE POLITICAL REGRESSION TO A NEW AUTHORITARIAN REGIME AND INSTITUTIONAL CHANGES

This section will analyse the following: how the state institutions had been changed after the emergence of the military regime; how the new military leaders reshuffled the existing state managers and social groups; and, particularly, how the new authoritarian regime changed institutions both between the state and big business, and between state and market, for the purpose of economic control over business groups.

The emergence of the junta-like repressive political organization

In May 1980, the political turmoil sharply decreased not only businessmen's confidence in their activities but also the interim government's capabilities to bring about a peaceful political transition to a civil government, thereby greatly increasing the possibility that a military coup for political power would occur.[1] On the night of 17 May the military cracked down on students, opposition leaders, and politicians. The Martial Law Command arrested a number of intellectuals, professors, and national assemblymen, as well as prominent politicians, including Dae-Jung Kim.[2] On the same day, it expanded the martial law, which transformed the existing limited martial law into one that imposed martial law on the entire nation. Immediately after the announcement of the full martial law, the military issued the Martial Law Decree No. 10 which banned all kinds of political activities and other politics-oriented assemblies and rallies, both indoor and outdoor.

Choy's government clearly had not expected this kind of military intervention in the nation's political affairs, for it was reported, on the same day, that Choy was to announce his determination to accept people's political demands for a constitutional amendment and for a quick transfer of political power to a civil government, by means of a legitimate election, in order to resolve the political turmoil.[3] Thus, the expansion of the martial law was part of the military leaders' plan to take over political power under the cover of devising security measures to counter North Korean threats and social unrest. In this way, the military intervention amounted to the new military leaders' second coup to grasp political power, whereas the mutiny within the military against their senior generals on 12 December 1979 was the same group's (junior generals) first coup to control military power.

On the next day, the Kwangju uprising against the military crackdown occurred. The protestors demanded the immediate withdrawal of martial law, speedy implementation of the democratic political transition, and the removal of Doo-Whan Chun, the most powerful coup leader. The military's harsh and cruel response to the uprising for democratization resulted in the Kwangju massacre.[4] Immediately after the Kwangju incident, the so-called reform-oriented military leaders embarked upon building their political organizations in order to gain political power. On 31 May, the Special Committee for National Security Measures (SCNSM) was established by the military. It was ostensibly to assist President Choy and the interim government in 'directing and supervising martial law affairs' and 'examining national policies' in order to 'facilitate the coordinating mechanism between the cabinet and the Martial Law authorities'.[5] In reality, the junta-like committee had operated through its Standing Committee and thirteen separate subcommittees as the ultimate, powerful decision-making organization for political, social, and economic affairs until 22 October 1980.

The massive reshuffling of state managers and social groups

First, the SCNSM began to implement a socio-political reshuffling for the so-called purification in order to legitimize its emergence at the early stage and to prepare for a new institutional building in state, society, and market. The committee announced that its four basic policy goals were 'reinforcement of the national security posture against internal and external situations, helping the government [to] actively overcome economic difficulties, maintenance of social stability for smooth political development, and establishment of a national discipline by eliminating various social evils'. Their implementation guidelines included measures to 'refresh the confused political climate and implement "ethical politics" under which free criticism is possible against injustice and immorality' and to 'rectify amoral business activities of enterprises and illegal activities by labour unions'.[6]

The Social Purification Subcommittee, one of thirteen subcommittees, enforced compulsory and audacious purges of bureaucrats, public employees, labour union leaders, politicians, church leaders, and journalists.[7] Targets of the purges were largely those who had amassed huge fortunes through abuses of power, incompetent and easy-going officials, opportunists, those who were accused of misconduct in their positions, and those who led disreputable public or private lives.[8] However, some old-timers were compelled to retire to make way for their juniors. In many cases, the criteria for purging were arbitrarily applied under unfair charges.

In July, the junta-like committee announced the purge of 4,760 low- to medium-level public employees from the central and provincial agencies, including policemen, firemen, tax collectors, and customs officials; it also dismissed 232 high government officials with the rank of the second grade and up, thereby including a cabinet minister and six vice ministers.[9] In November 1980, Chun's government purged 567 politicians and barred them from engaging in political activities for the following eight years.[10] In addition, purges were extended to bank and non-bank financial institutions and government-invested corporations; over 800 persons were dismissed in this sector.[11] Furthermore, 611 educational public service employees and 1,212 employees of the fisheries and agricultural cooperatives were dismissed.[12]

The process of ensuring political control through purification spread over both the labour and the business sectors. In the labour sector, shortly after the expansion of martial law, the Administration of Labour Affairs inspected such upper-level labour organizations as the FKTU, seventeen industrial labour federations, and 557 industrial labour chapters so as to select labour union leaders who had abused their power by ignoring workers' interests.[13] As a result, in August the SCNSM purged the Chairman of the FKTU and the chairmen of eleven industrial labour federations; it also dissolved 106 regional labour chapters in order to weaken the industrial labour system and limit labour disputes at the enterprise level. In September, the special committee purged 191 labour union leaders who had actively led the democratization movement of their labour unions and had sought the improvement of labour rights and strong collective actions at the firm level.[14]

The so-called reformist military leaders looked unfavourably on the big businessmen who had maintained the state-big business governing alliance during the period of heavy and chemical industrialization and had aggravated the economic situation of the late 1970s as a result of their excessive competition in the HCIs. As an instant response, as I will mention later, the SCNSM attempted to impose the compulsory and bold mergers of the big business firms in order to attain the investment adjustment that had been unsuccessful under the former governments. In the long run, the coup leaders planned to put big businessmen under government control, because their influence had grown to the extent that they could challenge and oppose government economic management. Furthermore, the leaders broke down the state-big business governing coalition with a view towards gaining public support to legitimize the military intervention.

Interestingly, however, the social purification drive did not purge businessmen who had accumulated their wealth through illegal means and benefited from privileged concessions, especially through their collusive connections with political leaders under the Park regime. As a matter of fact, young colonels among the military leaders had proposed a purge of large entrepreneurs in the name of 'corrupt ill-wealth accumulation'. But influential high government officials persuaded them to cancel their proposal, arguing that big businessmen had made positive contributions to economic development. The big businessmen themselves also desperately intensified their lobbying activities to prevent an implementation of the proposal and offered the military leaders political funds for social reforms.[15]

After all, the military leaders also worried about the possible harmful effects to the already depressed economy, which would result from purges of big businessmen and, thus, they changed their minds.[16] The special committee forced the four major peak business associations (the FKI, the KCCI, the KFTA, and the KFSMB) to declare and realize the 'Company Ethics Platforms'.[17] In July, the ethics platforms were adopted in the 'Company Climate Renovation Rally', which was led by the business interest groups. Their contents were as follows: improving productivity and quality of the goods for an increase in exports and price stability; separating ownership from management in terms of the social responsibility of companies; revitalizing the Factory *Saemoul* (New Village) Movement to reinforce labour-management cooperation; restraining big business firms' excessive business concentration, overlapped investment, and unfair trade; giving up the abnormal pursuit of profits by extreme reliance on external financing; and thus playing a leading role in the construction of a welfare state by realizing a just society.[18]

As shown above, the military's emergence as a force governing the crisis led to the complete breakdown of the remaining institutional structures of the state and between state and society. The military leaders regarded the massive reshuffling of major actors as the preliminary task for building new institutions. In fact, the purification drive amounted to an instrument for the military's political control over the ruling elites and social groups rather than a tool for socio-political reform in a real sense.

The institutional change for economic control over big business

Chun's interim government (from the military intervention on 17 May 1980 to the emergence of the Fifth Republic on 3 March 1981)[19] embarked on building new institutions both between the state and big business, and between state and market by means of strong state interventionist measures. The institutional building served as its short-term strategy to ensure economic control over big business irregularities and to prevent its dominance in the market. At the same time, the government began to form an economic plan and to take gradual steps for economic liberalization as part of its long-term reform strategy. This long-term policy orientation towards free market competition was also supposed to indirectly restrict big businessmen's privileged access to policy loans and their mono-oligopolized production in the market.

The movement for business ethics was detailed in the drastic policy proposal presented for a 'Monopoly Regulation and Fair Trade Act' on 19 September 1980. This policy measure expressed the new military leaders' strong determination to control big businessmen's unfair practices. During the 1970s, in contrast, the Park authoritarian regime had strongly encouraged the establishment of large enterprises to take advantage of scale economies in the HCIs based on the state-big business ruling alliance. The SCNSM actions marked a decisive turning point in the government's policy towards conglomerates. Park's government had attempted to enact monopoly regulation on several occasions; but in the face of strong big business resistance, it had failed to implement even the concerned laws that had been ostensibly established in the 1970s.[20]

The EPB had prepared for the economic act as part of the Comprehensive Measures for Economic Stabilization (CMES) of 1979 and the long-term economic liberalization policy. The EPB's main purpose was to control price manipulation of the market dominating companies in advance, and thus to attain price stability by leaving the prices to be determined by a liberalized market mechanism. In the process of policy formulation, the EPB faced sharp opposition from the peak business associations of the KCCI and the FKI, the other economic ministries of the MF and the MCI, and even some members of the SCNSM. The chairmen of the Subcommittee of Commerce, Industry, and Resources and the Subcommittee of Economy and Science within the SCNSM strongly supported the EPB's draft for mono-oligopoly regulation and mitigated the opposite views from the other organizations.[21] The draft was passed, with a little revision, through the Legislative Council for National Security in December 1980 and became effective in April 1981.

The monopolistic and oligopolistic market structure was most visible at the level of the commodity market. If we define the mono-oligopolistic market as a market where the top three firms account for more than 60 percent of the total share, the ratios of such markets in 1977 and 1982 were around 85 percent in terms of the number of products and 65 percent in terms of shipment.[22] This kind of market structure was the result of high business concentration. The unbalanced business structure, which existed between the large and small-medium firms, was one of the side effects that had resulted from the high economic growth strategy of export-oriented industrialization under Park's nearly two-decade regime. The market shares in manufacturing taken by the top 100 firms in terms of shipment were 44.9 percent and 46.8 percent in 1977 and 1982, respectively. The ratios of business concentration in Korea were higher than Japan's 27.3 percent in 1980 and Taiwan's 21.9 percent in 1980.[23]

The Monopoly Regulation and Fair Trade Act was established in order to rectify both the skewed market structure and the high business concentration. The major elements of the Act were as follows: it would prohibit undue price activities by market dominating firms; it would forbid such activities as consolidation, acquisition of stock-holdings, and appointments of new personnel that would impede normal market competition; it would prohibit unfair trade activities whose scope would include contracts or acts involving foreign capital or technology; and, furthermore, it would restrain unfair activities of business associations and would plan to establish a 'Fair Trade Committee'.[24]

Another astonishing measure for business purification was realized as the 'Strengthening of Business Firms' Financial Status' on 27 September 1980. This institutional change between state and big business enforced the state's economic control over big business irregularities and expansion in order to improve the large firms' financial structure. The presidential directives were

> expediting the disposal and restricting the possession of real estate for non-business use by large corporations; adjustment of affiliated companies of conglomerates; supplementing the corporation liquidation system and restraining relief financing; introduction of the external audit system to joint-stock corporations under the commercial code; and improvement of corporation tax systems to save business expenditure and support improvement of financial structure.[25]

Shortly after the announcement of the policy measures, business leaders decided to organize the 'Council for Measures to Strengthen Business Firms' Financial Status' as an ad hoc committee that would deal with the policy implementation.[26] In general, concerned business groups agreed to the government policy to enhance their financial structure, but they worried about the expected plummeting of business confidence in investment. In particular, they were compelled to cut off some of their marginal subsidiaries affiliated with their parent companies under the repressive authoritarian regime even though they had a feeling of strong resistance against the mandatory disposal measure.[27]

In contrast to the policy measures against big business, the Chun interim government tried to increase the small and medium business confidence in investment. While Park's regime, during the latter half of 1979, took the big business-oriented steps to stimulate the economy, Chun's interim government tried to promote the business activities of small and medium firms. Small and medium companies had suffered from big business firms' dominance of the financial and commodity market during the period of heavy and chemical industrial promotion and, subsequently, from Park's economic stabilization policies of the late 1970s. The Park regime had attempted to revitalize the HCIs by increasing financial supports for the HCIs in order to overcome the deep economic recession. In contrast, the new interim government focused on rescuing small and medium business firms that were experiencing financial difficulties and on promoting their activities; moreover, it tightly regulated big business investments and its financial structure, and reduced privileges for big business. The government offered only the rescue funds that were necessary for heavy and chemical industrial operation. Similarly, just as Park's regime had attempted to rectify the economic and political situation during the second half of 1979, Chun's interim government made desperate efforts to increase exports and revitalize the economy within the framework of stabilization.

The rate of economic growth during the first half of 1980 was –4 percent, the first negative growth rate since 1961.[28] This negative growth rate resulted from the high growth-oriented economic strategy, which was accompanied by high inflation (as a product of the overambitious heavy and chemical industrial promotion), the international oil-shock, and the economic externality of the socio-political instability. Big business firms' investments for facilities were reduced during the first half of 1980, in comparison to the same period of 1979, by 19.1 percent in the manufacturing industries and by 41.9 percent in the export industries, mainly because of financial difficulties and overinvestment in the HCIs.[29]

In addition to the non-corporatist economic control over big business firms, the government in September took measures to revamp the business organizational structure in order to promote tight corporatist control over general business through an institutional change between the state and employers' interest groups. A total of twenty-eight associations and cooperatives under the jurisdiction of the MCI were either dissolved or incorporated into upper level or similar organizations. Basically, the MCI intended to prevent business organizations' management irregularities and inefficiencies that resulted from overlapped functions. Therefore, 157 specialized interest groups would be under the direct control of the ministry. The measures were also aimed at protecting the interests of association members by readjusting their membership fees and regulating their operational guidelines.[30]

The economic reform-oriented planning

The military leaders intended to build new institutions for state-market relations, with the goal of economic liberalization, after they realized the short-term measures designed for economic stabilization. Most of the economic reform ideas were already announced by the EPB in January 1980 under Choy's interim government. At that time, the MF and the MCI were willing to follow the EPB-initiated policy measures for stabilization, but were reluctant to accept the EPB's policy goals for liberalization to achieve long-term economic stability. At this time, however, the SCNSM, with authoritarian leadership, propelled the economic reform based on the EPB's ideas and enforced its policy orientation on the other economic ministries.

Shortly after the emergence of the special committee, the EPB embarked on making the Fifth Five-Year Economic and Social Development Plan (1982–87) under the auspices of the new military group. In his presidential inauguration address on 1 September, Chun declared that his government would aim at building 'a society of democracy, welfare, and justice' in order to legitimate his new regime.[31] Here he put emphasis not only on economic stabilization but also on liberalization in line with the plan's policy reforms and guidelines.

The fifth plan was oriented towards building new institutions between state and market through 'indicative planning'. The plan was to implement the reform ideas for economic liberalization which were to achieve continuous growth based on long-term economic stability. The economic management was to shift the existing policy goals: from the growth-oriented economy to a stability-oriented economy; from unbalanced industrial policy to balanced industrial policy; and from the state-led economy to a private-initiated economy.[32]

Jai-Ik Kim (one of the leaders in the EPB's reform group, Director-General of the Planning Bureau in the EPB, and Chairman of the Subcommittee of Economy and Science in the SCNSM) played a major role in the formation of economic reform policy. In the process of making the fifth plan, he and Kyung-Sik Kang (one of the leaders in the EPB's reform group and the Assistant Minister of Planning in the EPB) presented Chun with interim progress reports on several occasions. These opportunities enabled them to 'educate him comprehensively on a wide range of policy problems and issues, instil in him a sense of economic policy priority, imbue him with their viewpoints, and to measure his responses'.[33] Finally, they convinced Chun of the necessity and importance of their reform ideas, which would evolve into the major economic policies of Chun's regime.

Nevertheless, until the end of 1980, the Chun interim government had not effectively implemented the policy measures for economic stabilization, including the investment adjustment in the HCIs. Rather, the interim regime tried to restore the business confidence by revitalizing the depressed economy. At the same time, the implementation of reform was pending because the strong state interventionist measures were taken for stabilization to form a sound basis for economic liberalization.

THE FAILURE OF THE SECOND HCIIA: THE UNSUCCESSFUL STATE-CONTROLLED CAPITALIST COLLECTIVE ACTION

The policy-making process

Shortly after the establishment of the SCNSM, the President of Hyundai International, In-Young Chung, sent a letter of recommendation to the special committee and the concerned ministries; he complained about the investment adjustment of power-generating equipment and argued for abolishing the first HCIIA of 25 May 1979. On the other side, many business groups lobbied, in a competitive manner, the Subcommittee of Commerce, Industry, and Resources (SCIR) of the SCNSM for an investment adjustment in ill-managed and depressed heavy and chemical industrial sectors.[34] Each business group put pressures on the bureaucrats with its own proposal that included strict monopoly or oligopoly in one heavy and chemical industrial sector or in the production of one item in order to maximize its privileged profits.[35]

Ironically, until then, the big businessmen had objected to any investment realignment via state intervention in their investment decision-making. However, they had no choice but to rely on the government's adjustment, for they were at the risk of going bankrupt under the worsening economic conditions existing at that time; they could not expect to be able to bring about their autonomous adjustment in light of the intensity of the big business competition for survival during the economic crisis. This case explicitly showed the big businessmen's ambiguous and arbitrary positions between state intervention for solving overinvestment and economic liberalization for increasing big business autonomy in investment decision-making. Finally, setting aside each group's private interests, the SCNSM took a bold and compulsory step; it decided that one business group would monopolize the production either of power plant facilities or of passenger cars, according to the independent judgements of the committee's military leaders and technocrats.

The concerned business groups were compelled to obey the investment adjustment plan. In mid-August, before an announcement of the policy decision, the Chairman of the SCIR called the owners and top managers of the Hyundai Business Group and the Daewoo Business Group to his office. There, the Hyundai Group chose the passenger car field, leaving the Daewoo Group to monopolize the power-generating equipment field.[36]

During the economic crisis, the special committee imposed the second heavy and chemical industrial investment adjustment (HCIIA) mainly in the fields of power-generating equipment and automobile manufacturing. As a result of the first HCIIA's policy failure, the military leaders took broader, bolder and more coercive measures than had the first HCIIA. The scheme of industrial realignment on 20 August 1980, detailed that the hitherto three-tier structure of passenger car manufacturing would be reorganized into one; after the policy failure in attempts at a two-tier structure, the existing four-tier industrial structure of power-generating equipment production would be reshaped into the monopolized one.[37]

On 20 August 1980, the SCNSM announced the scheme of investment adjustment and detailed the plan's policy background, purpose, and effect. It tried to justify the method of investment adjustment by claiming that the policy measure was an indispensable measure to rescue both firms and financial institutions. It was to reduce the firms' dependence on government support, especially policy loans and to rationalize the industrial structure towards a balance both between large and small-medium firms and between heavy chemical and light industry; thus, the investment adjustment was a preliminary task that would facilitate the long-term management of economic liberalization for economic reform. The concerned business groups were urged to develop their merged fields not for their own self-interests but for national interests. The plan further emphasized the necessity of the merger by referring to effective monopolies of power-generating equipment production in other countries (France and Germany). Finally, the special committee estimated the curtailed amount of policy loans until 1983 at some 1,200 billion won.[38]

The major elements of the adjustment scheme were as follows: the Daewoo Heavy Industries of the Daewoo Business Group would incorporate its Okpo Integrated Machinery Plants with the Changwon and Goonpo factories of Hyundai International in the power-generating equipment and heavy construction equipment fields; the Hyundai Motor Company, a subsidiary of the Hyundai Business Group, would take over the Saehan Motor Company, a subsidiary of the Daewoo Business Group, in the passenger car manufacturing field, and the Kia Motors Corporation was to give up its production of passenger cars and specialize in small trucks of less than five tons; and finally, the SCNSM expected the concerned big business firms to autonomously adjust their overlapped investments through consolidation or item specialization in other overinvested sectors, such as heavy electrical machinery, electronic switching systems, and diesel engines.

The dualistic institutional structure of policy-making

As I mentioned previously, Chun's interim government imposed the massive and coercive socio-political reshuffling by the junta-like political organization. The rise of the repressive authoritarian regime was expected to enable the state to exert strong enforcement power over big business firms in the policy-making and implementation of the investment adjustment. However, the government could not come up with an efficient and realistic policy measure even though it had imposed the policy decision based on the big businessmen's compulsory compliance. Furthermore, the inefficiency and ambitiousness of the plan later affected the failure of policy implementation.

More specifically, a dualistic institutional structure of policy formation led to the unreasonable nature of the merger scheme, which was to integrate the heterogeneous business entities by means of the discretionary command, without industrial laws. The dualistic decision-making structure was characterized both by political and economic rationales, and by the division between military and bureaucracy.

The policy-making was based on two logics. One was the economic logic that a major cause of the economic crisis was the excessive heavy and chemical promotion.[39] The other was the political logic that the government should demonstrate its coercive power over big businesses even though the investment adjustment was contradictory to its long-term strategy of economic reform towards a civilian-led economy. The junta-like committee under the strong leadership of General Chun and later, President Chun's new interim government, adamantly propelled economic stabilization as part of its struggle toward political legitimation, despite the gradual and incremental policy for economic revitalization.

The political logic outweighed the economic rationale for investment adjustment under the influence of the reform-oriented military leaders. The HCIIA was strongly propelled by the coup military leaders who gave priority to purification for the so-called 'justice society', which opposed Park's economic policy orientation, in order to justify the series of military coups. The leaders tried to quickly solve the side effects of state-led heavy and chemical industrial promotion for the purpose of economic stability. The military leaders blamed big businessmen for their overinvestments in the HCIs, which resulted from their excessive competition and business expansion based on such privileges as tax exemption, huge financial supports, and mono-oligopolized investment licensing. The Chun interim government made an effort to gain legitimacy for the military intervention by cutting off the symbiotic state-big business coalition that had operated under the Park regime. As a result, the scheme for investment realignment included the overambitious merger plan between the largest business groups' major subsidiaries; the plan did not take into serious consideration sufficient inducements for the concerned business groups and the foreign companies' positions involved in technological tie-up or in joint venture.

The military leaders instilled their political logic into the economic decision-making of dispatched technocrats within the SCNSM. The Standing Committee under the SCNSM in effect ran the government; it was the ultimate decision-making organization, based on *de facto* power of authority, and was composed of eighteen military generals and twelve civilian government officials, including the chairmen of its subcommittees. In general, its policy decisions on socio-political and economic affairs were implemented through the appropriate ministries. The subcommittees under the Standing Committee were composed of colonels, some lieutenant-colonels, dispatched bureaucrats from concerned ministries, and professors. One or two of the colonels were involved as members of each subcommittee; they exercised authority over the government ministries and directed substantial policy operations.[40]

The Subcommittee of Commerce, Industry, and Resources (SCIR) took charge of the second HCIIA. The subcommittee consisted of two lieutenant-colonels and one colonel (two professors of the Military Academy and one research fellow), one university professor, the Heavy and Chemical Industry Assistant Minister of the MCI, and the Chief of the Planning and Management of the MCI, who served as Chairman.[41] However, the merger scheme did not reflect the SCIR's original proposal of a duopolized production (two-tier structures) in the power-generating equipment and passenger car fields, which had been initiated by the dispatched Assistant Minister of the MCI in the subcommittee. Chairman of the Subcommittee of Economy and Science, Jai-Ik Kim (the Director-General of the Bureau of Planning in the EPB), argued for monopolizing the production in each field to one business group (one-tier structures). The MCI's bureaucrats in the SCIR opposed the monopolies in each sector. Their reason was that the merger plan was not compatible with the 'justice society', including fair markets, one of the military leaders' slogans that was used to justify the military intervention in politics.[42]

Since the emergence of the SCNSM, Jai-Ik Kim (one of the leaders in the economic reform group, who had taken the CMES of 1979), had greatly influenced its economic policy-making; he had convinced General (later, President) Chun of the necessity of economic stabilization and had received Chun's favour and confidence.[43] Ultimately, the coup leaders, headed by General

Chun, adopted Kim's scheme, which was more ambitious and unrealistic than the MCI's idea.[44] The SCNSM was highly centralized and had the close cooperation of its members from the military and the bureaucracy, as they dealt with political affairs and sought to consolidate political power. On the other hand, the institutional structure of the economic policy-making within the special committee was neither coherent nor coordinative between the military and the bureaucrat members and among the dispatched government officials.

The following subsections will deal with the following: how the institutional change of state institutions, of state-big business relationships, and of the financial system affected the state managers' and the big businessmen's bargaining power; and how the limits of the state's policy instruments, the big businessmen's demands, and conflicts among the big business firms involving a foreign company, determined the failure of the second HCIIA.

The dualistic institutional structure between policy-making and implementation

In addition to the institutional structure of policy-making within the SCNSM, the division of jurisdiction between policy formulation and implementation diminished the state managers' coercive enforcement power in their efforts to realize the scheme of investment adjustment. In general, economic policy decisions made in the subcommittees were implemented through normal channels of the economic ministries under Chun's interim government, until the SCNSM was replaced by the Legislative Council for National Security on 29 October 1980. Due to the dualistic institutional structure that existed between policy-making and implementation, the strong decision-making authority for realigning the investment allocation had not been reflected, to a large extent, in the process of implementation under the jurisdiction of the MCI. That is, the MCI's bureaucrats faced difficulties in resolving the big businessmen's demands for financial incentives, and met their foot-dragging resistance in resolving both technical and financial matters because they lacked the coercive power of economic penalties to prevent big business non-compliance.

Furthermore, the MCI rarely coped with emerging problems by cooperating with the EPB and the MF in the process of policy implementation. It could have dealt with financial issues by way of such existing organizations as the Economic Ministers Meeting and the Economic Ministers Consultation Meeting (Roundtable). Within these organizations, policy coordination could have been achieved among the MF, the EPB, and the MCI regarding such issues as financial support limits for the merging companies under the tight monetary policy and the amount of policy loans available for the merger. As a result, the MCI could not intervene effectively in the merger process in order to troubleshoot issues. In the end, the SCNSM gave up and changed the original merger scheme.

Business groups' unwilling compliance

In the initial stage, the repressive military-political organization of the SCNSM and the tight corporatist and non-corporatist control over big business firms led to the big businessmen's unwilling compliance and the state managers' increased coercive enforcement power for implementing the investment adjustment. The concerned business groups' compliance had different meanings in terms of their own interests.

Hyundai International, one of the companies to be merged, was forced to accept the merger scheme by its compulsory compliance. The company argued that the overlapped investment in the field of power-generating equipment was due to the government's inconsistent policy of allowing the other business groups' participation and that the government should observe the original contract among Hyundai International, the IBRD, and the Korean government.

The Hyundai Business Group was also compelled to engage in the merger process of the two fields by its non-voluntary compliance with the military leaders' order.[45] After the failure of the merger scheme in December 1980, the Chairman of the Hyundai Group, Joo-Young Chung, gave his straightforward opinions on the investment adjustment in the HCIs. He criticized the state managers' inconsistent and much too interventionist HCI policy, which had brought about overinvestment in production facilities and induced excessive competition among business groups; he argued that the government should have solved the overinvestment problem from the standpoint of the market competition principle; he thought that the domestic overcapacity in the two fields could be settled, through exports, in the international market.[46] In other words, he advocated the state's non-intervention in businessmen's investment decision-making so that only the strongest firms would survive in the market. His position reflected his calculations of the benefits and costs from the merger plan: in market competition, without any investment adjustment in the two fields, both subsidiaries of the Hyundai Heavy Industries and the Hyundai Motor Company would survive and have highly competitive edges based on their good financial status compared to the other highly debted companies.

In contrast to these two groups, the Daewoo Business Group held the following position: as the continuing economic crisis worsened, the government should solve the problem of overinvestment in order to avoid further big business competition in the small domestic market, for this side effect had stemmed mainly from the state's ambitious intervention in heavy and chemical industrial promotion.[47] At the initial stage, the group also had no choice but to acquiesce in the forced investment adjustment that it had opposed. But, after the Hyundai Group chose the passenger car manufacturing field, it intended to take advantage of the planned monopolized right of production after the planned merger in the power plant facilities field that was largest among the HCI sectors in terms of the amount of capital and sales. This would present a good opportunity for the Daewoo Group to become the largest conglomerate in South Korea, if the government was to guarantee to the Daewoo Heavy Industries the monopolized right of sales and sufficient financial support. Thus, the Daewoo Group's quasi-voluntary compliance with the investment adjustment was in response to both coercion and incentives.

The business groups' demands

However, as I mentioned, the enforcement power of the SCNSM did not transfer automatically to the techno-bureaucrats' bargaining power over big business because of the dualistic institutional split between policy formation and implementation of the investment adjustment. Furthermore, the MCI's inefficient bargaining power was affected by the dualistic institutional structure of policy-making within the SCNSM and by the bureaucratic incoherence. The institutional change of the state's tight control over big business heightened the state managers' enforcement power, but did not necessarily enhance their bargaining power over business groups in their struggle to implement the investment adjustment.

The state's coercive control over big business firms was not an effective means to stir up the collective action of merging. The state managers' threats of economic penalties for big businessmen's non-compliance may have been unrealistic and ineffective in the largest business groups-dominated market structure and at the time of economic crisis. For an extreme case, to make a large conglomerate go bankrupt by suspending policy loans would have had a very harmful influence on the whole economy, affecting many subcontracting small and medium firms and the employment of a number of workers. It would have brought a loss of Korean big business firms' credit from foreign lenders and joint-venture partners. Moreover, it would have been more difficult to dissolve a business group, which did not actually go bankrupt, by means of other business groups' acquisitions of its subsidiaries.

Additionally, the threats of economic penalties were not a sufficient condition for the concerned business groups' collective action of investment adjustment. Not only 'negative' (coercive elements) but also 'positive selective incentives' were necessary to compel the concerned business groups to bear the costs of the state-enforced mergers.[48] The heavy and chemical industrial promotion stimulated big business participation by providing high inducements and relatively high coercion at the initial stage, whereas the investment adjustment tried to force big business compliance by imposing low inducements and high coercion.

Indeed, the SCNSM instructed the business groups to follow basic guidelines for merging in accordance with the principle of 'first merging, later settling accounts': at first, the transfer and takeover of assets should be completed on the basis of book values for immediate management participation of the merging companies; along with these acquisitions, the concerned firms should obey the decisions of such government-designated agencies as the Korean Appraisal Board as to estimates of total assets and settlements of accounts; the Hyundai Group should return to Hyundai International what the former acquired from the latter according to the same principle of 'first merging, later settling accounts' of the first HCIIA on 25 May 1979; Hyundai International should repay in cash the amount that Hyundai Heavy Industries invested in the construction of Hyundai International's Changwon factory; and the Hyundai Group should absorb the capital share of the Daewoo Group in the Saehan Motor Company by first paying in cash on the basis of book values and then settling accounts at a later time.[49]

These guidelines were compulsory measures for the merger procedure until the end of August 1980. As for possible measures of inducement in settling accounts, the guidelines only said: in principle, the merging companies would pay for the loss that the corporations to be merged would suffer as a result of abandoning facilities; but, in these cases, the government would take supplementary compensating measures for the loss when the company to be merged would suffer from its financially difficult management.[50] Even this kind of feasible financial incentive was not applied to the merging companies.

As in the case of the first HCIIA, the concerned business groups were not prepared to sacrifice their private interests for the mergers without the rewards of sufficient financial incentives. At most, they intended to maximize their interests through the mergers. At least, they were reluctant to implement the mergers without sufficient financial support or an exclusive sales contract. As the authority of adjustment transferred from the SCNSM to the MCI for the policy implementation, the big businessmen seemed to perceive less risk in resisting the mergers. They began to demand prerequisites before completing the consolidations.

On 13 September 1980, the Chairman of the Daewoo Business Group, Woo-Joong Kim, took over management authority of Hyundai International and established the Korean Heavy Industrial Corporation (KHIC) as the integrated company.[51] Although the Daewoo Group would take responsibility for the management, the government would have shareholders' voting rights for the time being. In fact, the amount of authorized capital for Hyundai International's factories was 80 billion won. Forty-two billion won of paid-in capital was composed of Hyundai International's 20 billion won, the Korea Development Bank's 17 billion won, and the Korea Exchange Bank's 5 billion won. The state-owned and managed banks shared 52.7 percent of the total stocks. Thus, the government planned to guide the Daewoo Group to share stocks of over 50 percent, except for the state capital because the Daewoo Group was not able to invest the whole amount of paid-in capital. To help Daewoo's financial difficulties, the government would allow the KHIC to monopolize the production of all power plant facilities, including construction works in some cases, for forthcoming hydroelectric, thermoelectric, and nuclear power plants.[52]

However, the Daewoo Group required that the government should supply a huge amount of capital in order to normalize the financially ill-managed Hyundai International's factories for power-generating and heavy construction equipments (an interest repayment of 100 million won per day was needed even before completion of the Changwon factory's construction). The Daewoo Group announced an ambitious plan of investment and procurement of necessary capital: until 1985, 800 billion won would be spent on finishing the construction works and normalizing the operations of Hyundai International and the Okpo Integrated Machinery Plants (500 billion won for the former and 300 billion won for the latter); and it would invest 100 billion won in power-generating equipment by financing its internal funds, which would be mobilized by the transfer of its stocks in the Saehan Motor Company to the Hyundai Motor Company (26,500 million won), the sale of its headquarters building (50,000 million won), and a disposal of its affiliated companies' real estate (23,500 million won).[53] As a consequence, for the KHIC, the government would have to supply financial support of 400 billion won, adding to the internal financing. Furthermore, the business group asked the government for its permission to monopolize construction works on orders of power plants; it also demanded a sharp decrease of bank interest rates, which would help to mitigate its heavy burden of debt service.[54]

Daewoo's position was that it would deserve the privileged supports from the government and that it was qualified to absorb Hyundai International's factories not because of its abilities of financial mobilization but because of those of management.[55] As a matter of fact, before merging, the Daewoo Heavy Industries invested only 15 billion won, while Hyundai International and the Hyundai Heavy Industries invested 260 billion won and 50 billion won in the field of power-generating equipment, respectively. At that time, the Hyundai Group had better financial status than the Daewoo Group: the former had total assets of 2,016,200 million won (equity capital: 578,000 million won; liabilities: 1,438,000 million won) and a debt-equity ratio of 249 percent, whereas the latter had total assets of 1,579,700 million won (equity capital: 278,800 million won; liabilities: 1,300,900 million won) and a debt-equity ratio of 470 percent.[56]

Later, on 21 October 1980, the government announced its plan of financial support for the KHIC after seriously considering Daewoo's demands. The government would make it possible for the KHIC to induce cash loans from overseas banking institutions to help finance the power plant equipment manufacturing industry. It also planned to extend some 45,000 million won in relief funds to the KHIC. Additionally, matured loans owed by the KHIC would be allowed to be rolled over as a means of supporting its financially troubled situation.[57] Still, the MCI came up with only these temporary policy instruments for rescue financing, but had not made a decision on long-term financial aid to the KHIC, which could have covered Daewoo's request of 400 billion won.

Conflicts among big business firms, including the multinational company

Hyundai versus Daewoo

Interest conflicts between the concerned business groups and those between a domestic business group and an involved foreign company reduced the state managers' bargaining power over individual firms and augmented the business groups' individual bargaining power. The policy measures for merging led to the business groups' competition for their own interest maximization within the limits of investment adjustment. As a result, the concerned big business firms faced sharp conflicts in settling accounts. The state could not avoiding intervening in these cases. Furthermore, in some cases, the firms took advantage of the government in order to improve their competitive capabilities. That is, they induced the state managers, through lobbying, to take steps that would serve their interests.

First of all, the Daewoo Group could not reach an agreement with the Hyundai Group on an estimate of the Hyundai Group's assets that had been invested in Hyundai International in accordance with the first HCIIA. According to the merger guidelines, the government was supposed to solve this problem by an assets estimate of Hyundai International, which would be investigated by the Office of National Tax Administration and the Korea Appraisal Board.[58]

Another problem existed regarding the Daewoo Group's acquisition of the Hyundai Group's ongoing power plant projects since the investment adjustment on 25 May 1979. The two groups had largely different estimates for the amount that the Hyundai Group had invested in building several thermoelectric and nuclear power plant facilities. The Daewoo Group argued for repaying 1 percent of planned total investment amounts to the Hyundai Group while the latter insisted on 10 percent; later, the government tried to bring about a compromise between them by suggesting 5.5 percent.[59] These incidences of state intervention, however, were expected to face many difficulties in settling the conflicting property rights of these business groups by means of coercive power.

Hyundai versus GM

In the meantime, in its merging process to form a monopoly in the passenger car manufacturing industry, the Hyundai Group was in a prolonged conflict with the General Motors Corporation (GM: the foreign partner of the Saehan Motor joint-venture company, a subsidiary of the Daewoo Group). The issues of friction concerned GM's equity ratio in the newly merged company and the different marketing strategies of GM and the Hyundai Motor Company (HMC: a subsidiary of the Hyundai Group).

According to the merger guidelines of the SCNSM, the Hyundai Motor Company was supposed to absorb Daewoo's equity shares (13,250 million won: 50 percent of the total capital in book value) of the Saehan Motor Company (SMC). Following this measure, the Hyundai Group tried to establish the newly integrated company which would be capitalized by 64,750 million won (38,250 million won as its equity capital of the HMC and 26,500 million won as the total capital of the SMC). In this case, the Hyundai Group would own 80 percent (51,500 million won) of the newly merged company's total equity capital, while GM would hold 20 percent (13,250 million won: 50 percent of the SMC's total capital). In this scenario, GM could no longer exercise veto power in management, as its ratio of shares would be below one-third of the total stocks.[60]

However, GM opposed these merger plans and instead presented an idea for increasing its equity capital up to 50 percent in the proposed integrated joint venture in which it would be an equal business partner. Shortly after the second HCIIA, on 22 August, a delegation of GM negotiators, led by GM Vice-President John P. McCormack, came to Korea, and GM's special task force joined this group on 28 August. The HMC also formed its practical group for acquisition and it negotiated with GM on ten different occasions concerning their merger.

The Vice-President of GM made the following arguments regarding the reasons for GM's desire for an equal voice in the proposed merger and about what advantages it could bring to Korea:

> GM wants an equal equity share in the proposed merger to assure an equal voice in management. That does not mean dominance, it means equality, just as we have today in Saehan. Neither partner has veto power, it is a powerful stimulus to both parties to make the necessary compromises to assure that the interests of the merged company always take precedence over everything else. GM has a fully developed worldwide network of major car producers and a distribution system to match these facilities. Korea could benefit from this fact in many ways ranging all the way from training personnel to lending its expertise to support and develop worldwide distribution.[61]

The Hyundai Group, however, insisted that GM should not own more than 30 percent in equity shares of the would-be joint venture so that GM would be prevented from gaining a virtual management dominance based on its veto power. President of the HMC, Se-Young Chung, explained Hyundai's position in terms of the multinational corporation's dominance over the Korean automobile industry: 'If and when GM is assured of 50 percent equity share in the proposed joint venture tied up with Hyundai, the auto company would be a multinational business interest which is beyond the managerial influence of the Korean business partner'; 'the joint venture is destined to become a mere part of GM's worldwide automobile assemblyline for the "World Car" which GM plans to develop as a fuel-efficient subcompact' instead of Hyundai's own Korea Model passenger car. Firmly saying that the equal equity participation requested by GM was nonsense in consideration of the importance of the auto industry to the national interest, Chung disclosed 'Hyundai Group plans to invest some 150,000 million won to the merged auto company if Hyundai Motor can have the controlling interest of the automobile firm in a joint venture with the GMC'; and for this, the Hyundai Group was prepared to dispose of its key subsidiaries, if necessary, while making its major companies of the Hyundai Construction Co. and the Hyundai Heavy Industries go public.[62]

Finally, the government intended to put an end to the tug-of-war between the HMC and GM in the merger of the SMC and the HMC at the end of October. The MCI was determined to accomplish the planned merger in the passenger car industry by resolving the dispute of equity and management rights through exercising its influence. It asked the parties to submit their respective reports about their final positions on the merger issue before the end of October. But it did not find any ideas of settlement to make the companies reach a compromise.[63]

The government was in a dilemma. It could not force GM to follow the merger plan according to the original guidelines of the SCNSM, which the Hyundai Group had defended. It could not persuade the multinational company to make a concession to the HMC because the United States had influence on the SCNSM regarding GM's involvement in the passenger car merger.[64] On the other hand, the interim government had much difficulty in making the HMC accept GM's demands in several issue areas where both the state and the HMC had common interests.

Primarily, the purpose of the investment adjustment was not only to reduce overinvestment in the domestic market in the short run, but also to improve the concerned companies' export competitiveness in the international market in the long run. Second, the marketing management of GM, through auto part specialization of its own model in foreign countries, would make it difficult to develop Korean model cars through localization. Finally, it was not desirable that the multinational company would intervene much in the automobile industry, one of Korea's key industries, which had high forward and backward industrial effects.[65] As a result, the MCI failed to settle the interest conflicts between the domestic business group and the multinational corporation.

The failure of policy implementation

As shown above, the state interventions in the merging cases were unsuccessful. The MCI, which had jurisdiction over the policy implementation of investment adjustment, could not impose the original SCNSM guidelines for merging on the big business conflicts. Moreover, it was not able to solve the private asset conflicts through compulsory mediation because the SMC and Hyundai International to be merged did not go bankrupt.

In particular, GM, as the foreign actor, had a decisive impact on the failure of the car industry merger by nullifying the state managers' enforcement power under the repressive authoritarian regime. In the end, the attempt to merge the automobile companies was unsuccessful; on 28 February 1981, the government announced the policy change that directed that both the HMC and the SMC would monopolize production of passenger cars according to the Automobile Rationalization Measure.[66]

GM's objections to the merger plan indirectly affected the merger failure in the power plant industry. When the Hyundai Group faced the abandonment of negotiations between Hyundai and GM, it attempted to absorb only Daewoo's equity shares in the SMC instead of giving up the proposed merger between the HMC and the SMC. However, GM opposed even the equity acquisition by suddenly bringing up the GM-SMC joint-contract conditions dictating that the Daewoo Group should give GM notice and gain GM's agreement 180 days before disposing of its equity capital.[67] Because of this conflict, the Daewoo Group was in a position where it could not finance the planned internal funds for the KHIC without selling its equities in the SMC.[68] In addition, the Daewoo Group was confronted with difficulties in financing a huge amount of funds in the process of merging power-generating facilities, for the state had not guaranteed a specific plan for sufficient financial supports to satisfy its demands.

The business group also asked the government to give it the right to monopolize not only equipment production but also construction works of all forthcoming power plants. To make matters worse, the government could not allow its monopoly right of power plant construction works. In the behind-the-scenes decision-making process, construction companies of other business groups, including the Hyundai Group, desperately lobbied the state managers so as to prevent the Daewoo Group from gaining the exclusive right. The state-run Korean Electric Power Corporation (KEPC), which took charge of power plant construction, also objected to Daewoo's demands for the monopolized construction works.[69]

Furthermore, both the Hyundai Group and the KEPC induced the government to change the KHIC under the Daewoo group into a public enterprise. Since the first HCIIA, the Hyundai Group had argued that it would be more desirable to establish a state-run company in order to normalize the financially troubled Changwon factory of Hyundai International.[70] The KEPC, under the Ministry of Power and Resources, had objected to the formation of a private monopoly in the production of power-generating equipment because it wanted to protect its privileged right to give an order to any domestic or foreign company through open bidding. The state-run company lobbied one of the most powerful military leaders in order to merge the concerned companies into a public enterprise that would be run under the KEPC's management.[71]

In the end, on 29 October 1980, shortly after the dissolution of the SCNSM,[72] the government announced that the KHIC would change from a private enterprise, under the Daewoo Group, to a public one.[73] Its paid-in capital would be composed of 100 billion won of state fiscal investment, 45 billion won from the Korea Development Bank (KDB), and 65 billion won from the Korea Exchange Bank in 1980; subsequently 100 billion won from the state and 50 billion won from the KDB would be added in 1981. The Minister of the MCI said that the government would also supply the would-be public enterprise with a financial support of 50 billion won and a foreign cash loan of 100 billion won.[74] The financing funds of over 500 billion won, which was as much as the Daewoo group's planned amount for normal operation, were to be invested in the merged state-run company.

The major reason for this policy change was Daewoo's difficulty in financing its own funds to finish the construction and normalize the operation of the KHIC.[75] If the government had accepted Daewoo's financial demands, it could not have mobilized sufficient domestic and foreign loans without state subsidies of fiscal investment within the limits of the tight monetary policy. Here, the institutional change for economic stabilization in the financial system made economic technocrats reluctant to supply huge policy loans. To establish a financially improved, merged company, it had to increase the KHIC's paid-in capital through fiscal investment up to a lower debt-equity ratio. In this case, the state, not the Daewoo Group, would share over 50 percent of KHIC's total equity capital. Thus, the government preferred direct investment of state capital to unfair and privileged supports of huge capital for one business group, even though the establishment of the public enterprise would contradict the long-term policy goal of economic liberalization. Here, the institutional change for strict state control over big business affected this policy choice.

The investment adjustment in the marginal HCI sectors

In an exceptional case, the government succeeded in implementing the policy measures of investment adjustment on 7 October 1980, by means of investment designation, in most cases, with specialized groupings. The MCI imposed investment designations on each business group in detailed items of such heavy and chemical products as heavy electrical equipment, electronic switching systems, and diesel engines; it also enforced mergers in the two fields of ultra-high-power transformers with more than 154 kV capacity, and copper smelting.[76]

The secondary phase of HCIIA was originally devised by the Subcommittee of Commerce, Industry, and Resources in the SCNSM. In contrast to the two previous major HCIIAs, the government gave the business groups concerned one month's time to achieve a voluntary investment adjustment through their mutual consent.[77] However, the business groups failed to adjust their investments by themselves, without state intervention. Later, the MCI made specific decisions for the adjustment in the less seriously overinvested and marginal HCI sectors. The policy decisions were based on contents discussed in the process of big business autonomous realignment.

In addition, the following factors in this adjustment accounted for the differences between the previous major cases of policy failure and this case of policy success. First, the MCI alone had made the scheme of investment reallocation without bureaucratic conflicts and implemented it after negotiating with the business groups. Second, the concerned big businessmen were, to some degree, determined to suffer a kind of investment revamping by bargaining among themselves in these financially depressed sectors, even though they opposed a compulsory investment adjustment imposed by the government. The first and second factors reduced state-big business conflicts in the process of policy implementation. Finally, the way in which this investment adjustment was realized depended heavily on investment designations according to specific criteria in the subfields of each sector; in part, it used a small merger within the oligopoly in the heavy electrical equipment industry, and the privatization of the public enterprise merged to a private company in the copper smelting sector. These kinds of investment adjustments hardly put a financial burden on the government and they reduced potential conflicts among the specific interests of the business groups involved. For these reasons, the companies were confronted with little cause for opposition in the decision-making process as well as in the specifics and methods of adjustment.

As shown also in Chapter 5, during the economic and political crises, the decay, disorder, and change of the state institutions for the policy-making and implementation, of the institutions (particularly policy networks) between the state and big business, and of the institutions (particularly the financial system) between state and market, had affected the state managers' and the big businessmen's bargaining power in the implementation of the first and second HCIIAs.

The lack of bureaucratic coherence and coordination under President Park's influence, and the dualistic institutional structure of the policy formation and implementation under the new military leaders' control over the Chun interim government, had decreased the state managers' capacities (bargaining power over the big business firms) for their efficient implementation of the investment adjustments. In contrast, despite the relatively centralized and coordinated bureaucracy, the state institutions' lack of coercive enforcement power resulted in the failure of the first investment adjustment under Choy's interim government. The political logic of the state's strict control over the business groups under Chun's interim regime led to the unrealistic and ambitious method of the second HCIIA.

The Park government's economic strategy to maintain the state-big business ruling coalition had made it very difficult for the technocrats to strictly implement the first investment adjustment. Under Choy's regime, the institutional disorder between the state and big business, which had been accompanied by the dissolving state-big business governing coalition, brought about the big businessmen's opposition, strong demands, and conflicts. Under Chun's regime, in the institutional change between the state and big business (the state's tight control over the business groups by means of the breakdown of the state-big business ruling coalition), the state managers failed to resolve the business groups' demands and conflicts in association with the foreign company.

Additionally, the state managers' bargaining power had been reduced, and the big businessmen's bargaining power had been enhanced, by the decay of the state-controlled financial system under Park's regime, and by its disorder under Choy's and Chun's interim regimes. Under the Park, Choy, and Chun governments, the financial system within the limits of the economic stabilization policy and the policy orientation towards economic liberalization had nullified the state managers' policy instruments for their financial support; it had also reinforced the big businessmen's individual bargaining power for their opposition or interest maximization in the implementation process of the HCIIAs. As a result, the weak institutional capacities of the state could not provide the business groups either with the selective incentives of strong enforcement (coercion) and sufficient financial support (inducements) under Park's and Choy's governments, or with sufficient financial incentives under Chun's government, which could have induced their collective actions of the planned mergers.

NOTES

1 Faced with a series of violent labour troubles and student demonstrations, the President and the Martial Law Command issued several warnings, saying that an overheated political atmosphere would not be tolerated. During this political crisis, General Chun became Acting Director of the KCIA and thus, on 29 April, dominated the security agencies of the Defense Security Command and the KCIA; he could exercise a great political and military influence through these organizations.
2 *The Dong-A Daily News*, 19 May; and *The Korea Herald*, 18 and 20 May 1980.
3 *The Dong-A Daily News*, 17 May 1980.
4 For the Kwangju incident, see the National Assembly Records, *Special Hearings on the Kwangju Incident* (Seoul: 1989) (in Korean).
5 See Young Whan Kihl, *Politics and Policies in Divided Korea* (Boulder: Westview Press, 1984), pp. 80–83; and the SCNSM, *White Paper on the Special Committee for National Security Measures* (Seoul: 1980), Chap. 1 (in Korean). The idea and detailed plan to establish the SCNSM were made by young colonels of the Defense Security Command among the coup leaders and then approved by General Doo-Whan Chun before the imposition of the full martial law (Kyung-Sik Sun, 'The SCNSM', *Monthly Joong-Ang* [March 1988], pp. 286–87 [in Korean]). The special committee was chaired by President Choy and composed of eight government officials, fourteen military generals and two top presidential aides. The members were divided into the two categories of sixteen ex-officio members and ten presidential

appointees. Under the special committee, there was a standing committee to deliberate and coordinate matters entrusted by its members. The Standing Committee was headed by General Chun and composed of eighteen military officers and twelve civilian government officials. It had sixteen appointees and chairmen of its thirteen subcommittees. The subcommittees comprised 108 field-grade officers, government officials, and professors. These subordinate committees 'exercised authority over the government ministries and directed operations of all phases of government). In doing so, they bypassed the Cabinet and reported directly to the thirty-man Standing Committee. Thus with the help of its thirteen subcommittees, the Standing Committee in effect ran the government. Indeed, many Korean specialists likened the Standing Committee to the Supreme Council for National Reconstruction set up by the late Park after the 1961 coup; ... the Standing Committee was the supreme organ of power in the country and its chairman Chun was in effect the most powerful man in South Korea.' Koon Woo Nam, *op. cit.* [Chapter 4, note 61], pp. 232–33; and *The Dong-A News*, 1 and 5 June 1980.

6 *The Dong-A Daily News*, 8 June 1980; and *The Korea Herald*, 14 June 1980.

7 See Jong Sup Jun, 'The Paradoxes of Development: Problems of Korea's Transformation', in Bun Woong Kim, David S. Bell, Jr., and Chong Bum Lee, eds., *Administrative Dynamics and Development: The Korean Experience* (Seoul: Kyobo Publishing Inc., 1985); and Young Whan Kihl, *op. cit.*, pp. 74–89.

8 *The Chosun Daily News*, 10 July 1980.

9 *The Chosun Daily News*, 10 and 16 July 1980.

10 See *The Dong-A Daily News*, 3, 7, 12, 15, and 25 November; and *The Chosun Daily News*, 9 November 1980. The Political Renovation Committee, which was a nine-member screening committee established under the Political Climate Renovation Law, prohibited 567 politicians, mainly from the former ruling and major opposition parties, and intellectuals from playing any role in politics until 30 June 1988.

11 *The Chosun Daily News*, 19, 20, and 22 July 1980. Notably, 211 public employees were purged from the Korea Electric Power Corporation alone.

12 *The Dong-A Daily News*, 1 August 1980. In the meantime, the repressive purification campaign reached the mass media. See the National Assembly Records, *Special Hearings on the Measures of Purging Journalists and Merging Newspapers and Broadcasting Stations* (Seoul: 1989) (in Korean).

13 *The Chosun Daily News*, 21 May 1980.

14 Jang-Han Kim *et. al.*, *80s' History of Korean Labour Movement* (Seoul: Jogook Press, 1989), pp. 39–41 (in Korean); and June-Sik Park, 'Labour Movement around 1980 and State Intervention', in the Korean Industrial Society Research Council, ed., *Today's Korean Capitalism and the State* (Seoul: Hangil Press, 1988), pp. 332–33 (in Korean).

15 Interviews; Sang-Hyun Choi, 'Quasi-Taxes on *Jaebols* and Behind the Scenes of Privileges', *Monthly Kyunghyang* (December 1988), p. 217;

and 'Special Roundtable Talks: The Fifth Republic Irregularities and Politics-Business Collusive Alliance', *Monthly Chosun* (September 1988), p. 132 (in Korean).

16 See *The Chosun Daily News*, 7 June 1980; and *The Dong-A Daily News*, 18 June 1980.

17 See the National Assembly Records, *Special Hearings on the Ilhae Foundation* (Seoul: 1989) (in Korean). The panel probed the collection of money for the establishment of the foundation, as part of the Fifth Republic irregularities; Ilhae is the pen name of ex-President Chun. In the hearings, Joo-Young Chung, the former Chairman of the FKI, testified as to the pressures from the military leaders on the ethics declaration.

18 The SCNSM, *op. cit.*, pp. 124–25.

19 I will refer to the Choy government (from the political dominance of the junta-like committee on 17 May 1980 to the resignation of Choy, the formal President on 16 August 1980), which had been controlled by the military, as Chun's interim government because General Chun was the real ruler. Afterwards, Chun succeeded Choy as President of the interim government, in accordance with the Yushin constitution under the Park regime, on 1 September 1980. The new interim government amended the old constitution in October 1980. Chun was elected President of the Fifth Republic according to the new constitution on 25 February 1981.

20 For the general survey of laws concerned with monopoly regulation and fair trade under Park's regime, see the Graduate School of Public Administration at the Seoul National University, ed., *A Collection of Policy Cases in South Korea* (Seoul: Bub Moon Press, 1989), pp. 232–67 (in Korean).

21 For the process of policy-making, see ibid., pp. 268–70; and the Graduate School of Public Administration at the Seoul National University, *A Research on Cases of Policy Implementation* (Seoul: Seoul National University, 1983), pp. 10–11 (in Korean).

22 Kyu-Uck Lee, 'Recent Development in Industrial Organizational Issues in Korea', *KDI Working Paper* 8609 (1986), p. 4 and Table 3.

23 Ibid., Tables 1 and 2.

24 *The Maeil Kyungje Daily News*, 19 September 1980; *The Hyundai Kyungje (Korea Economic) Daily News*, 20 September 1980; *The Chosun Daily News*, 20 September 1980; and Sang-Min Sin, 'The Background of the Establishment of the Fair Trade Act', *Sin Dong-A* (December 1980) (in Korean).

25 *The Korea Herald*, 28 September 1980; *The Maeil Kyungje Daily News*, 27 September 1980; and *The Dong-A News*, 27 September 1980.

26 *The Hyundai Kyungje Daily News*, 1 October 1980.

27 For the reaction of business firms and the result of the policy instrumentation, see the FKI, *Twenty Years' History of the FKI* (Seoul: 1983), pp. 294–98 (in Korean); *The Dong-A Daily News*, 4 and 24 October 1980; *The Hyundai Kyungje Daily News*, 28 September 1980; *The Korea Herald*, 31 December 1980; and Yong-Bum Cho *et. al.*,

Korea's Monopoly Capital and Jaebols [*Business Groups*] (Seoul: Pool Bit Press, 1984), pp. 214–22 (in Korean).

28 *The Dong-A Daily News*, 18 August 1980.
29 *The Maeil Kyungje Daily News*, 31 May 1980. Actually, the growth rates of fixed investment were 40.5 percent in 1978, 9.7 percent in 1979, and −14.8 percent in 1980. Especially, the total amount of investment in 1980 in the manufacturing industries reduced from that in 1979 by 45.8 percent (FKI, *A Survey of the Korean Economic Development* [Seoul: FKI, 1987], p. 489 [in Korean]).
30 *The Korea Herald*, 23 September 1980; *The Dong-A Daily News*, 17 September 1980; *The Hyundai Kyungje Daily News*, 18 and 23 September 1980; and *The Maeil Kyungje Daily News*, 22 September 1980.
31 The Secretariat for the President, *The 1980s Meeting a New Challenge: Selected Speeches of President Chun Doo Hwan*, Vol. 1 (Seoul: Korea Text Book Co., 1981), pp. 3–11.
32 See Kyung-Sik Kang, *op. cit.*, pp. 45–48; EPB, *Economic Policy of Development Period*, pp. 234–40; and Bela Balassa, 'Korea During the Fifth Five-Year Plan Period', Roger D. Norton, 'The Korean Economy in 1980 and the Fifth Five-Year Plan', and Wilhelm Hankel, 'Some Comments and Recommendations to Macro-Issues, Sectoral Priorities and Selective Incentives with Regard to the Fifth Five-Year Development Plan of Korea', all in Il Sakong, ed., *Macroeconomic Policy and Industrial Development Issues* (Seoul: KDI, 1987).
33 Byung-Sun Choi, *op. cit.* [Chapter 7, note 7], pp. 174–75.
34 Interviews. Exceptionally, however, we can guess from a speech of the Chairman of the Hyundai Business Group, Joo-Young Chung, that the Hyundai Group may have objected to any investment adjustment. In his speech on the heavy and chemical investment adjustment in December 1980, as I will quote later, Chung firmly advocated a private-initiated economy based on free market competition against the policy measures of investment adjustment. Behind his argument, he implicitly assumed that financially well-managed companies should survive through natural selection based on free market competition (Bum-Sung Chun, *Chung Joo-Young* [Biography] [Seoul: Su Moon Dang Press, 1984], pp. 415–17 [in Korean]).
35 Even the KCCI, a peak business association, urged the government to realign heavy and chemical industrial overinvestment through merging and to delay planned investments (*The Hyundai Kyungje Daily News*, 19 August 1980). The business organization has officially represented general business interests, but frequently supported and recommended big business interests, mainly due to its leadership structure that was dominated by large firms. Interestingly, the FKI, the representative association of big business interests, frequently expressed its desire for a private-initiated economy without government intervention and thus indirectly opposed the investment adjustment policy. As a result, although concerned big business firms among FKI's members wanted a government investment adjustment under the worst economic situation, the organization could not consider a collective recommendation of state intervention that would be contradictory to its former

position of free market competition. In fact, they were not able to make a collective action of autonomous adjustment because of their different strategies for profit maximization based on their specific costs and benefits.

36 There was a doubt about why the Hyundai Group chose the automobile industry despite its privileged position in the power plant industry in light of its experience and technology of production, investment scale, and financial capacity for merging. The group had experience in constructing several power plants and had developed the engineering technology required. Furthermore, according to the first HCIIA, it had almost merged with Hyundai International. However, the choice was based on the company's rational calculation to maximize benefits and minimize costs within the limits of the compulsory merger. The conglomerate expected to continuously undertake domestic and international power plant construction works and to greatly develop its strategic automobile industry for domestic and international demand. Additionally, from its experience in the policy failure of the first HCIIA, it seemed to hesitate to take over financially trouble Hyundai International without any government guarantee of sufficient financial support in the tight monetary situation. (My interpretation is based on interviews and the following sources: for different interpretations of Hyundai's choice, see Bum-Sung Chun, *op. cit.*, 1984, p. 418; Bum-Sung Chun, *Kim Woo-Joong* [Biography] [Seoul: Su Moon Dang Press, 1987] [in Korean], pp. 398–99; Byung-Hyu Bae, 'Is the Daewood Group in Good Shape?', *Sin Dong-A* [March 1981], p. 160 [in Korean]; and for the official position of the Hyundai Group, see the Hyundai Motor Company, *Twenty Years' History of the Hyundai Motor Company*, pp. 380–82 [in Korean].)

37 For the contents of the second HCIIA, see *The Dong-A News*, 20 August 1980; *The Chosun Daily News*, 21 August 1980; *The Korea Herald*, 20 August 1980; *The Maeil Kyungje Daily News*, 20, 21, and 22 August 1980; and the Subcommittee of Commerce, Industry, and Resources in the SCNSM, 'The Investment Adjustment for Merging the Power-Generating Equipment and Automobile Fields', 19 August 1980, in KDI, *op. cit.*, Vol. 2.

38 See the Subcommittee of Commerce, Industry, and Resources in the SCNSM, ibid., pp. 1201–2, 1204–14.

39 Doo-Whan Chun, the most powerful leader, gave an answer to economic problems in an interview: '. . . we have been experiencing some economic difficulties. I have come to the conclusion that there are two main sets of factors involved – external and internal. The chief external factor, as you have noted, is the fact that the nations of the world are being greatly affected by increases in oil prices. Domestically, the chaotic situation following the assassination of 26 October last year also had a major adverse impact on the economy. The relatively excessive investment in heavy industry of the recent past is yet another problem plaguing our economy.' The Secretariat for the President, *op. cit.* (1981), Vol. 1, p. 212.

40 See Kyung-Sik Sun, *op. cit.*

41 Ibid., p. 292.
42 An interview.
43 An interview; and Sook-Kil Kim, *op. cit.* [Chapter 7, note 23], pp. 258–60.
44 An interview.
45 An interview.
46 Bum-Sung Chun, *Chung Joo-Young*, pp. 415–17.
47 An interview.
48 Olson's concepts of 'selective incentives' and his arguments about collective action in a large group are applicable to the state-imposed collective action of investment adjustment in the small group of big business firms. See Mancur Olson, *op. cit.*, pp. 44, 51.
49 The Hyundai Motor Company, *op. cit.*, pp. 379–80.
50 Ibid., p. 380.
51 *The Hyundai Kyungje Daily News*, 13 and 14 September 1980.
52 *The Maeil Kyungje Daily News*, 20 August 1980; and Eui-Kyun Kim, 'Hyundai and Daewoo', *Sin Dong-A* (November 1980), p. 130 (in Korean).
53 *The Maeil Kyungje Daily News*, 30 August 1980; and Byung-Hyu Bae, 'Is the Daewoo Group in Good Shape?', *Sin Dong-A* (March 1981), pp. 162–64 (in Korean).
54 Interviews.
55 An interview; and Byung-Hyu Bae, *op. cit.*, p. 162.
56 Eui-Kyun Kim, *op. cit.* (November 1980), pp. 130, 133.
57 *The Hyundai Kyungje Daily News*, 21 October 1980; and *The Korea Herald*, 21 October 1980.
58 Eui-Kyun Kim, *op. cit.* (November 1980), p. 130; and *The Hyundai Kyungje Daily News*, 21 October 1980.
59 Eui-Kyun Kim, *op. cit.*, p. 130; and Byung-Hyu Bae, *op. cit.*, p. 163.
60 *The Maeil Kyungje Daily News*, 8 and 9 January 1981; and Eui-Kyun Kim, *op. cit.* (December 1980), pp. 260–61.
61 *The Korea Herald*, 23 October 1980.
62 Ibid. In fact, the Hyundai Group worried about GM's participation in management in light of the bankruptcy of General Motors Korea (GMK). GMK was established in 1972 when the GM joined the Shinjin Motor Corporation (SHMC). As a joint-venture firm, the GMK suffered from a lack of sales because of GM's poorly-managed marketing strategy. It produced a revised model of the unpopular Chevrolet 1700 as part of GM's world market policy instead of developing an independent car model. One of the major reasons of the bankruptcy was that GM had made an unequal contract with the SHMC by including its profit guarantee and dominance in management. In the end, GMK went bankrupt in 1976 and became the Saehan Motor Company (*The Maeil Kyungje Daily News*, 23 October 1980).
63 According to a government mediation, GM and the HMC had agreed to form a joint-service company that was supposed to adjust and determine such management problems as the ratio of joint venture, mobilization of financing funds, choice of car model, and development of auto parts and technology. But the plan was not realized because of

their different positions (the Graduate School of Public Administration at the Seoul National University, *op. cit.*, 1989, p. 161).

64 An interview.

65 The Hyundai Motor Company, *op. cit.*, pp. 383–84; Graduate School of Public Administration at the Seoul National University, *op. cit.* (1983), p. 125; and *The Maeil Kyungje Daily News*, 9 January 1981.

66 See *The Korea Herald*, 1 March 1981; *The Dong-A Daily News*, 28 February 1981; and the Hyundai Motor Company, *op. cit.*, pp. 385–86. In particular, the policy measures were directed towards merging the Kia Motor Company with the Dong-Ah Motor Company as a means of reinforcing their financial standing and management rationalization. The merged company was supposed to monopolize the production of specially equipped cars and trucks such as fire-fighting engines and cement mixers, and small-medium buses and trucks. However, the government failed to implement the compulsory merger in the face of the big businessmen's opposition, interest conflicts, and criticism from the press. On 25 July 1982, it announced the cancellation of the measure for merging. (For the process of the policy implementation, see the Graduate School of Public Administration at the Seoul National University, *op. cit.* [1989], pp. 170–73.)

67 The Hyundai Motor Company, ibid., p. 384.

68 Byung-Hyu Bae, *op. cit.*, p. 164.

69 An interview.

70 *The Maeil Kyungje Weekly News*, 6 November 1980.

71 An interview.

72 The SCNSM lasted until 27 October 1980, and members of the special committee enacted a law to establish the new eighty-one-member Legislative Council for National Security (LCNS) on 27 October. On 29 October 1980, council members were appointed from former SCNSM members, former ruling and opposition party members, academics, lawyers, and leaders of social organizations. The LCNS played the role of an interim legislature, enacting laws for the legal order of new institutions under the Fifth Republic (1981–87). The legislative council existed until April 1981 when the new National Assembly emerged following the March 1981 general election (see *The Chosun Daily News*, 29 October 1980; and Dong-Il Ahn, 'The True Character of Reform Legislation: Activities of the LCNS', *Monthly Chosun* [April 1988] [in Korean]).

73 Jai-Ik Kim, who had determined the merger scheme in the second HCCIA, argued for the establishment of public enterprise (an interview).

74 *The Maeil Kyungje Daily News*, 29 October 1980.

75 For the limits of Daewoo's financial mobilization, see Byung-Hyu Bae, *op. cit.*

76 For the contents of the investment adjustment, see *The Dong-A Daily News*, 7 October 1980; *The Maeil Kyungje Daily News*, 7 October 1980; *The Korea Herald*, 8 October 1980; and MCI, 'The Heavy and Chemical Industrial Investment Adjustment', in KDI, *op. cit.*, Vol. 2, pp. 1215–25.

77 *The Dong-A Daily News*, 13 September 1980; *The Maeil Kyungje Daily News*, 13 and 15 September 1980; and *The Korea Herald*, 14 September 1980.

Chapter 7

The politics of economic reform

Chapters 7 and 8 will analyse how Chun's government had installed new institutions for economic reform; why the government failed to realize the economic reform (financial reforms and regulations of business groups) in face of the limits of economic liberalization; and how Chun's regime returned to a collusive state-big business governing coalition through another industrial adjustment. In particular, Chapter 8 will focus on why and how, in contrast to the failed HCIIAs, the new authoritarian government made it possible to dispose of financially ill-managed large firms by means of political and financial control over big business in order to achieve industrial adjustment. The new authoritarian government had built new institutions for liberal economic reform within the state, between state and society, and between state and market.

THE STATE INSTITUTIONS FOR ECONOMIC LIBERALIZATION

During the early 1980s, the reform-minded group, which had been led by Presidential First Economic Secretary Jai-Ik Kim, had restored the EPB's leadership in making and implementing not only macroeconomic policies but also industrial policies. During the 1970s, the Planning Office of the HCIPC took the initiative in planning and promoting the HCIs, including the defence industries, by centralizing and coordinating the practically subordinate ministries, including the EPB. However, during the first half of Chun's regime (1981–84), the EPB had played a crucial role in economic stabilization, liberalization, and industrial policy.

After the massive and repressive reshuffling, which was carried out in the socio-political arenas, the Fifth Republic of President Chun embarked on actively implementing economic stabilization and liberalization; this programme was led by the EPB in cooperation with other economic ministries and in consultation with the First Secretary of the Presidential Economic Secretariat. In general, the EPB's leadership under Chun's regime played a greater role in coordinating economic policy proposals undertaken by other operating economic ministries. In contrast, during the 1960s, the EPB's role under Park's regime had concentrated on centralizing the economic ministries in order to make and implement, in a coherent and effective manner, economic development plans for the export- and growth-oriented industrialization.

Jai-Ik Kim contributed to the renaissance of EPB leadership in economic policy-making and implementation. Since the emergence of the SCNSM, he had been the most influential technocrat and had received the full confidence of President Chun until his sudden death in October 1983.[1] Kim firmly asserted that the government should strive for a market-oriented reform through economic stabilization and liberalization so as to achieve continuous growth within economic stability. He also argued for the reform of the state institutions for economic policy formation and implementation with a view towards restoring the EPB's leadership. Finally, the presidential secretary persuasively explained his reform ideas to Chun, even though he and the EPB had met with the strong resistance of the MCI and the MF during the early 1980s. The President committed himself to supporting Kim's economic and administrative reform.[2] This presidential commitment made it possible to realize the EPB's leadership and enabled the EPB to propel reform policies for economic liberalization based on economic stability.[3]

Bureaucratic conflicts between conservatives and reformists, and the resurgence of the EPB leadership

On 7 January 1981, President Chun presided over the Economic Policy Meeting to discuss the general orientation of economic policy. On the same day, the ruling Democratic Justice Party announced its platforms and basic policies. In the two meetings, the ruling elites confirmed that the Chun regime's goal of economic management would be a private-initiated (market-oriented) economy.[4] In the latter half of 1980, the new military leaders and military-turned politicians had intervened strongly in the market by imposing the investment adjustments, the anti-monopoly and fair trade act, and the regulations of business groups, as I mentioned previously, which were to construct a firm base of economic stability and reform. Afterwards, during the early 1980s, the government had actively made stabilizing efforts to prevent high inflation within the tight monetary policy and had pursued a gradual recovery of economic activities. In fact, substantial growth based on stability had been achieved during this period: the growth rates for 1980, 1982, and 1983 were 6.4 percent, 5.3 percent, and 9.2 percent, respectively; the GNP deflators for 1981, 1982, and 1983 were 16.2 percent, 7.7 percent, and 2.8 percent, respectively.[5]

However, the liberalization policy of economic reform had been delayed and not effectively implemented until 1982. The policy implementation of economic stabilization had been pushed within a high degree of consensus among the economic ministries, whereas that of economic liberalization was expected to face considerable conflicts among them. As a matter of fact, the state managers, including the politicians and technocrats, agreed to the goal of economic management towards a market-oriented economy, but they had different views in terms of the way and degree of economic liberalization. In particular, the MCI and the MF did not want to lose their own organizational interests and vested policy instruments (or rights) in the process of policy implementation (the ministries had already acquired these rights during the heavily state-led industrialization of the 1970s). Furthermore, during the early period of Chun's regime, President Chun himself did not completely understand and make full commitment to the reform-minded group's ideas as to how the liberalization policy should be realized in the short term, although he had strongly supported the strict economic stabilization policy and the economic management's long-term policy goal towards a liberalized economy.

In this policy environment, the Presidential Economic Secretariat and the EPB had made strenuous efforts to construct new state institutions for EPB leadership in the economic policy-making and implementation. The reform leaders thought that their strategic institutional building would enable them to grasp their leadership for integrated policy coordination not only in formulating but also in implementing the economic liberalization.

First of all, the EPB, in cooperation with Jai-Ik Kim, took seriously the distorted industrial strategy of the 1970s that had allocated excessive resources to the HCIs. They claimed that Park's unbalanced (favouring the HCIs) and big business-oriented industrial policy resulted in the underdevelopment of small and medium-sized business firms and the underinvestment of many labour-intensive and light-industrial sectors, where price and wage increases caused their deteriorating export competitiveness. The reform group decided to change the existing industrial assistance system that had promoted the HCIs under Park's regime. They intended to reform the industrial policy that had been characterized by state interventions of discretionary field manipulation and command. To build a new industrial support system, they also keenly felt the necessity of an institutional reform that would grant the EPB the authority of integrated coordination in industrial policy-making and implementation. At the same time, the administrative reform for economic management was expected to pre-empt the resistance of other concerned ministries that had enjoyed their vested rights of such policy instruments as credit allocation and investment licensing.

On 17 September 1980, the EPB, in cooperation with Jai-Ik Kim, made a report of its plan for rearranging the existing industrial assistance system. At that time, the EPB's initiative was strongly challenged by the MF and the MCI. Before the EPB's report, in an interview with journalists on 3 September, Minister of the MCI Suk-Joon Suh announced a different planned industrial assistance system that would focus on the HCIs. The MCI proposed to promote the HCIs as the leading export industries in the long term, to prepare for a heavy industrial fund of 1 trillion won until 1985, and to unify the eight heavy industrial promotion laws.[6] The MCI's plan still pursued the HCIs-oriented unbalanced industrial strategy that would be supported by a huge amount of state-controlled policy loans. Basically, the MCI and the MF had different views from those of the reformist group of the Presidential Economic Secretariat and the EPB in terms of industrial strategy and the degree of state intervention and policy instruments to be used in industrial policy. The bureaucratic conflicts had continued until November, when Prime Minister Duck-Woo Nam stepped in and shored up the EPB's proposal.[7] On 12 November, the MCI and the MF received the Prime Minister's direction that the EPB should establish an 'Industrial Assistance Law' integrating the various existing industrial laws.

On 26 November, the EPB made some revisions of its original proposal and reported it to President Chun. The major contents of the EPB's proposed law were as follows:[8] industrial assistance would be offered not on an industry basis but according to different 'investment activities' for facilities, technology development, and manpower development; the type of assistance would be limited to tax incentives (either special depreciation or investment tax deduction), excluding policy loans and tariff exemption or reduction; exceptionally, such types of assistance as preferential policy loans (various policy loans would be unified as an 'investment assistance fund'), and tax and tariff assistance would be provided for 'promising strategic industries'; the promising industries would be protected only for a specified period; and the 'Investment Deliberation Council' (later, the Industrial Policy Deliberation Council), chaired by the Deputy Prime Minister (the head of the EPB), would be established to strengthen the effective and integrated coordination of industrial policies and give the EPB the right of coordination among the ministries concerned.

The EPB's intention was to reduce state intervention in the economy by controlling the MF and the MCI that had been deeply involved in the market. In fact, according to the planned law,

> the EPB could request change in policies initiated by the [MF] (in regard to tax and financial assistance, tariff rate adjustment, etc.) and the MCI (in regard to import liberalization, for example) when the EPB considered them in accordance with its overall industrial policy objectives.[9]

Faced with vehement opposition from the MCI, the MF, and other presidential secretaries, the EPB's proposal could not be legislated through the normal channels of compromise and coordination among the state organizations even after several revisions.

In the middle of the sharp conflicts among the concerned ministries, Presidential First Economic Secretary Jai-Ik Kim and Planning Assistant Minister of the EPB Kyung-Sik Kang (who were also the reform leaders within the EPB who were involved in making the CMES of 1979) skilfully realized their proposal by convincing Chun to announce presidential directives that contained the major contents of the EPB's proposed law:[10] one was the 'Presidential Special Directives Concerning Operation of Industrial

Assistance System' of August 1981, which included the establishment of the Industrial Policy Deliberation Council (IPDC) to
allow the EPB to play a leading role in industrial policy; the
other was the Presidential Directive of December 1981, which
determined that 'each economic minister ought to get the Deputy
Prime Minister [of the EPB]'s prior sanction on every major economic policy proposal requiring the President's or the Prime Minister's final approval'.[11] Therefore, the EPB was able to exercise its
right of coordination, on this institutional basis, in making and
implementing economic policies for economic liberalization.

The industrial support system would use a functional approach
rather than the existing industry-specific and individual firm
approach. The reform group asserted that the functional approach,
based on general industrial laws, would be compatible with the
general policy of economic liberalization because, within government industrial guidelines, business firms could autonomously
adapt themselves to industrial adjustment without direct state
intervention. After determining the orientation and the instruments
of industrial policy, the EPB recognized that a specified industrial
law should be established in response to the pressure of international competition and the need for industrial rationalization in
declining industries.

Finally, the Industrial Development Law (IDL) was approved
by the National Assembly in December 1985. It abolished and
integrated, on the basis of a functional approach, the seven existing
individual promotion laws regarding machinery, electronics, textiles, iron and steel, non-ferrous metals, petrochemicals, and shipbuilding industries. The IDL's main objectives were to minimize
the scope and degree of state intervention for industrial adjustment
in industries and to encourage voluntary efforts of the private
sector by avoiding arbitrary government decisions in the industrial
policy-making process.[12]

However, this industrial law remained in rhetoric rather than in
reality and was wrongly used in declining industries, as I will
mention later, because the reform-oriented EPB leadership had
declined since 1985 as a result of the conservative ministries' (the
MF and the MCI) rising organizational power and the politicized
economic decision-making.

Administrative reforms and personnel exchanges among the economic ministries

In addition to the state institutional reform for the EPB's leadership, the government made general administrative reforms in 1981. The general reforms of the state institutions were aimed at the improvement of bureaucratic efficiency and the reduction of government regulations, and thus were compatible with the policy orientation towards a private-initiated economy. The government took measures on 15 October 1981 for reducing the administrative organizations. The original plan for this reform was derived from the ideas of the SCNSM, which took the drastic measure of purging government officials. The junta-like committee ordered each government administrative organization to make its reform plan. The massive administrative reform reduced 531 positions held by officials with the rank of the fourth grade and up, as well as three offices, forty-one bureaus, and 135 divisions and branches, which included some parts of the EPB, the MF, and the MCI.[13]

In 1981, another administrative reform was introduced in the revision of the Civil Service Law. The basic aim of the revision was to improve efficiency in 'personnel administration, job security for the career civil servants, and professional independence of the civil service system'.[14] In particular, according to the law, a personnel exchange system among government ministries was established to increase inter-ministry cooperation and coordination. Later, interestingly, Jai-Ik Kim took full advantage of this personnel shift system in order to pre-empt the other ministries' resistance against the EPB's economic liberalization policy.

As a matter of fact, despite the institutional reform for the EPB's leadership, serious bureaucratic conflicts regarding a choice between state intervention and market orientation still took place. In other words, the structural change was not a sufficient condition for propelling the economic liberalization policy. The conservative actors (mainly, the MCI's and the MF's technocrats) tenaciously resisted the EPB's leadership for economic liberalization. Jai-Ik Kim had a great influence on Chun's decision to replace the state interventionist leaders of the main economic posts. The First Economic Secretary persuaded the President to fill the high-level seats with persons who had shared beliefs in economic liberalization. The typical way in which the cabinet was reshuffled involved the interchange of high government officials between the EPB, and the MCI and the MF. In January 1982, the personnel exchange between the EPB and the MF occurred in order to push the MF's financial deregulation and tariff reform.[15] In late 1983, an EPB man was appointed the Vice-Minister of the MCI in order to accelerate the MCI's import liberalization.[16] The new appointees of the MF and the MCI were either one of the reform group's leaders or staunch economic liberalists.

THE AUTHORITARIAN REGIME WITHOUT A SUPPORTING COALITION

Financial deregulations and government regulations of business groups: the political process

As I mentioned in Chapter 6, the reform leaders took the drastic measures for the economic control over business groups. Basically, the reform-oriented technocrats and the new military leaders firmly believed that the reform of economic liberalization for long-term stability would not be successful without preventing further business concentration. The new military and military-turned political leaders felt the necessity for state control over big business in order to legitimate their new authoritarian regime. The Chun regime put emphasis on its political goal of the 'welfare and justice society' against Park's collusive state-big business ruling coalition. Thus, the government enacted the fair-trade and anti-monopoly law to establish a sound condition for free market competition; it also ordered the highly indebted business groups to strengthen their financial structure with a view towards prohibiting the financial supports of further privileged rescue funds.

By 1979, the EPB began to pursue financial deregulations for economic stabilization and liberalization because the state-controlled credit allocation had brought about the unbalanced industrial structure, many financially ill-managed and highly indebted business firms, high currency inflation, and the high business concentration of the late 1970s. This ministry announced a reform of the financial system, including a reduction of policy loans and a readjustment of interest rates to a realistic level, in the CMES. Furthermore, in September 1979, the EPB, in cooperation with the Bank of Korea and the KDI, reported to President Park general recommendations for financial liberalization, including liberalization of interest rates, privatization and management autonomy of commercial banks, independent management of the Bank of Korea, and the Monetary Board's takeover of the monetary and credit policy from the MF.[17]

Until then, the MF had been sceptical about financial liberalization; it felt that the financial liberalization policy would be implemented too early because the government would have to maintain the state-led credit allocation to support forthcoming heavy and chemical industrial construction and export promotion. Moreover, the MF did not want to lose its powerful policy instruments so as to maintain its vested organizational interests of financial control over business firms by means of credit and investment allocation.

After the emergence of Chun's regime, however, the MF could not help giving up, to some degree, its privileged rights of financial control under Chun's economic reform policy, although there was a big gap between the MF's and the EPB's proposal. The proposal of the MF agreed with that of the EPB in terms of the reduced adjustment of policy loans, the cut-off of further rescue funds for financially ill-managed firms, the restraint of excessive financial support for strategic industries, and the gradual privatization of commercial banks.[18]

The MF precisely recognized the limits of state-controlled financial intervention in financially depressed big business firms, particularly in the overinvested and distorted HCIs during the period of economic crisis. The ministry had a frustrating experience in its failure of financial control over big businessmen's investment decision-making in the HCIs. In the late 1970s and 1980, the state managers were not able to prevent the big businessmen's competitive overinvestments in the HCIs and had failed to implement the HCIIAs. During that period, the government's financial policy had been trapped by the financial demands of the highly indebted and financially suffering big business firms. The government could not reject the huge financing loans because it had to prevent the bankruptcies of large firms, which would result in the insolvency of the concerned banks. In fact, the MF was suffering from a sharp decrease in its financial bargaining power over business groups. Interestingly, thus, the ministry decided its way of financial deregulation to restore its financial power over big businessmen in a sense. In December 1980, the report of the MF's proposal to President Chun was approved in the Economic Policy Meeting at the Blue House (the presidential office).

In September 1981, the MF revised the General Banking Act for the privatization of commercial banks and autonomy of bank management, which was supposed to be sent to the National Assembly in December. The Act's major contents were to provide denationalized banks with a freer hand in dealing with their own managerial affairs and to prevent banks from being influenced by a few large shareholders by imposing ceilings on conglomerates' ownership and borrowing. Suddenly, however, the MF gave up introducing the revised bill. Instead of the ministry, the main opposition party (the Democratic Korean Party: DKP) submitted its version, which was similar to the MF's bill. The opposition national assemblymen criticized the government; the MF's cancellation of the revised bill was caused by lobbying pressures from business groups that worried about the credit ceiling on big business firms.[19]

In early 1982, as I mentioned previously, in order to actively propel the financial liberalization policy, Jai-Ik Kim persuaded President Chun to reshuffle the MF's high government officials with the EPB's men. Afterwards, the personnel exchange contributed greatly towards bringing about a collective action for financial liberalization among the conflicting economic ministries.

The largest curb market loan scandal occurred in May 1982. Young-Ja Chang, who was one of the large curb loan lenders and distantly related by marriage to President Chun (her sister's husband was Mrs Chun's uncle), and her husband, former Deputy Chief of the KCIA, Chul-Hi Lee, illegally manipulated the commercial papers of almost $1 billion (about 17 percent of South Korea's entire money supply) by defrauding the involved big business firms.[20] The couple netted a huge sum of $250–300 million. It was alleged in one rumour that part of the money had entered the political funds of the ruling Democratic Justice Party (DJP). At that time, many big business firms suffered from a lack of external financing funds from banks because of the tight monetary policy. Thus, the companies relied heavily on the curb market (the informal and unregulated financial sector) to meet their quick fund requirements.

This loan incident offered the reform leaders (Jai-Ik Kim and the EPB's technocrats) a good opportunity to convince President Chun of the benefits of their economic reform for economic liberalization and to pre-empt the other economic ministries' passive attitudes towards the liberalization policy. President Chun himself firmly declared that he would not tolerate the creation of such an environment where big businessmen could abuse political power for illegal financial gain; he added that the government would spare no effort to extend positive support to any sound small-medium industrial firm. Thus, he seriously felt the need for a reform of the financial system. Subsequently, he reshuffled his cabinet members and the ruling party leaders.[21]

Shortly after the scandal, the government took measures to deregulate the formal financial system and regulate the informal financial sector. On 28 June, to prevent an expected slowdown of economic activities, the government decided to lower bank interest rates by an average of 4 percent and to abolish preferential interest rates of various policy loans with a view towards gradually phasing out policy loans; it also announced that the three nation-wide city banks would be owned by the private sector. In July, the MF announced a drastic proposal requiring all financial trans-actions to be made in the real names of the persons concerned, which was intended to reduce the scope of the curb market and to establish a more equitable tax system.[22] The real-name system had been secretly devised and initiated by Jai-Ik Kim (the Presi-dential First Economic Secretary). The policy decision for this financial reform measure had been supported by Chun.

Until then, nevertheless, Jai-Ik Kim had received much criticism regarding his leadership of the economic liberalization plan from political leaders, including the military-turned power group as well as from the MF's and the MCI's bureaucrats. The opposition groups basically had a consensus on economic reform, especially in terms of the economic control over big business among them, but they argued for a gradual approach to the liberalization policy of import, tariff, financial, and industrial assistance systems rather than for a rapid reform progress. For instance, the Presidential Secretary for Audit and Investigation and the Presidential Secretary for Political Affairs (the two were young colonels among the core military coup) attempted to attack Kim's drastic economic liberalization policy by secretly instructing the KDI and the Bank of Korea to provide data generation that would criticize and oppose Kim's policy.

However, taking the loan scandal as a turning point, the EPB and Kim held an advantageous position in the policy-making conflicts because they received Chun's approval and support. President Chun replaced the other presidential secretaries. The former colonels were removed from the political power bloc and then sent to foreign countries.[23] Thus, Chun's firm position regarding economic reform solved the serious conflicts within the Presidential Secretariat and prevented opposition from the state managers, including the other economic ministries' government officials.

In addition, the government took measures to merge the 'underground economy' with the institutionalized formal financial sector in order to mobilize as much money as possible from the informal (curb) financial sector. Thus, the establishment of non-bank financial institutions, including investment and finance companies, had been promoted. In December 1982, the aforementioned General Banking Act was passed in the National Assembly; the Act restricted single shareholders of nationwide commercial banks to 8 percent of total ownership so as to prevent the banking industry from being controlled by business groups. It also limited the maximum ceiling of guarantees and loans for a single beneficiary to 50 percent of a bank's net worth.

Big business firms complained about the real-name system and the credit ceiling because of the restrictions they imposed on businessmen's growth-oriented investment decision-making and financial demands.[24] Basically, big businessmen objected to a rapid progress of tariff reform and import liberalization in order to protect their monopoly markets. Although, in general, the big businessmen actively favoured the financial deregulations, they were reluctant to accept the anti-monopoly and fair-trade Act and financial regulations of their investments and borrowings for establishing a sound basis for the reforms of economic liberalization.

Finally, after the largest loan scandal, the EPB, in cooperation with Jai-Ik Kim, was able to push the reform policy towards economic liberalization, which would be accompanied by government regulation over big business, by securing the full confidence of President Chun and by pre-empting the opposition of political leaders, other economic ministries' technocrats, and big businessmen. In December 1983, the EPB revised the Fifth Five-Year Economic and Social Plan under the condition of stabilizing and liberalizing the economy. The revised plan (1984–86) put more emphasis on economic liberalization, restructuring the industrial assistance system, and technology development.[25]

The repressive state control over labour

As I mentioned in Chapter 5, under Park's and Choy's regimes during the crisis period of 1979–80, the state managers and the big businessmen had reacted to the explosive labour disputes by minimizing the scope of workers' collective action and nullifying their collective bargaining power. Likewise, the new political leaders of Chun's regime made an effort to impose tighter state control over labour by installing a new institutional structure between the state and labour. Faced with the expected increasing labour pressures, Chun's government clearly understood that the state corporatist arrangements, which had been established by Park's authoritarian regime during the 1970s, had limits in controlling labour disputes, particularly restraining wage increases in accordance with the economic stabilization policy.

In the end, in December 1980, the government revised the four existing labour laws – the Labour Union Law, the Labour Dispute Adjustment Law, the Labour Committee Law, and the Labour Standard Law – and enacted the new Labour-Management Council Law.[26] Basically, in order to reinforce the already established state corporatist structure, the authoritarian regime intended to tightly control the FKTU and its industrial federations of labour unions, which would be prohibited from playing an intervening role in the collective bargaining of unit labour unions. It also aimed to prevent rank-and-file labour-management conflicts in advance, which had incapacitated the state's repressive control over labour unions, through non-corporatist arrangements.

More specifically, one of the major amendments to the Labour Union Law was as follows: in order to prevent the collective bargaining actions of labour unions at the industrial or national level, the labour unions' organizational structure changed from industry-based to enterprise-based unions and collective bargaining systems. That is, the locus of organizing and negotiating authority shifted from the FKTU and its industrial federations to the enterprise-level unions. For this purpose, the labour law forbade the so-called 'third parties' from intervening in labour disputes at the enterprise level. The government interpreted the third parties not only as political, student, social, and religious organizations but also as these peak labour organizations.

In addition, the new Labour-Management Council Law required all business places to establish a Labour-Management Council that would be composed of equal numbers of representatives of workers and management. The law's announced goal was to seek industrial peace and make a contribution to the development of the national economy through cooperation and understanding between employers and employees. Although the formal objective was to deal with labour-management matters, except for collective wage bargaining, the government's real intention was to supplant the existing labour unions' roles and prohibit the founding of new labour unions in plants without unions.[27] In other words, this state's non-corporatist control over labour was intended to ultimately incapacitate even the unit labour unions' collective bargaining power at the enterprise level.

The dualistic institutional structure for the state's control over labour minimized workers' abilities to undertake collective action within all business firms either with or without labour unions. As a result, the repressive labour policy contributed to the economic stabilization by restricting wage increases. As a matter of fact, real wages decreased by 0.5 percent in 1981, although labour productivity increased by 10.4 percent in the same year.[28]

In brief, the emergence of the EPB's reform leadership was accompanied by the government's control over big business and labour. The EPB's leadership enhanced state capacities to propel the economic reform in terms of bureaucratic coherence and coordination. The authoritarian regime without a favoured supporting coalition could increase state autonomy from social groups' opposition in pushing economic stabilization and liberalization.

NOTES

1 Kim died in the Rangoon bomb blast in Burma during Chun's diplomatic tour.

2 There is a question as to why the new military-turned politicians adopted and relied heavily on the EPB among state organizations, to spearhead the economic reform. The answer can be found in terms of the legitimation of the new authoritarian regime and the EPB's institutional autonomy from particular interest groups and flexibility.

3 During the period of the Fifth Republic, economic policies for liberalization had been pursued in the following categories: reshaped price mechanism based on free market competition and fair trade, import liberalization, financial deregulation, and industrial assistance system.

4 *The Maeil Kyungje Daily News*, 7 January 1981.

5 Sang-Woo Nam, op. cit. [Introduction, note 3], p. 77. For the detailed

　　analysis of the Korean economic situation during 1981–86, see the
　　FKI, ed., op. cit. (1987), pp. 510–716.

6　*The Maeil Kyungje Daily News*, 4 September 1980.

7　Byung-Sun Choi, 'Institutionalizing a Liberal Economic Order in
　　Korea: The Strategic Management of Economic Change', Ph.D. Diss.,
　　Harvard University (1987a), p. 274.

8　For the contents of the proposed law, see the EPB, *op. cit.* (1982),
　　pp. 225–27 and EPB, 'The Orientation of Changing Investment Assist-
　　ance System', on 26 November 1980, in KDI, *op. cit.*, pp. 1267–83.

9　Byun-Sun Choi, *op. cit.* (1987a), p. 275.

10　Ibid., pp. 276–77.

11　Ibid., pp. 172–73.

12　See Ji Hong Kim, 'Korean Industrial Policies for Declining Industries',
　　KDI Working Paper 8910 (January 1989), pp. 33–37.

13　For the purpose, contents, and effects of the administrative reform,
　　see Jang-Kyu Lee, 'Anti-Democratic Government Organizations',
　　Monthly Joong-Ang (March 1988) (in Korean) and Keun-Ho Park, 'A
　　Study on the Korean Administrative Reform', M.A. Thesis (Seoul:
　　Dong-Kook University, 1985) (in Korean).

14　Jong Sup Jun, 'The Paradoxes of Development: Problems of Korea's
　　Transformation', in Bun Woong Kim *et. al.*, *Administrative Dynamics
　　and Development: The Korean Experience* (Seoul: Kyobo Publishing
　　Inc., 1985), p. 65.

15　The EPB's Assistant Minister for Planning, Kyung-Sik Kang, was
　　appointed the Vice-Minister of the MF. At the same time, the MF's
　　Vice-Minister became the EPB's Vice-Minister. The MF's two assistant
　　ministers went to the EPB and the EPB's Director-General of the
　　Planning Bureau became the MF's Director-General of the Finance
　　Bureau. Later, shortly after the largest curb loan scandal in May 1982,
　　the Minister of the MF resigned and was replaced by the Vice-Minister
　　of the MF (Byung-Sun Choi, op. cit. [1987a], p. 293).

16　President of the Korean Development Institute (KDI: a government-
　　invested institute affiliated with the EPB) Ki-hwan Kim (a former
　　Senior Adviser to the EPB's Deputy Prime Minister) was appointed
　　the MCI's Vice-Minister (ibid., p. 294).

17　The Graduate School of Public Administration at the Seoul National
　　University, op. cit. (1989) [Chapter 6, note 20], pp. 91–94.

18　For the contents of the MF's proposal, see the MF, 'The Liberalization
　　of Commercial Banks' Management', in November 1980 in the KDI,
　　op. cit., pp. 699–717 and *The Chosun Daily News*, 5 December 1980.
　　The proposal recommended that one commercial bank would be priva-
　　tized in 1981. The Hanil Bank was chosen to become the nation's
　　privately controlled bank in April (*The Korea Herald*, 28 April 1981).

19　The Graduate School of Public Administration at the Seoul National
　　University, op. cit. (1989) [Chapter 6, note 20], pp. 108–18.

20　For the detailed contents of the large curb loan scandal, see *The Korea
　　Herald*, 12, 13, 18, 19 and 21 May 1982; *Wall Street Journal*, 25 May
　　1982; and 'The Special News Coverage for Chang Young-Ja Incident',
　　Sin Dong-A (June 1982) (in Korean), pp. 72–120.

21 *The Korea Herald*, 15, 21, and 22 May 1982. Vice-Minister of the MF, Kyung-Sik Kang (former EPB's Planning Assistant Minister and Jai-Ik Kim's close colleague), became Minister of the MF. Afterwards, he strongly pushed the banking liberalization policy and a reform-of-tariff system.

22 For these financial deregulations, see Joong-woong Kim, 'Economic Development and Financial Liberalization in Korea: Policy Reforms and Future Prospects', *KDI Working Paper* 8514 (December 1985), pp. 18–28; and The World Bank, *Korea: Managing the Industrial Transition*, Vol. 1 (Washington: The World Bank, 1987), pp. 79–90.

23 Soo-Kil Kim, 'Kim Jai-Ik and Moon Hee Kap: Presidential Economic First Secretaries of the Fifth and Sixth Republics', *Monthly Joong-Ang* (September 1989), pp. 262–63 (in Korean) and see also Jang-Kyu Lee, *You are Economic President: The Inside Economic Story of Chun's Regime* (Seoul: Joong-Ang Daily News Press, 1991), pp. 303–8 (in Korean).

24 *The Korea Herald*, 30 July 1982. Big businessmen argued that the firm foundation for absorbing the curb money into the institutionalized financial system must precede the real-name system. Actually, the real-name system was intended to crack down on the informal financial market by prohibiting anonymous financial transactions. However, the proposal had been delayed and not legislated in face of the opposition from the upper classes and the ruling party.

25 See the Government of the Republic of Korea, *The Revised Fifth Economic and Social Development Plan, 1984–86* (Seoul: 1983) (in Korean).

26 For the contents of the labour laws, see *The Dong-A Daily News*, 4, 6, and 26 December 1980; Alexander Irwin, 'Real Wages and Class Struggle in South Korea', *Journal of Contemporary Asia* 17 (No. 4, 1987), p. 403; Michael A. Launius, 'The State and Industrial Labor in South Korea', *Bulletin of Concerned Asian Scholars* 16 (October-December 1984), pp. 5–7; and In-Ryung Sin, *Labour Laws and Labour Movement* (Seoul: Il-Wal Press, 1987), pp. 132–53 (in Korean).

27 During the period of 1981–86, the ratios of organized workers to all employees had been below 20 percent: 19.5 percent in 1981, 19.0 percent in 1981, 18.0 percent in 1983, 16.8 percent in 1984, 15.7 percent in 1985, and 16.9 percent in 1986 (23.1 percent in 1987) (Ministry of Labour, *The Labour Statistics Yearbook* [Seoul: 1987] [in Korean]).

28 *The Dong-A Daily News*, 8 April 1982.

Chapter 8

The return to a collusive state-big business governing coalition
The disposals of financially ill-managed firms

Despite the institutional building, the new institutions for the economic reform began to crumble easily in the face of the economic cost of liberalization and the political cost of economic stabilization. Along with the financial deregulation, the government was losing its financial control over big business and thus could not prevent big business dominance in the market. Labour disputes increased against tight wage restriction for economic stabilization. Opposition forces were reactivated against the repressive authoritarian regime. In the end, the government failed to reform the financial system, and the politicized institutions had brought the state-controlled disposals of financially ill-managed large firms in line with industrial adjustment.

THE LIMITS OF GOVERNMENT REGULATION OF BIG BUSINESS

As I mentioned previously, Chun's government had tried to solve the problem of big business dominance both by expediting the economic liberalization policy and by regulating business groups. The tariff reform and import liberalization were to reduce big business firms' monopoly markets; the financial deregulations were to minimize the big businessmen's privileged access to preferential policy loans. In order to guarantee free market competition against big business dominance in the market-oriented economy, the government intended to regulate big business activities by means of the Fair Trade Act and credit control.

However, the financial deregulations led to the business groups' dominance in the ownership of financial institutions. Moreover, the government regulations had not been effective in preventing the business groups' dominance in financing funds and high business concentration in the industrial organization.

The business groups' financial dominance

As part of the economic reform, along with the financial liberaliz-ation policy, the government tried to correct the high concentration of bank loans to large companies (subsidiaries of business groups). The largely skewed credit allocation had been one of the side effects of the heavily state-led heavy and chemical industrialization of the 1970s. Since 1980, the Chun government had ordered the banks to allocate more credits to small and medium firms; it mandated that 55 percent of any local banks' total credit and 35 percent of the nationwide city banks' total credit should be loaned to small and medium firms. In addition, in 1984, the government froze the share of the thirty largest conglomerates in total bank loans at the end-of–1983 level and did not allow the large firms, whose debt-equity ratio exceeded 500 percent, further access to bank loans.[1]

Nevertheless, since 1983, the share of small and medium firms' borrowing in the net increase of the nationwide city banks' total credit had begun to decrease from 33.6 percent in 1983 to 27.0 percent in 1986, which did not reach the above-mentioned obligatory credit ratio (35 percent).[2] The concentration of credit allocation was increasing: the ten largest business groups in 1984 were the ten largest borrowers of bank loans; the share of the thirty largest business groups in the domestic total credit (bank loans and payment guarantee) increased from 43.2 percent as of the end of August 1983 to 48.0 percent as of the end of March 1984.[3]

In addition, after the government's liberalization policy of financial institutions, the largest business groups dominated both ownership of commercial banks (nationwide city banks and local banks) and non-bank financial institutions (short-term finance companies, securities corporations, insurance companies, etc.).[4] As of the end of September 1984, the thirty largest business groups borrowed about 70 percent of the short-term finance companies' total credit as a result of the government's decontrols on entry into and ownership participation in the non-bank financial institutions.[5]

The deepening business concentration

The degree of business concentration had been growing despite the establishment of the Fair Trade Act and the measures of 27 September 1980, to restrict big business expansion through mergers and acquisitions. In 1983, 70 percent of Korea's exports was generated by the top ten business groups. The average annual growth rates of sales and assets of the nine largest business groups were 34.5 percent and 27.8 percent, respectively, during the 1979–85 period, while the average growth rates of the real GNP and the GNP deflator were 5.4 percent and 9.9 percent, respectively, for the same period. The average number of member companies of the ten largest business groups had not been reduced from twenty-four between 1979 and 1985. According to the 27 September measures, the largest conglomerates disposed of their non-mainstream subsidiaries, but later they absorbed bigger business firms.[6] As a result, the business groups' financial structure had been worsening; 83.5 percent of the ten largest business groups' asset growth was financed by debt during the 1979–80 period; their average debt-equity ratio increased from 356 percent in 1979 to 464 percent in 1985; the average debt-equity ratio of the thirty largest business groups was 498.5 percent in 1983 in spite of the continuous regulatory credit management policy to the conglomerates, while the average ratio of the overall companies was 364.9 percent.[7]

As shown above, the government failed to restrain further business concentration and to improve big business firms' financial structure.

THE POLITICAL UNGOVERNABILITY OF THE AUTHORITARIAN REGIME

The crisis of legitimacy

Since the end of 1983, Chun's regime had groped for an appeasement policy towards opposition groups. The ruling political leaders thought that they had succeeded in installing a stable authoritarian regime through their repression of anti-regime forces, including opposition politicians, religious groups, labour unions, and students. To consolidate the authoritarian regime, the ruling group had to do something to legitimize its political power. The state managers felt the need to tempt the middle classes into becoming a pro-regime group; they planned to win more popular votes for their regime in the National Assembly election of early 1985. The political strategy had been manifested in a series of political openings to the opposition forces.[8]

In December 1984, the government allowed student activism within school boundaries, removed the police from universities and used policemen only to restrain demonstrations outside the campuses, and approved the re-admission to universities of expelled students and dismissed faculty members. In December 1984, President Chun lifted the ban on political activities from eighty-four of the ninety-nine banned persons; thus, the remaining fifteen politicians were left under the political ban, among the 567 who were excluded from political activities in 1980. In order to prepare for the national election, some of the formerly banned opposition politicians rebuilt the New Korea Democratic Party (NKDP), whose predecessor (New Democratic Party) had been the major opposition party under Park's regime and had been dissolved by the military coup leaders in 1980. One of the prominent opposition leaders, Dae Jung Kim, was allowed to return to Seoul before the scheduled election. Another most influential opposition leader, Young Sam Kim, was released from house arrest.

The two opposition political leaders had a great influence on the NKDP's successful re-emergence through the national assembly election, even though they were still under the political ban. The revived opposition party gained 29 percent of the total vote one month after its creation and became the major opposition party. The other two minority parties, which had been tamed by the authoritarian regime, lost their former voters of 1981. The three opposition parties won 58 percent of the popular vote. Although the ruling party (DJP) received only 35.4 percent, it could occupy 55 percent of the National Assembly seats because of the proportional representation system in favour of the government party.

Obviously, the outcome of the national election reflected the people's dissatisfaction with Chun's government and their support for political liberalization. In addition, contrary to the ruling party's strategy to separate the opposition party forces, the party system changed from the existing multi-party system to the two-party system of the DJP and NKDP. Intensive power struggles between the ruling party and the hard-line opposition party were expected. Opposition leaders launched their campaign for a constitutional revision that would provide a direct presidential election system in order to achieve a democratic transition to a civilian regime.

Labour pressures

In this situation of political opening, the opposition groups' democratic movement, the labour movement, and student activism outside the political institutions began to recur along with the newly formed opposition party's strong challenges against Chun's authoritarian regime. Since the end of 1983, the labour movement in particular had been reactivated in opposition to the government labour policy of restricting wage increases in the name of the economic stabilization policy. Two hundred and twenty-five labour disputes occurred in 1985; that number was twice that of 1984.[9] Like the institutional decay between the state and labour under Park's regime in the late 1970s, neither the corporatist nor the non-corporatist arrangements for labour control were effective in preventing labour disputes.

A number of state-controlled labour unions were reorganized into autonomous unions through the rank-and-file struggles. Furthermore, the movement for democratic labour unions, which had been led by labour activists, was relatively organized under Chun's regime, while the rank-and-file labour activism in workshop units was not organized under Park's regime. Additionally, the Korean labour movement under Chun's regime was linked with both student activists and outside (*Jaeya*) political activists. Thus, the labour activism became part of the political liberalization movement.

The Korean Workers' Welfare Council (KWWC), one of several voluntary labour organizations formed by labour movement activists, was established in 1984. The KWWC's establishment offered a basis for unity and solidarity of the labour movement among unit labour unions. It had also participated in the democratic movement as a part of the National Council for the Promotion of Democracy. In 1984, a national front for democratic struggles, the Unified People's (*Minjoong*) Movement for Democracy and Unification (UPMDU), was formed against the authoritarian regime. The coalition was composed of twenty-three organizations that represented banned labour activists, farmer groups, intellectuals, poets, dismissed journalists, and church and temple activists.[10]

Moreover, the FKTU leaders attempted to revise the Labour Union Law in order to intervene in wage bargaining at the enterprise level. As a matter of fact, the Labour Union Law, enacted in 1980, had constrained wage increases by prohibiting upper-level labour organizations from exercising industrial collective bargaining power on business firms. Basically, the institutional structure of wage settling had been formed by bargaining between workers and employers, based on an unequal power structure within the framework of the government's and the KEA's (Korean Employers' Association) wage guidelines.[11] Usually, at the year's outset, the wage guideline of the KEA was much lower than that of the FKTU; then, the government implicitly imposed its wage guideline that was little higher than that of the KEA.

During 1984–86, along with the increasing labour disputes for higher wages, the FKTU frequently demanded wage increases and protested against the state managers' and businessmen's wage restriction because the real rates of wage rises were only 6–7 percent, far below its expected rates. Finally, at the end of 1986, the peak labour organization succeeded in enacting a bill for a minimum wage and achieved a revision of the Labour Union Law, which would allow the FKTU and the industrial labour federations to intervene in collective bargaining at the enterprise level.[12] In particular, during 1987, the year of political democratization, both the upper labour organizations' intervention in collective wage bargaining and the enormously increased labour disputes brought a substantial wage rise by some 9 percent. Besides, Labour-Management Councils had made little contribution towards solving labour-management problems due to the employers' insincere attitudes towards, and the workers' non-confidence in, the councils.[13]

In brief, the failure of the government regulation on high business concentration had increased the economic cost of the economic reform; in the process of the opposition forces' pressures for political opening, the increased labour activity had greatly reduced the political governability of the authoritarian regime. In this political and economic situation, the government tried desperately to maintain the regime's stability for dictatorship by giving up the economic reform.

THE LIMITS OF FINANCIAL REFORM

The deregulation of business goups' credits

In 1985, the Korean economy met with a temporary slowdown: the lowest export growth rate (2.7 percent) since 1961 in face of the Western advanced countries' new protectionism and economic depression; increasing unemployment; and dissolutions of big business firms through the disposals of financially ill-managed big business firms (particularly, the collapse of one of the top ten business groups, the Kukje Business Group).[14] Faced with this economic depression, a group of the most influential business groups' owners visited President Chun in April. They requested that Chun relax the squeeze on credits to business groups and ease the ongoing tight money supply in order to boost investments. They directly asked the President for policy changes, after failing to convince the Minister of Finance, claiming for the economic rationale that business confidence (the investment climate) had worsened due to the recent government monetary and financial policies.[15]

Chun took their requests seriously and accepted the big businessmen's demands, disregarding the existing reform policies of the liberal-minded technocrats. The business groups' business interests coincided with the political leaders' interests in regime security. The power group's political rationale needed a supporting coalition with big business, which was to maintain the authoritarian regime against challenges from the new opposition party through the national election and the labour pressures. Thus, just as Park's government had made every effort to overcome the economic crisis by adopting the big business-oriented economic policy in the middle of economic stabilization in the latter half of 1979, so did Chun's government try to overcome the economic slowdown by loosening the existing anti-monopoly capital regulations and the tight money policy.[16]

The Office of Bank Supervision and Examination (OBSE), which had enforced the credit regulations, waived one regulation that required credit control-targeted business groups to sell their real estate or other non-mainstream member companies in cases of raising funds for new investments in its mainstream companies. The OBSE also exempted the top thirty largest business groups' credits for facilities investment and exports from the credit control.

In addition, the government released more funds for industrial plants and export financing at the expense of the strict stabilization policy.

Later, during 1986–87, the Korean economy had fully recovered high economic growth within stability in the international economic atmosphere of low oil prices, low interest rates, and the depreciated dollar.

The limits of financial liberalization

The regulated financial sector had been rapidly growing during the first half of the 1980s: the total credit from this sector had increased from 68 percent of GNP in 1980 to 94 percent in 1984. The cause of the financial acceleration was mainly due to the explosive expansion of non-bank financial institutions in the investment and insurance market, the commercial paper market, and the securities market of stocks and bonds. The share of bank credit in the total credit had dropped from 63 percent in 1980 to 55 percent in 1984, while that of non-bank financial institutions (NBFIs) credit had increased from 37 percent in 1980 to 45 percent in 1984.[17] Thus, the much less controlled NBFIs had contributed much more to the liberalization of the financial system than had the still highly controlled banks under the limited effort of deregulation of credit allocation, despite the transfer of government ownership to the private sector.

In fact, the government continued to control interest rates and offer a substantial part of policy loans among bank loans despite such policy measures for financial deregulation as the privatization of the nationwide city banks, the reduction of policy loans, and the abolition of preferential interest rates. In particular, the industrial policy through direct state intervention had been justified as it facilitated the rescue or disposal of highly indebted big business firms in declining industries.

The government had been in a dilemma between financial control and decontrol over banks. The reform-oriented policy-makers fully recognized that the Korean financial market had been underdeveloped and distorted because of the state-controlled financial system for the heavily state-led industrialization under Park's regime. They realized that the government should liberalize the financial sector towards a market-oriented economy in order to expand financing funds in accordance with the rapidly growing economic scale.

However, they were increasingly trapped by the banks' enormous non-performing loans, which had been accumulated during the heavy and chemical industrial promotion of the 1970s and aggravated due to such declining industries as shipping, shipbuilding, and overseas construction. The non-performing assets of the commercial banks as well as of state-owned banks such as the Korea Exchange Bank and the Korea Development Bank were 4 trillion won ($5 billion).[18] In the 1970s, the government had intervened to efficiently allocate credits to companies and industrial sectors that it regarded as promising. On the other hand, in the 1980s, the government intervened to correct the distortions created by the past state interventions. The state managers made desperate efforts to prevent bankruptcies of financially depressed banks through strong state interventions in credit allocation. As a result, the private-owned commercial banks were still vulnerable to the state's credit management because of their heavy dependence on the Bank of Korea for low-cost funds to cover their outstanding non-performing loans.

There is a question of how the authoritarian government tried to overcome the weakening financial institutional capabilities. Under the big business-oriented government, the government's choice for industrial adjustment was to rescue financially ill-managed big business firms and commercial banks at the expense of small and medium firms in the short term, and the low and middle classes in the long term. The process of financial reform had been determined not only by economic logic but also by political logic. The failure of the financial reform for credit control over business groups as well as for financial liberalization led to politicized state intervention in businessmen's investment decision-making by means of massive disposals of financially ill-managed firms. The politicized financial system was deeply connected with political donations, thereby forming a symbiotic relationship between the state and big business.[19] The next section will show how the authoritarian regime had covered the economic cost of industrial adjustment and the political cost of regime maintenance under the collusive state-big business governing coalition.

THE DECLINE OF EPB LEADERSHIP AND THE POLITICIZED BUREAUCRACY

The government was compelled to rescue the financially depressed banks, which had suffered from the large business firms' huge non-performing loans in the declining industries; thus the state managers had to prevent financially ill-managed firms from going bankrupt in addition to providing financial aid to the banks. In order to save the highly indebted business groups, the government chose to employ state interventions in investment decisions; it was to use the policy instruments of discretionary command to dispose of financially depressed firms. Chun's regime abandoned its earlier economic reform will towards a private-initiated economy. The big business-oriented economic adjustment was also a political choice that was undertaken to cover the increasing political costs that would be required for the maintenance of the unpopular authoritarian regime.

The decline of EPB leadership

The EPB's reform leadership had declined since 1985. The rising organizational interests of the conservative economic ministries (the MF and the MCI) had been reflected more than those of the EPB in economic policy decisions. The EPB could not take the initiative and was busy with coordinating different organizational interests in policy-making and implementation. The top executive, President Chun, became less committed to the EPB's reform leadership. Jai-Ik Kim, the most influential and firm reformist, who had been most favoured by Chun, died in the Rangoon bomb incident in October 1983; the other reformists were replaced by liberal-minded but gradual market-oriented technocrats – Mahn-Je Kim (the Finance Minister in 1985 and the EPB's Head in 1986), In-Young Chung (the Finance Minister in 1986 and the EPB's Head in 1987), and Il Sakong (the Presidential First Economic Secretary in 1986 and the Finance Minister in 1987). The two Finance Ministers were promoted to the Deputy Prime Minister (the Head of the EPB) in 1986 and 1987. The three technocrats took charge of disposing of the financially weak large firms in the name of industrial rationalization.

The new technocrats supported the economic stabilization policy in the short term and the economic liberalization policy in the long term. They tried to push import liberalization and reinforce regulations on business and credit concentration for free market competition. However, unlike the former reformists, the new, liberal-minded policy-makers were hesitant to actively implement the financial liberalization to achieve bank autonomy, including non-state intervention in credit allocation. Rather, they chose a gradual approach to financial reform. They argued that the government should not lose the policy instrument of financial control over firms, so as to rectify the distorted financial system from the past state intervention. Ironically, their logic was that it would be indispensable to impose the state's even compulsory financial intervention in the commercial banks and declining industries in the short term, in order to achieve the financial reform and apply a functional approach (state interventions at a minimum) to industrial policy in the long term.

The MCI had been more conservative in terms of the economic liberalization policy than the MF, even though it recognized the ultimate long-term goal of a market-oriented economy. In 1984, in the middle of institutionalizing a private-initiated industrial policy, the ministry began to cautiously prepare legal bases for industrial adjustment in the declining industries, particularly financial policy instruments for rescuing or disposing of financially weak firms.[20] The plan to establish an industrial adjustment law faced serious resistance both within the bureaucracy and from the big business circle. The controversial issues were how to define a 'declining industry' and to specify detailed criteria for the law's implementation, which would prevent possible abuses of the planned law.[21]

At that time, the EPB was creating new rules and organizations to set up a private-led industrial policy. In August 1985, the IPDC created the Industrial Development Civil Council (IDCC), which would be composed of businessmen, scholars, and journalists. Civil participation in industrial policy-making was to be expanded to achieve a harmonious policy cooperation between bureaucrats and civilians.[22] Finally, in place of the MCI's planned law, in September 1985, the EPB enacted the IDL (as I mentioned in Chapter 7) to stipulate the new liberalized industrial assistance law.

However, the new industrial law remained in rhetoric only. By 1985, the EPB had lost its reform leadership role in industrial policy. Since 1984, the state had already intervened to rescue and dispose of financially depressed firms in the name of industrial rationalization. During 1984–85, the state interventions had occurred based on administrative measures without legal authority. During 1986–87, the MCI and the MF found the legal basis in the IDL; they abused the IDL's exceptional rules for state interventions in declining industries.

The politicized bureaucracy

In addition, the state institutions for economic policy-making were politicized in two ways. First, the political power elite, including the top executive, were deeply involved in industrial policy. Policy measures for industrial adjustment came largely from political decisions rather than economic rules and criteria. In other words, the financial supports for and disposals of financially weak firms had been arbitrarily and politically decided to a large extent since 1985; the policy measures had been largely related to political funds and donations. Ironically, as a result, the IPDC, which was supposed to sustain and reinforce the EPB's reform leadership for economic liberalization, became a politicized organization for propelling the strong state intervention in industrial policy.

Second, the institutional channels between the government and the business groups were politicized. The business groups' owners had frequent, direct contacts with political leaders of the regime by bypassing the top-level bureaucrats. Under Park's regime during the 1970s and Chun's regime in the early 1980s, big business interests were represented through regular channels of the FKI's roundtables and the monthly export promotion meeting in the Blue House; individual business groups' interests were channelled through irregular meetings with economic ministers. During the latter half of Chun's presidential term, however, owners of the largest business groups often directly contacted the top of the government, while hired top managers of business groups met with the minister- or vice-minister-level bureaucrats, in order to represent big business interests and to demand individual conglomerates' interests.

The reasons for this shift of interaction channels between the government and big business were as follows: in general, under Chun's regime of the early 1980s, the techno-bureaucrats' basic policy guidelines for economic stabilization, liberalization, and industrial adjustment had brought about many conflicts with big business interests. More importantly, President Chun himself controlled political funds through the unified direct channel between the President and the business groups' owners, a large part of which was made of concerned business groups' kickbacks given in return for their enormous benefits from acquisitions and/or mergers of financially ill-managed business groups' large firms.[23] As a result, the politicized institutional structure between the government and big business had greatly reduced the bureaucracy's autonomy from the political leaders. Thus, the bureaucrats were vulnerable to political pressures in their decision-making for policy formation and implementation.

In 1985, the government enacted specific laws for institutional designs to facilitate the disposals of financially suffering large firms in the declining industries. The government amended the Bank of Korea regulations to let the central bank provide the commercial banks with long-term soft loans (3 percent annual interest rate). The so-called 'special loan' would help the city banks increase interest income and offset losses generated by the non-payment of loans and interests from almost-bankrupt companies in the declining industries.[24] Additionally, the government promulgated the Tax Reduction and Exemption Law. Under this law, the state would force acquisitions and/or mergers of poorly managed and near-bankrupt firms with well-managed and profitable firms. The law included the exemption of capital gains and withholding taxes in cases where firms had to sell assets while disposing of insolvent enterprises.[25] Later, despite the opposition parties' strong protest, this bill was passed in the National Assembly, where only the ruling party (the DJP) attended.

THE DISPOSALS OF FINANCIALLY ILL-MANAGED FIRMS: THE SUCCESSFUL STATE-CONTROLLED CAPITALIST COLLECTIVE ACTION

In the midst of economic liberalization, the disposals of poorly managed firms began in 1984, after the government realized the limits of pouring endless rescue funds into the declining industries of overseas construction, shipbuilding, and shipping. Under the favourable economic conditions of high growth with stability, the full-scale disposals took place on the basis of the new industrial assistance laws during 1986–87. The declining export-oriented industries had suffered from overcapacity and huge debts in the face of the depressed international market. More importantly, the financially depressed firms failed to achieve a voluntary self-adjustment (capitalist collective action) to reduce their investment and production as a result of their profit-maximizing market competition.

Under Chun's regime, thus, the disposals of the financially depressed firms were forced not only for the economic goal of industrial adjustment in the declining industries but also for the political goal of political leaders' control over business groups. Ultimately, the government was to rescue both almost-bankrupt business groups' companies and financially depressed banks by means of mergers with or acquisitions of other business groups' companies. At the same time, the political power elite intended to politically control business groups under an unequal symbiotic partnership. That is, in order to consolidate the state-big business governing coalition, the state managers wanted big businessmen to remain a dependent and loyal supporting group, under both political and financial control. The supporting group would pay the increasing political expenses for maintaining the authoritarian regime in return for the government's granting of privileged financial benefits to business groups.

Major policy instruments for the policy implementation were both coercive enforcement by political and financial control and positive selective incentives by financial supports. These instruments of coercion and inducement greatly enhanced the state managers' bargaining power over the planned merged and merging firms, which led to the successful collective actions for industrial adjustment (the disposals of financially ill-managed firms).

Coercive enforcement power: political and financial control

The state managers' coercive enforcement power had been exercised in decision-making on the following issues because there were no specific detailed rules for practical criteria in the process of policy formulation and implementation: which firms would be designated as financially ill-managed objects for industrial rationalization; which ones among designated financially weak firms would be rescued by financial supports or dissolved into mergers or acquisitions; and, finally, which business groups would take over the financially depressed firms. There were two typical cases where political coercion was heavily involved in disposing of the financially depressed business groups.

First, surprisingly, in February 1985 the government dissolved the Kukje Business Group, which was the seventh largest business group in 1984, with a total turnover of 1.8 trillion won and a debt-equity ratio of about 1600 percent (the group's total assets at 1.7 trillion won and liabilities at 1.6 trillion won).[26] In fact, the Kukje Group had faced serious financial difficulties since 1984. The group would have already gone bankrupt in December 1984 when about 30 billion won worth of notes rebounded. According to the government's order, the creditors' banks provided emergency loans to prevent bankruptcy just before the National Assembly election. Nevertheless, the matter of the dishonoured cheques led concerned short-term financial institutions to believe that the government might suspend its financial supports and let the group go bankrupt. Thus, the short-term creditors rushed to recall their loans to the group and forced the group into a corner.[27]

However, many businessmen had doubts about Kukje's dissolution case concerning the following reasons: why the banks did not honour the Kukje's cheques, as it was the established practice to consult with the group before bouncing cheques, and why the government selected the Kukje Group for dissolution, even though other financially ill-managed business groups had similar or greater financial difficulties. After the government announced the decision to dissolve the Kukje Group in the name of management rationalization, the President of the major creditor bank forced the chairman of the group to sign papers by threatening the owner with political penalties in the event of his disobedience. The signature would force the owner to give up his business group and sell his stocks to other firms at far below-market prices.[28] The public prosecutors' inspection into the Kukje case revealed that the Minister of Finance at that time had made an effort to recommend a scheme for the group's disposal of some member companies only without dissolving the whole group, as in other cases of financially ill-managed business groups, but that President Chun had instructed the minister to collapse the group.[29]

It was alleged that political rather than economic reasons were involved in the decision-making on the Kukje Group's collapse. In 1988, Chairman Chung-Mo Yang filed a suit to recover ownership of the Kukje Group and also testified regarding Chun's forced dissolution in the National Assembly's Inspection of the Government Administration and in the Special Hearings on the Fifth Republic Irregularities. He claimed that the Kukje Group was victimized by Chun's regime because he had infuriated President Chun and his loyal associates by donating relatively small amounts of money to the New Community fund[30] and by complaining about the government's collection of large contributions for the establishment of the Ilhae Foundation.[31]

The second case was the disposal of the Korean Shipping Corporation (KSC: one of the largest shipping companies and the mainstream company that formed a business group with four affiliated subsidiaries). Although the government had provided emergency loans for, or disposed of financially weak shipping firms in 1984, the financial state of the shipping companies had deteriorated. In February 1987, the government took the second measure for rescuing the surviving shipping companies by means of privileged financial support. Exceptionally, the government decided to dispose of only the KSC, which had liabilities of 1.2 trillion won, while the state managers continued to support the Pan Ocean Shipping Corporation (POSC), which had a debt of 1.6 trillion won.[32]

The disposal of the KSC was also the result of a political choice, undertaken in an unfair and arbitrary manner, rather than an economic choice. In 1984, the KSC was subjected to a frightening tax investigation by the Office of the Tax Administration in association with the scandal of the Acting President of the ruling party.[33] Since Park's regime, tax investigation had been one of the government's most powerful coercive policy instruments – one of the penalties used against businessmen's non-compliance. Companies under tax investigation suffered a sharp decrease in indirect financing funds from financial institutions, regardless of the investigation results. Since the investigation, as was usually the case, the KSC had faced serious financial difficulties.

The KSC's owner protested against the government's compulsory disposal by refusing to sign the contract to give up his ownership. The Chief of the KCIA, the Minister of Finance, concerned bankers, and the Head of the Office of Bank Supervision and Examination (OBSE) (Chun's friend and powerful close aide) forced him to abandon his company by threats, which was fully supported by President Chun. The owner claimed that he had never signed the contract, opposing the political oppression, but that the IPDC had approved the KSC's disposal on the basis of a forged contract document.

Finally, political decisions of enforcement affected, in part, which business groups would take over the financially weak large firms. At first, bureaucrats designated candidates among the large business groups and then President Chun chose a business group. Specific rules and criteria were hardly applied to the process of decision-making, which was vulnerable to the lobbying of concerned business groups through political funds and donations. At the initial stage of disposals, designated business groups hesitated to accept the government's offer but later actively took over almost-bankrupt firms after the government promised privileged financial incentives. In many cases, furthermore, large business groups tried to competitively absorb or merge dissolved large firms on the condition of privileged benefits. They intended to expand their business lines and scales by taking advantage of firms' disposals.

In the Kukje Group's case, the government chose Hanil Synthetic Fibre, of the Hanil Business Group, as the merger partner of the general trading and footwear divisions of the Kukje-ICC Corporation (the mainstream company of the Kukje Group), even though the Hanil Group's company had no track record in management of the footwear business. The government allowed Dongkook Steel to take over Union Steel of the Kukje Group by repressing the Union Steel workers' strong protest.[34] Chul-Hyun Kwon (a former majority owner and chairman of the company before the Kukje Group acquired Union Steel as a result of the Union Steel Group's political dissolution in 1977) strongly requested that he take over the company. But the government rejected his demand, although he still held 30 percent of Union Steel's stocks. Furthermore, it was highly questionable whether Dongkook Steel's performance had been better than Union Steel's. In fact, Union Steel had shown a good performance in terms of real profits among Kukje's member companies.

In the KSC's case, Minister of Finance, In-Young Chung, recommended to Chun three government-designated candidates (the Choyang Shipping Co., the Hyundai Merchant Marine Co., and Hanjin Container Lines) for the merger. The Choyang Group offered a better contract condition than the other two groups by planning to sell its member company. Hanjin Container Lines had deficits of over 40 billion won in 1984 and 1985. But President Chun ultimately decided that the KSC be taken over by the Hanjin Group.

By 1984, Chun's loyal aides prepared a scheme of political manipulation to enable Chun to exercise political influence after he stepped down.[35] They compiled a report entitled, 'Preparations for a Peaceful Power Transfer in 1988'. Afterwards, in the middle of economic liberalization and political opening, Chun's regime seemed to strongly feel the necessity of coercive political and financial control over big business in order to get more political donations. Chun himself wanted to control political funds in order to exercise his influence on ruling party members even after he would finish his presidential term. He politically controlled the big business sector by means of coercion in the disposals of financially ill-managed firms, in line with the above-outlined political strategies. In a special hearing, Jung-Mo Yang, the former chairman of the now-defunct Kukje Group, directly testified that President Chun had invited him and ten major business group leaders to a dinner in 1984: '[a]t the meeting, Chun, under the influence of alcohol, told the businessmen [that] he could destroy or help businesses'.[36]

Privileged financial incentives: the politicized financial system

Whenever the government was determined to break down a business group, it could do so by telling the state-controlled commercial banks to suspend additional loans to the company. This measure could happen to any business group. However, there should be limits on coercive financial instruments for political and financial control over big business. To achieve the firms' disposals, the authoritarian regime could not depend solely on coercive financial threats, even under the favourable economic conditions of 1986–87. The government had to give merger or acquisition business groups positive financial incentives to prevent them from becoming more financially depressed.

Until 1985, bureaucratic factions within the government had not agreed on policy means although there was consensus on the need for rationalizing troubled companies and industries. The EPB's position was to avoid direct state intervention in accordance with the new private-initiated industrial policy. On the other hand, the MF's and the MCI's position for the most effective industrial management was to directly intervene in firms and banks.[37] During 1984–85, the MCI and the MF had already intervened in industrial adjustment by means of financial rescues and compulsory disposals of financially weak firms, which had been approved and supported by the top executives. In early 1986, Finance Minister Mahn-Je

Kim became Deputy Prime Minister (the Head of the EPB) and subsequently actively propelled the troubled firms' disposals. Thus, the effective coherence within the bureaucracy, including the EPB, was attained in terms of the means for industrial adjustment – state-controlled financial instruments supported by the new banking and tax laws.

Concerned business groups received such privileged supports as tax reduction and exemption, repayment by instalments of liabilities over ten to fifteen years after a grace period of ten to fifteen years, partial exemption of debts, and new loans at low interest rates with a long maturity period (seed money), when they took over the highly indebted firms, most of which had more liabilities than assets. The government had used these kinds of abnormal financial measures to transfer ownership and management without letting the financially poorly managed firms go bankrupt. The huge financial supports would also reduce the creditor banks' financial loss in the short term and delay their financial burden in the long term. Additionally, the Bank of Korea provided huge special loans with a very low interest rate to the commercial banks in order to cover the privileged financial supports.[38]

In fact, during 1986–87, the government disposed of the seventy-eight financially weak firms by means of fifty-seven acquisitions (including mergers) of business groups, trustee management of banks, self-disposals of business groups, and two bankruptcies. The total amount of support for firms and banks was over 9 trillion won (7,282.4 billion won of financial support, 241.4 billion won of tax reduction and exemptions, and 1,722.2 billion won of the Bank of Korea's special loans).[39] The finally designated business groups desperately requested, even over one year in some cases, that the government offer privileged supports since they began to manage the dissolved firms, in accordance with the government's 'first take over, later settle account' rule. The big businessmen made every effort to squeeze as many concessions from the government as possible.[40]

In principle, the financial supports were to offset the financially weak firm's liabilities, which surpassed their assets. There had been two types of financial support. One was to exempt a large part of the existing bad loans, either with or without new loans. The other was to offer new loans (seed money) without exempting part of the non-performing loans. As for one of the former cases, when Hanil Synthetic Fibre took over the Kukje-ICC Co., the govern-

ment exempted existing loans of 180.8 billion won and offered the
seed money of 58.1 billion won; and it allowed the Hanil company
to repay a 180.8 billion won debt over fifteen years, after the grace
period of fifteen years, and another 217.5 billion won debt over
twelve years, after the maturity period of ten years. In the KSC's
case, the government exempted existing loans of 420.7 billion won
and allowed the Hanjin Group to repay another 373.1 billion
won debt over fifteen years free of interest, after the fifteen-year
grace period. As for one of the latter-type cases, when the Daewoo
Group took over Kyungnam Enterprise (a large overseas construction company), the government provided the seed money of 200
billion won, which would be repaid by instalments with the 10
percent interest rate over five years, after the fifteen-year grace
period, and permitted the Daewoo Group to pay back a 474.1
billion won debt over fifteen years, after the fifteen-year grace
period.

Business groups' political investment and rewards

The government had disposed of many financially ill-managed
firms in an unfair and arbitrary manner by means of political
decisions, in association with political contributions to state-run
foundations – the New Generation Education Foundation and the
Heart Foundation, led by Mrs Chun; the Ilhae Foundation, led
by President Chun; and the New Community (*Saemaul*
Movement), led by Chun's younger brother.[41] The political power
elites imposed contributions on business groups in the form of
quasi-compulsory 'quasi-taxes'. Big businessmen responded to the
fund-raisings either in a voluntary or in an involuntary manner:
at most, they competitively donated money for privileged favours,
or in return for privileged benefits, or at least they contributed
out of fear of any unfavourable treatment.

In particular, selective coercive enforcements by political power
leaders were apparent in the fund-raising efforts for the establishment of the Ilhae Foundation. Se-Dong Chang, a former Chief of
the Presidential Security Office, abused his political power by
forcing business groups to donate large sums to the foundation.[42]
In a special hearing on the Ilhae scandal, Joo-Young Chung, the
owner of the Hyundai Business Group and a former Chairman of
the FKI, testified that he and other businessmen were forced to

donate money to the foundation for fear of any unfavourable treatment.[43]

The amount of political donations to the foundations, along with the disposals of the financially weak firms, rapidly increased, particularly after the Kukje's collapse.[44] Some business groups competitively donated large sums, expecting or rewarding their privileged benefits in the firms' disposals for industrial adjustment. For instance, Dongkook Steel donated 1,250 million won to the Ilhae Foundation in 1985 shortly after it took over the Kukje Group's Union Steel; but the company made a contribution of only 200 million won to the foundation in 1986 and contributed nothing in 1984.[45]

In addition, the business groups' direct political contributions to the political power group had had a correspondingly positive effect on their privileged benefits.[46] During the period of 1982–88, the formal political funds of 58.1 billion won were contributed to the Central Election Management Committee; 98 percent (58 billion won) of the amount went to the ruling party (the Democratic Justice Party: DJP).[47] Many business groups made individually designated contributions of 54 billion won to the DJP. The aforementioned business groups, which benefited from the financial supports from the government in association with the firms' disposals, contributed large sums to the party. The Hanil Group, the Daewoo Group, the Hanjin Group, and Dongkook Steel made larger donations than the Hyundai Group (the largest Korean business group).[48] Furthermore, it was alleged that a large part of the donations to the state-led foundations was wrongly used as political funds. For an instance of informal political funds, the former owner of the KSC claimed that the Hanjin Group gave President Chun over 100 billion won in return for its takeover of the KSC.[49]

In conclusion, there were similarities and differences between the disposals of financially ill-managed firms (DFIFs) during 1986–87 and the investment adjustments in the HCIs (HCIIAs) during 1979–80, in terms of the following issues: context, goal, and manner of industrial adjustment; institutional change within the state, between the state and big business, and in the financial system; state managers' bargaining power for and big businessmen's bargaining power against state intervention in investment decision-making; and the state's policy instruments.

First, the HCIIAs and the DFIFs were state-controlled industrial adjustments where the state intervened strongly in the businessmen's investment decision by means of discretionary command. In a broad sense, the HCIIAs were another way of disposing of financially weak firms, although the concerned largest business groups could save their financially depressed subsidiaries. The HCIIAs were to solve overcapacity in the distorted heavy and chemical industries during the economic crisis period, in the middle of the business groups' competitive investment, while the DFIFs were to overcome the same problem in the declining industries during the period of favourable economic conditions. The HCIIAs and the DFIFs were the temporary emergency policy measures in the midst of economic stabilization policy and of long-term economic liberalization policy, respectively.

Second, the institutional decay or disorder in the policy-making and implementation processes, in state–big business relations, and in the financial system, had affected the general policy failure of the HCIIAs. In contrast, the new politicized institutions for industrial adjustment had increased the state managers' capacities for state intervention and had led to the policy success of the DFIFs. In both cases, the state managers tried to overcome their financial institutional incapabilities in order to restore financial control over big business: before the HCIIAs, the government had increasingly lost its financial control over business groups as a result of the heavily controlled credit allocation in the HCIs; on the other hand, before the DFIFs, the policy-makers were losing their financial control due to the financial deregulation. In addition, in both cases, the authoritarian regime wanted to restrict the increasing big business power. Ultimately, the DFIFs coopted the big business circle as the dependent and loyal support group of the authoritarian regime, while the HCIIAs either kept a distance from big business or broke down the existing state–big business governing coalition.

Finally, the state managers in the HCIIAs had weak bargaining power over the big businessmen under the institutional constraints in association with foreign capital, compared to those in the DFIFs. The former lacked the policy instruments either of both strong coercive enforcement and adequate financial support, under Park's and Choy's governments, or of sufficient financial incentives, under Chun's government. On the other hand, the latter had both highly coercive instruments for financially weak large firms and financial instruments of highly privileged supports for the takeover business groups.

In the HCIIAs, the takeover business groups exerted strong bargaining power over the state managers by demanding privileged financial benefits; the business groups, which had their member company to be merged, resisted the compulsory mergers by means of foot-dragging on implementation through the conflicts among the business groups and the foreign actors' opposition. In contrast, in the DFIFs, the financially weak business groups had no choice but to accept their dissolution in the face of threats of bankruptcy and/or political threats for non-compliance. Unlike the HCIIAs' state managers, the DFIFs' state managers could provide the business groups' financial demands, in an excessive manner, in exchange for political donations. Thus, unlike the HCIIAs' merging business groups, the DFIFs' acquisition and/or merger partners had weak bargaining power against state intervention in their investment decision-making because the government allowed them to request huge financial supports and benefits, in return for their risk-taking in acquiring the highly indebted firms.

NOTES

1 The World Bank, *op. cit.* (1987) [Chapter 7, note 22], Vol. 1, pp. 92–93. Small-medium firms are defined as follows: total assets are less than 1 billion won, and the total number of employees is less than 300 in a manufacturing industry and 200 in a service industry (ibid., p. 93).

2 *The Dong-A Daily News*, 20 February 1987. For the small and medium firms' financial difficulties, see *The Dong-A Daily News*, 6, 9, and 19 January 1984; and *The Hankook Daily News*, 23 March 1987.

3 Seok-Ki Kim, 'Business Concentration and Government Policy: A Study of the Phenomenon of Business Groups in Korea, 1945–85', D.B.A. Diss. (Harvard University, 1987), pp. 259–60. See also *The Chosun Daily News*, 27 October 1984; and *The Maeil Kyungje Daily News*, 28 November 1986. As of the end of May 1985, the share of the thirty largest business groups in the total bank loans was 35.8 percent (*The Dong-A Daily News*, 2 June 1986). For the list of the thirty largest business groups' and the fifty largest companies' borrowings from banks, see *The Dong-A Daily News*, 2 June 1986.

4 For the detailed list of the business groups' ownership, see *The Maeil Kyungje Daily News*, 12 June 1984; and *The Daegoo Maeil Daily News*, 30 October 1984.

5 *The Dong-A Daily News*, 22 November 1984.

6 See Seok-Ki Kim, *op. cit.*, pp. 251–53, 287–90; Hang Yul Rhee, 'The Economic Problems of the Korean Political Economy', in Ilpyong J.

Kim and Young Whan Kihl, *Political Change in South Korea* (New York: The Korea PWPA Inc., 1988), pp. 203–7; *The Dong-A Daily News*, 14 April 1984; *The Maeil Kyungje Daily News*, 27 April 1984; and *The Hankook Daily News*, 13 July and 27 September 1984. The share of the five largest business groups of value-added in GNP grew from 9.7 percent in 1980 to 12.1 percent in 1984. During the four years following the 27 September measures of 1980, the twenty-six conglomerates, which had been designated under government supervision, purchased new real estate twenty times greater in value than what they had been required to sell. Many business groups expanded through skilful interlocking investment within the limits of their financial capital. They increased their capital by investing mutually in bookkeeping among their member companies without new capital input. Likewise, a member company also invested in stocks to acquire a new company and the rest of new actual capital was funded by bank loans. To make matters worse, the concentration of ownership had been very high: in typical cases, a business group (*Jaebol*) has been directly and indirectly owned and controlled by a single family; shares of the group's equity are dispersed to family members, holding companies, and its foundation for social works; and the holding companies and the foundation are owned and controlled by the family.

7 Seok-Ki Kim, ibid., pp. 253, 254; *The Maeil Kyungje Daily News*, 25 March 1985; and Eui-Kack Hwang, 'The Principal Offender of Ill-Financing: Skewed Credits to Big Companies', *Sin Dong-A* (September 1988), pp. 472–76 (in Korean). The average debt-equity ratio of Korean companies had been higher than that of other countries' companies: during 1981–84, 385 percent in Korea, 105 percent in the U.S., 167 percent in Taiwan, 219 percent in West Germany, and 348 percent in Japan.

8 For the process of political opening, the national election, the popular sector's activation and pressures, and the struggles for constitutional amendments during 1984–86, see Ralph N. Clough, *Embattled Korea: The Rivalry for International Support* (Boulder: Westview Press, 1987), Chap. 5; and Ilpyong J. Kim and Young Whan Kihl, eds., op. cit.

9 *The Dong-A Daily News*, 5 November 1985. One hundred and twenty-nine cases among those disputes were caused by demands for wage increases and payments of delinquent wages.

10 Suk Joon Kim, *The State, Public Policy & NIC Development* (Seoul: Dae Young Moonwhasa, 1988), pp. 456–59.

11 As for the collective bargaining in labour-management relations under Chun's regime, see Mario F. Bognanno, 'Korea's Industrial Relations at the Turning Point', *KDI Working Paper* 8816 (December 1988), pp. 28–31.

12 See *The Federation of Korean Trade Unions*, 25 April 1986; *The Hankook Daily News*, 13 November 1986; and *The Dong-A Daily News*, 11 December 1986.

13 *The Federation of Korean Trade Unions*, 25 April 1986.

14 *The Hankook Daily News*, 24 December 1985.

15 'Monolith of a Problem', *Business Korea* (May 1985), p. 14.

16 See *The Maeil Kyungje Daily News*, 22 July 1985; *The Dong-A Daily News*, 13 April, 2 July, and 16 August 1985; and *The Hankook Daily News*, 17 July, and 6 and 17 August.

17 See Yoon Je Cho and David C. Cole, 'The Role of the Financial Sector in Korea's Structural Adjustment', *KDI Working Paper* (December 1986), pp. 10–14. The growth ratio of NBFIs' credit to GNP doubled that of bank credit to GNP between 1980 and 1984.

18 'Monolith of a Problem', *Business Korea* (May 1985), p. 14. The amount of non-performing loans was equal to 5.5 percent of GNP and 11.8 percent of total lendings in loans. For non-performing assets to impede bank reforms, see 'Banking is Public Service', *Business Korea* (May 1986) and 'Non-Performing Assets Slow Bank Reforms', *Business Korea* (October 1985).

19 The term 'politicized' is used to indicate that the operation of the financial system was heavily based on political decisions.

20 See *The Dong-A Daily News*, 18 October 1984; and *The Chosun Daily News*, 4 October 1984.

21 See *The Maeil Kyungje Daily News*, 17 December 1984; and *The Chosun Daily News*, 22 December 1984.

22 *The Maeil Kyungje Daily News*, 1 August 1985.

23 See Jong-Ryul Park, 'The Fifth Republic's Political Funds', *Sin Dong-A* (January 1989) (in Korean). Under Park's regime, several powerful political leaders loyal to President Park collected political funds through different channels, including the Chief of Presidential Secretariat and the Finance Chairman of the ruling party (the DRP).

24 *The Dong-A Daily News*, 18 June 1985; and 'Banking is Public Service', *Business Korea* (May 1986).

25 *The Maeil Kyungje Daily News*, 13 December 1985; and 'No Major Surgery Due on Policies', *Business Korea* (October 1985).

26 The business group had twenty-three member companies with 38,000 employees, which were widely diversified, with business lines of textiles, shipping, engineering, electronics, overseas construction, machinery, securities, steel manufacturing, and chemical manufacturing. Its Kukje-ICC Corporation was a privileged, government-designated general trading company. For the Kukje's situation, see 'Kukje K.O.'d', *Business Korea* (March 1985); 'Kukje: A Lesson for Many', *Business Korea* (April 1985); 'Poorly Managed Companies Could Face Kukje's Fate', *Business Korea* (July 1985); and *The Dong-A Daily News*, 21 February 1985.

27 'Fighting to Regain an Empire', *Business Korea* (May 1988), p. 20.

28 See *The Weekly Chosun*, 17 April 1988.

29 See *The Weekly Chosun*, 22 January 1989.

30 'Fighting to Remain an Empire', *Business Korea* (May 1988), p. 19.

31 Big businessmen agreed to donate large sums of money to bereaved family members of the Rangoon victims shortly after the brutal North Korean bomb attack in Rangoon that killed seventeen senior government officials. Afterwards, the Chief of the Presidential Security Office (one of the most powerful men loyal to Chun) and the leading business groups' owners decided on the establishment of the Ilhae (Chun's pen

name) Foundation, which would be engaged in research into economics, diplomacy, and national security in addition to providing compensation to the victims' families. The Hyundai Business Group, the POSCO (the state-run Pohang Iron and Steel Company), and the Samsung Business Group were the biggest contributors, donating 15 billion won, 4.5 billion won, and 4.5 billion won respectively. Joo-Young Chung (owner of the Hyundai Group and Chairman of the FKI) served as the chairman of the foundation. The total amount of fifty-two businessmen's donations to the founndation was 57.8 billion won. For the Ilhae scandal, see *The Dong-A Daily News*, 3 November–9 December 1988.

32 See *The Maeil Kyungje Daily News*, 16 and 19 February 1987.

33 The father-in-law of the owner's younger brother (the Vice-Chairman of the KSC) sent the government an anonymous note that revealed the Acting President's illicit wealth accumulation. As a result, the accused was forced to resign. Shortly after, the government ordered tax investigation into the company as part of its political revenge. Furthermore, the Chairman (owner) of the KSC, Suk-Min Yun, was the Vice-President of the Korea National Party (a minor opposition party). For Yun's testimonies in the National Assembly's investigation and special hearings on the Fifth Republic Irregularities, see *The Dong-A Daily News*, 29 October 1988; Suk-Hwan Kim, 'The Collapse of the KSC and Political Manoeuvring', *Monthly Joong-Ang* (January 1989) (in Korean); and Young-Kil Kwack, 'Lee Won-Cho and the Suspicious Disposal of the KSC', *Monthly Chosun* (March 1989) (in Korean).

34 See 'Union Steel Workers Say "No" ', *Business Korea* (July 1986).

35 The report was made public in special hearings on the Ilhae Foundation scandal. Opposition party members claimed that the establishment of the Ilhae Foundation was part of the report's planned political manipulation (see *The Korea Herald*, 9 December 1988). There was other evidence that Chun made every effort to exercise real political power even after his presidential term was over. Just before he stepped down, he revised the law of the Senior Advisory Committee for the Government Administration, which would be chaired by himself and composed of former presidents, to exercise more political influence. He also filled powerful military positions with his core of loyal generals.

36 *The Korea Herald*, 10 November 1988.

37 See 'In Search of the Right Stuff', *Business Korea* (March 1985).

38 For the financial supports, see Sang-Min Sin, 'Business Concentration as a Result of the Disposals of Financially Weak Firms', *Sin Dong-A* (November 1986) (in Korean); and Soon-Jik Kwon, 'The Inside Story in the Disposals of Financially Weak Firms', *Sin Dong-A* (May 1988) (in Korean).

39 For the detailed list and the amounts of financial support, see *The Dong-A Daily News* 7 and 21 July 1988. The financial supports were composed of bank-loan exemptions of 986.3 billion won, new loans of 460.8 billion won, graces and reductions of interest repayment for

the principals' amount of 4,194.7 billion won, and graces of only the principal repayment for the principals' amount of 1,640.6 billion won.

40 See *The Maeil Kyungje Daily News*, 16 February 1987; and 'Corporate Mergers Raise Questions', *Business Korea* (July 1986).

41 For characteristics of the foundations and funds, and the business groups' political donations, see the National Assembly Records, *Special Hearings on the Ilhae Foundation)* (Seoul: 1989) (in Korean); *The Dong-A Daily News*, 1 November 1988; Sang-Hyun Choi, 'Quasi-Taxes on *Jaebols* and the Behind-the-Scenes Story of Privileges', *Monthly Kyunghyang* (December 1988) (in Korean); Yong-Jung Kim, 'The Inside Story of the Companies' Quasi-Taxes to be Transferred to the Consumer', *Sin Dong-A* (January 1987) (in Korean); and Jong-Ryul Park, 'The Ilhae Foundation', *Sin Dong-A* (October 1988) (in Korean). The total amount of political donations (which were revealed to the public) to the foundations was about 270 billion won under Chun's regime (149.6 billion won to the New Community fund, 22,351 million won to the New Generation Education Foundation, 42,296 million won to the Heart Foundation, and 59,850 million won to the Ilhae Foundation).

42 See *The Korea Herald*, 8 November 1988 and 26 January 1989.

43 *The Korea Herald*, 10 November 1988 and 18 January 1989.

44 See Se-Hoon Park, 'The Fifth Republic's Collusive State-Business Coalition', *Monthly Chosun* (December 1988) (in Korean).

45 The following are the amounts of large donations to the Ilhae Foundation from the aforementioned business groups that benefited from the firms' disposals: the Hanil Group, 900 million won; Dongkook Steel, 1,450 million won; the Daewoo Group, 4 billion won; and the Hanjin Group, 2.2 billion won (see Jong-Ryul Park, *op. cit.* [1988], p. 347).

46 Under Chun's regime, there were formal and informal channels for political funds. In December 1980, the Legislative Council for National Security passed the revised 'Laws about Political Funds' to make public sources of political funds. According to the laws, the scope of the political funds was limited to open political contributions through business associations, government subsidies, individual designations, and party supporters' organizations. However, the amount of political funds collected through the above-mentioned formal channels was much smaller than that of illicit funds obtained under the table.

47 Sang-Hyun Choi, *op. cit.*, p. 218.

48 The Hanil Group (the second largest donator), 1,300 million won; the Daewoo Group (the thirteenth largest donator), 700 million won; the Hanjin Group (the eighteenth largest donator), 600 million won; Dongkook Steel, 600 million won; and the Hyundai Group, 520 million won. For the formal political funds, see Jong-Ryul Park, *op. cit.* (1989).

49 *The Dong-A Daily News*, 29 October 1988.

Conclusion

THEORETICAL IMPLICATIONS

Institutional arrangements within the state, between state and society, and between state and market are structural conditions affecting the success or failure of state-led or controlled capitalist collective action to achieve industrial adjustment. Institutional capacities of the state fluctuate according to the constraints of institutional decay, disorder, and new institutional building. Faced with bureaucratic conflicts, political power struggles, and social groups' resistance and opposition, in particular, a winning group of state managers intentionally builds new institutional mechanisms to increase state capacities for effective state intervention in the market. Here, it is important for state managers to design institutions in the area of capitalist collective action problems, which would provide the government with specific policy instruments. In general, policy instruments are characterized by coercive enforcement and financial incentives.

Institutional capabilities of the state affect state managers' and business firms' interests and bargaining power over industrial policy formulation and implementation. More specifically, the degree of both coercive punishment and financial rewards, which are constrained by a successful or unsuccessful institutional design, either facilitates or prohibits state managers' policy choices and abilities (bargaining power); ineffective or effective policy instruments also either increase or decrease businessmen's bargaining power for both resistance against coercive enforcement and demands for financial benefits. Finally, these instruments affect businessmen's rational choices (interests) between cooperation and non-cooperation either among business firms or with the government's policy choices. Ultimately, the successful or unsuccessful policy implementation of state-led or controlled economic adjustment depends on whether or not the state can create capitalist collective action in compliance with the state's policy choices.

These theoretical arguments in this study explain why and how state intervention succeeds or fails. This study can give several theoretical implications to new institutional approaches, which focus on analysing the politics of state intervention in the market. First, institutional arrangements within the state, between state and society, and between state and market, strongly affect interests and capabilities of the actors involved in economic adjustment and strategic interactions among these actors. Existing state-centred, society-centred, or market-centred approaches offer only partial explanations for state intervention in economic management. In particular, specific characteristics of the financial system are very important institutional constraints that greatly influence bargaining power struggles between state managers and businessmen.

The second implication is concerned with levels of analysis. In other words, this issue is how to synthesize structural (macro-level) variables with actors (micro-level). The new institutional approach in my study shows not only how institutional variables constrain actors' interactions, but also how collective action problems among actors bring about the establishment of new institutions, which result from state managers' institutional design. That is, my new institutional approach explains both institutional origins and maintenance (functions).

Finally, my approach provides a dynamic analytical framework. Institutional arrangements may differ according to economic issues and change over time. During the periods of economic stabilization and liberalization, the so-called strong states intervened, in a selective and limited manner, in the industries. Institutional change (institutional decay, disorder, and new institutional building) over time resulted in fluctuating state capacities for economic adjustment. In particular, it is important to analyse who (a governing coalition) installed what kind of institutional design in the process of new institutional building. In these countries, more importantly, the effective institutional arrangements for high economic growth themselves became sources for institutional decay and subsequently led to weakening state capacities along with the economic slowdown or recession.

THE LIMITS OF KOREAN STATE-CONTROLLED INDUSTRIAL ADJUSTMENT

The dilemma between state intervention and liberal economic reform: lessons from Japan and France

As I mentioned previously, Japan and France pursued high economic growth with the state-led industrial adjustments during the 1960s. The state-led industrial adjustments were formulated and implemented by bilateral interactions between the state and big business. The successful cases of economic growth in Japan and France have usually been discussed in ways that demonstrate state autonomy *vis-à-vis* interest groups and that illustrate the ability of the bureaucracy to implement economic policies. Traditional explanations primarily concentrate on proving the superiority of state capacities as compared to other developed countries. South Korea as a newly industrializing country is mentioned as a successful case of high economic growth under an authoritarian regime. The success story is frequently explained by underscoring state capacities in macroeconomic and industrial policies based on the state-controlled industrial adjustment, which repress popular sectors.

However, the state-led industrial adjustments in Japan and France had faltered in their implementation of economic stabilization and liberalization since the first oil-shock of 1973 and, especially, during the world economic recession of the 1980s. Likewise, the state-controlled industrial adjustments in Korea did not work effectively to achieve economic stabilization and liberalization during the late 1970s and the 1980s. Existing institutions within the state, between state and society, and between state and market had been withering and changing in both the developed and developing countries. Institutional decay or disarray had reduced governmental capabilities and the effectiveness of industrial policy instruments. The side effects or limits of state intervention in economic management had increased.

In general, Korea, Japan, and France took advantage of more market-oriented and less state-interventionist instruments (less discretionary field manipulation in France and Japan, and less discretionary command in Korea) than before; the financial instruments for state intervention changed from direct to indirect subsidies and private funding. Despite the policy changes towards market-oriented management, however, the three countries still continued to support some industries that had a comparative edge and other declining industries. The countries also tried to keep a high level of business activities under government guidance or control.

The new Korean authoritarian government, unlike France and Japan, still had compulsory instruments for state intervention. The new Korean government was able to control business associations with inducements and constraints, and to suppress labour unions with repression under the strict political control. In the cases of business firms' non-compliance, the government could still keep big business under the financial control with the threats or penalties of withdrawing loans.

As shown above, there were 'tensions between state and market' in economic management. Thomas M. Callaghy argued that African states failed to achieve economic reforms because of the weakness of both the state and the market. Interestingly, South Korea, France, and Japan became 'lost between state and market', despite the strength of both the state and the market.[1]

The limits of authoritarian state capacities

In conclusion, the ultimate theme of this study is the limits of authoritarian state capacities either for state intervention in the market or for liberal market reform, which have been proved in the process of explaining why and how the Korean state-controlled industrial adjustment did or did not work. The Korean authoritarian regimes became fragile, in terms of economic and political governabilities, without the collusive state-big business governing coalition.

First, during the period of 1979–80, the authoritarian governments failed to attain the state-controlled investment adjustments in the process of provoking the state-big business conflicts and the breakdown of the state-big business governing coalition. Furthermore, in the late 1970s, the government began to be overwhelmed by big business influence and to lose state control over big business. As a result, the Park regime had to pay the huge economic cost of overcapacity. The unsuccessful state-controlled industrial adjustment could not solve, in the short term, the side effects of the ambitious heavy and chemical industrial promotion. The economic inefficiency within the limits of the state-big business ruling coalition could not offset the increasing political cost for regime security. Ultimately, Park's regime collapsed as a result of the political pressures of excluded social groups.

Second, Chun's authoritarian government attempted to achieve the liberal economic reform, including state control over big business dominance. But the repressive government, without a supporting coalition, faced the failure of its reform policy. The political leaders seemed to be based on military power alone, excluding even big business as a social base of political power. Chun's regime did not want to maintain the governing coalition between the state and big business that had existed during the 1970s. It intended to prevent an increase of big business influence and high business concentration in order to achieve the liberal economic reform for fair market competition. The attempts to achieve economic control over big business during the early period of Chun's regime were undertaken as part of the goal of legitimating the authoritarian regime.

However, the government failed to reduce big business domi-nance and then gave up the market-oriented reform in the mid–1980s. Later, it could not avoid implementing the stronger state intervention to dispose of the financially depressed companies within the declining industries; in these cases, it was alleged that big businessmen gave political funds to the government and contri-butions to the state-led foundations, in return for enormous privi-leges of financial benefits from the government, in the latter period of Chun's regime. That is, Chun's regime concentrated huge eco-nomic resources in the hands of a small group of big businessmen and at the expense of small- and medium-sized firms and the popular sectors. The authoritarian regime tried to pay the increas-ing political cost for regime security by exploiting the state-controlled industrial adjustment. In the end, after the failure of liberal economic reform, Chun's regime was forced to return to the collusive alliance between the state and big business that Park's regime had created in order to legitimate the dictatorship in the name of high economic growth.

LOST BETWEEN STATE AND MARKET DURING 1988–92: DEMOCRATIZATION AND ECONOMIC LIBERALIZATION

During the first half of 1987, the authoritarian government had been crumbling in the face of democratic forces' strong pressures.

A mass uprising in June forced the ruling party to agree to democratic transition. The 29 June declaration by the Chairman of the ruling party, Tae-Woo Ro, included a direct presidential election system, and amnesty and restoration of civil rights for dissidents. The December 1987 presidential election took place under a democratic constitution. He was elected President of the Sixth Republic (1988–92).[2]

Under Ro's regime, the political management of the economy led to the failure of liberal economic reform in the unstable process of political democratization. In other words, the government's politically rational (rather than economically rational) economic policy choice resulted in the shelving of market-oriented reform. The aborted institutional building for economic reform was accompanied by an unstable state-big business governing coalition in institutional disorder. The weakening institutional capacities of the state achieved neither state-controlled nor market-initiated industrial adjustment. In the end, the government could not stir up capitalist collective action of investment to enhance the international competitiveness in manufacturing industries. That is, Ro's government could not efficiently intervene in businessmen's investment decision-making. Moreover, it failed to induce capitalist investments in fair market competition by regulating big business firms.

The policy choice of economic reform

During 1988–89, the government attempted to achieve both measures (deregulations for state decontrol) for economic liberalization and regulations for fair market competition (particularly regulations of big business). After the dramatic transition from authoritarian dictatorship, the process of political liberalization had been accompanied by efforts at liberalizing and deregulating the economy. During the early period, the government's political interests tended to satisfy growing political and social demands for welfare and equality.

The main goals of economic management were maintaining economic and social stability, balanced development between different classes and areas, accelerating liberalization and internationalization, reducing government intervention and promoting economic fairness. The government's most important strategy was to mitigate such growing destabilizing forces as inflation, widely spreading

labour disputes, and rising speculative investment in real estate.[3]
Within this economic policy strategy, the orientation of industrial
adjustment was set up in two ways. First, the government's role
should be limited to assisting in the development of technology
and human capital and the government must suspend giving support to declining industries and to poorly performing firms.
Second, the power of the Fair Trade Commission should be
strengthened to diffuse the concentration of economic power by
regulating business groups.[4]

The failure of institutional building for economic reform

During 1988–89, reform-oriented bureau-technocrats (particularly
the EPB and the Economic Presidential Secretariat) had made an
effort to take reform measures under the *yeo-so ya-dae* (the ruling
minority and the combined opposition majority) party structure.
The core of economic reform was the 'public land ownership' and
the real-name financial transaction. The former included a ceiling
on residential property, tax on earnings accrued from regional
development, tax on profits from excessive land ownership, and
adjustment of assessment standards for property tax.[5] The latter
was a drastic proposal requiring all financial transactions to be
made in the real names of the persons concerned which was
intended to reduce the scope of the curb market, to establish a
more equitable tax system, and to prohibit political funds under
the table.

However, the economy's sharp downward slide and the dramatic
change of party structure brought about a sudden shift of Ro's
economic policy. Korea's economic performance began to slow
down in late 1988 due to increasing wages in labour disputes and
the appreciation of the won.[6] Meanwhile, Ro's regime faced with
accelerating political pressures from opposition parties and social
groups. In this situation, the ruling elite was not able to cope with
both increasing political cost and short-term transition cost for
economic reform. Finally, in January 1990, the ruling party (the
Democratic Justice Party) merged with the two opposition parties
(the Reunification Democratic Party and the New Democratic
Republican Party). A grand conservative majority party was
created to overcome political instability and weak business confidence in investment.

The new Deputy Prime Minister of the EPB and the new First

Economic Secretary adopted a growth-oriented economic strategy by calling for economic-boosting measures. They weakened or aborted the existing reform measures in support of large business firms' demands. The regulations for the public concept of the land ownership were eased or delayed. Additionally, the planned introduction of the real-name system for financial transactions was suspended. During the period of Chun's regime, the proposal had been delayed and not legislated in face of the opposition from business groups and the ruling party because of the restrictions they imposed on businessmen's growth-oriented investment decision-making and politicians' political funds.

The weakening government capacities in institutional disorder

The failure of institutional building for liberal economic reform made it impossible for the government to install institutional arrangements either for state-led or for market-oriented economic adjustment. The institutional capacities of the state had been crumbling and weakening in institutional disorder.

First, the state institutions for economic policy formation and implementation had been incoherent and inefficient for economic adjustment. The bureaucratic autonomy from politics had been decreasing in the process of democratization. The Party–Government Council aborted or mitigated the reform measures of the EPB's and the Presidential Economic Secretariat's proposal. The growth-oriented party policy-makers' political logic (rationality) surpassed the stability-oriented government technocrats' economic logic (rationality).[7]

By 1990, as a result, Head of the EPB Soon Cho and First Secretary of the Presidential Economic Secretariat Hi-Gab Moon were replaced by the party's chief policy-maker Seung-Yun Lee and a former party policy-maker Jong-In Kim, respectively. Furthermore, the institutional structure of the bureaucracy was characterized by a low degree of coherence and coordination. President Ro had not put full confidence in the EPB's leadership for economic adjustment. The EPB's role of coordinator had reached its limits as the voices of other ministries were getting stronger.[8]

Second, the democratic transition had shaken the state corporatist (through the state's control over functionally differentiated business organizations) and non-corporatist (through direct interactions between the government and business groups) arrangements under the authoritarian regime. The national business associations' autonomy from government control had been increasing with respect to leadership selection and collective interest representation. In particular, the big business organization (FKI) had actively lobbied national assemblymen in order to abort the government regulations of the public land ownership and the real-name system.[9] During the early period of 1988–89, the business circle seemed to be nervous about the new era of uncertainty and unpredictability and adopted a defensive, wait-and-see investment strategy. Bilateral direct policy networks between the government and business groups had not worked efficiently for the growth-oriented policy under the unstable state-big business governing coalition based on the conservative supercoalition party. Korea's leading business groups had been obsessed with *zai-tech* – profits engineered solely from financial dealings. Instead of capital investments in production facilities, they had competitively invested in securities and real estate, earning record amounts of non-operating profits.

Finally, institutional arrangements of the financial system had been in disarray between the state-controlled and a market-oriented financial system. The process of financial reform (government regulations for fair market competition and deregulations for financial liberalization) had been retarded. After the emergence of the supercoalition party, as I mentioned previously, the plan to implement the real-name system was shelved in the face of politicians' and big businessmen's opposition. With the ongoing financial liberalization,[10] the country's banks were allowed more autonomy and freedom in their internal management. The Bank of Korea had asked the MF for an independent and autonomous role in monetary and credit policy. However, the government was still intervening in banking activities by means of interest rate regulation and policy loans in order to maintain monetary and credit control. The ministry had rarely given up its existing jurisdictional rights.[11]

The unsuccessful capitalist collective action for industrial adjustment

As shown above, the institutional capacities of the state were appropriate neither for a state-led nor for a market-oriented industrial adjustment. Despite the attempt at establishing a cooperative state-big business governing coalition in order to stimulate the economy by 1990, tensions and conflicts within state–big business relationships had been increasing for lack of policy instruments in institutional disorder. The state managers could not offer the policy instruments of strong coercive enforcement and privileged financial incentives with a view towards intervening in big businessmen's investment decision-making.

In addition, they failed to strengthen regulations of business and credit concentration to restrain unfair market competition.[12] Many large bank loans had been used for unproductive fields – investments in securities, real estate, and leisure businesses. The nation's thirty leading conglomerates (business groups) held $15 billion in real estate at home and abroad and $9 billion in securities on their books at the end of 1988. The financial structure of the conglomerates had worsened. The government set a specific net-worth target-ratio for each business group to improve its financial structure.[13] According to the regulation of core business specialization, each of the thirty largest business groups was required to specify the group's core business lines. The selected companies had been freed from credit controls imposed on other subsidiaries.[14] As a result, however, the credit regulation of business groups had hardly been successful because the business groups took advantage of the core business programme to increase their bank loans rather than to enhance their international competitiveness.[15] Exceptionally, the drastic regulation of real-estate speculation was effectively imposed on conglomerates. The forty-nine largest business groups were ordered to sell their non-business land and buildings within six months. They were also banned from purchasing real estate for non-business purposes until June 1991.[16]

In general, Ro's government could provide neither policy instruments of highly coercive punishment for big business firms' non-compliance (such economic penalties as suspending new loans, withdrawing old loans, tax investigation, and political revenge),[17] nor those of sufficient incentives to reward firms' compliance (preferential interest rates, tax reduction and exemption, direct and indirect government subsidies, privileged access to policy loans, and mono-oligopolized rights of production and sale). Furthermore, it had not been effective to control business groups by means of the government regulations for fair market competition, except for the real-estate regulation. As a result, the state managers had weak bargaining power over big businessmen. The state managers failed to induce business groups to concentrate on investing in manufacturing industries with a view towards enhancing the international competitiveness based on technology, manpower, and research development. Thus they had much difficulty in reducing the transaction costs of industrial adjustment for promoting capital-knowledge-technology-intensive industries. In the end, the democratic government failed to stir up a successful capitalist collective action to achieve industrial adjustment in a way either of state intervention or of government regulations for market competition.

As shown above, Korea's state became lost between state and market in the process of political and economic liberalization. The weak government capacities had accelerated conflicts between business groups and the state. The dilemma between state intervention and market-oriented reform had brought about firms' prevalent rent-seeking investments and thus resulted in the failure of investment adjustment for reinvigorating profit-seeking business activities.

NOTES

1 See Thomas M. Callaghy, 'Lost between State and Market: The Politics of Economic Adjustment in Ghana, Zambia, and Nigeria', in Joan M. Nelson, ed., *Economic Crisis and Policy Choice: The Politics of Adjustment in the Third World* (Princeton: Princeton University Press, 1990) and also Thomas M. Callaghy, 'Toward State Capability and Embedded Liberalism in the Third World: Lessons for Adjustment', in Joan M. Nelson *et al.*, *Fragile Coalitions: The Politics of Economic Adjustment* (Washington: Overseas Development Council, 1989). Interestingly, David Friedman denied the state-centred and market-centred approaches that had explained Japan's successful economic development; he argued that the economic success was a result of the dramatic expansion of small manufacturers, continuous production innovation other than economies of scale for efficiency, and the rapid and flexible responses of firms to changing market opportunities (see David Friedman, *The Misunderstood Miracle: Industrial Development and Political Change in Japan* [Ithaca and London: Cornell University Press, 1988]). It seemed to me that his arguments based on flexible industrial strategies may explain how the Japanese government tried to overcome the dilemma between state interventionist and market-oriented economic policy during the period of economic stabilization and liberalization (the 1970s and the early 1980s).

2 For the detailed process of democratic transition, see Manwoo Lee, *The Odyssey of Korean Democracy: Korean Politics, 1987–1990* (New York: Praeger, 1990), Chaps. 2, 3, and 4.

3 'The Phoenix Ascends', *Business Korea* (February 1989).

4 'Reassessing Development Strategies', *Business Korea* (October 1988).
5 'Can the Circle be Broken?', *Business Korea* (November 1989); and also, see Jae-Young Son, 'Analysis of and Reform Proposals for "The Land Problem" in Korea', *KDI Working Paper* 9013 (September 1990).
6 The growth rate of exports was nearly halved from 12.2 percent in 1988 to 6.5 percent in 1989. The current account surplus declined from $14.2 billion in 1988 to $5.5 billion in 1989. See Soogil Young, 'New Challenges to the Korean Economy and Their International Implications', *KDI Working Paper* 9004 (April 1990).
7 See Back-Man Lee, 'Deputy Prime Minister Cho Soon's Frustration for One Year and Three Months', *Sin Dong-A* (March 1990) (in Korean).
8 See Back-Man Lee, 'The Crumbling Economic Planning Board', *Sin Dong-A* (May 1990) (in Korean); and Jung-Gil Jung, 'Successive Presidents' Economic Policy: Ro Tae Woo', *Sin Dong-A* (November 1992) (in Korean).
9 Ji-Do Eum, 'A War between President Ro and *Jaebols* (Business Groups)', *Monthly Chosun* (June 1992), pp. 334–35 (in Korean).
10 'A New Era: Interview with Finance Minister Rhee Young-Man' and 'Toward Greater Banking Competition', *Business Korea* (October 1991).
11 See Gwon-Hi Hong, 'The Finance Ministry and the Bank of Korea: Thirty Years' Jurisdictional Dispute', *Sin Dong-A* (April 1991) (in Korean).
12 The combined turnover of the nation's thirty leading conglomerates reached $161 billion that was equivalent to 94.8 percent of Korea's 1988 GNP. Their bank credits were $55 billion ($28 billion in bank loans and $27 billion in payment guarantees) in August 1989. 'Debt Builds, Performance Sputters', *Business Korea* (November 1989).
13 'Debt Builds, Performance Sputters', *Business Korea* (November 1989).
14 See Byung-Hyu Jung and Young-Sik Yang, *An Economic Analysis of Korea's Jaebols* (Seoul: KDI, 1992), pp. 253–304 (in Korean).
15 See Man-Hee Lee, 'The Political Economy of Korea's Regulation Policy of *Jaebols*: The Focus on Fair Trade Institutions', *Korea and International Politics (Hanguggwa Googjejungchi)* (Spring-Summer 1993) (in Korean).
16 'Testing Roh's Determination', *Business Korea* (June 1990).
17 Exceptionally, the government still had a controlling grip on bank and non-bank financial institutions and, to a lesser degree, on the stock market. Though the grip was not as tight as it once was, it was sufficient to punish conglomerates' political non-compliance by means of credit control and tax investigation. In 1992, conflicts between the state and big business reached the highest point at the time of regime change. In particular, Ro's government had tried to restrain business groups' political participation. Joo-Young Chung, the owner of the Hyundai Business Group, entered politics, created the Unification National Party, and became a presidential candidate. The Office of National Tax Administration imposed $180 million in back taxes and fines on Joo-Young Chung, eight relatives, and fourteen Hyundai

affiliates in the name of irregular stock transactions for inheritance and donation. At that time, such illegal share transactions were not uncommon among a number of large conglomerates. Additionally, the Hyundai Business Group had much trouble in raising capital in the domestic market – borrowing new bank loans and issuing corporate bonds. Later, Woo-Joong Kim, the owner of the Daewoo Business Group, attempted to participate in the upcoming presidential election. However, he failed to join presidential candidates due to a possible government backlash of punishment. See 'Democracy's Growing Pains', *Korea Economic Report* (May 1992); 'Hyundai Forced into Loan Sharks' Arms', *Business Korea* (May 1992); and 'The Flip-Flop Presidential Candidate', *Business Korea* (November 1992).

Appendix A

INTERVIEWEES: NAMES AND THEIR BRIEF CAREERS RELATED TO THIS STUDY

Mr Soo-Myung Cha

1976–78: Director-General for the Machinery Industry in the Ministry of Commerce and Industry (MCI)
1978–80: Director-General for the Heavy Industries in the MCI
1980–81: Assistant Minister for the Heavy Industries in the MCI

Mr Gak Kyu Choi (Kak-Kyu Choi)

1977–79: Minister of Commerce and Industry

Mr Myung-Kul Choi

1976–82: Vice-President of the Daewoo Heavy Industries
1982–85: President of the Daewoo Motor Company (Saehan Motor Company)

Mr Kyong Shik Kang (Kyung-Sik Kang)

1977–82: Assistant Minister for Planning in the Economic Planning Board
1982: Vice-Minister of Finance
1982–83: Minister of Finance

Mr Woun-Gie Kim

1972–78: President of the Korea Development Bank
1978–80: Minister of Finance
1980:   Deputy Prime Minister and Minister of the Economic
          Planning Board

Mr Moon-Young Kwon

1977–84: Chief of the Section of Investment Investigation in the
          Economic Planning Board (EPB)

Mr Choon Lim Lee

1978–82: President of the Hyundai Heavy Industries
1982–87: Chairman of the Hyundai Heavy Industries

Mr Soo-Kon Pae

1975–79: President of the Korean Commercial Bank
1979–82: President of the Office of Bank Supervision and
          Examination

Appendix B

Changes in exchange rate between Korean won and US dollar, 1973–92

End of Period	Exchange rate of $1 to
December 1973	397.5
December 1974	484.0
December 1975	484.0
December 1976	484.0
December 1977	484.0
December 1978	484.0
December 1979	484.0
January 1980	580.0
December 1980	659.9
December 1981	700.5
December 1982	748.8
December 1983	795.5
December 1984	827.4
December 1985	890.2
December 1986	861.4
December 1987	792.3
December 1988	684.1
December 1989	679.6
December 1990	716.4
December 1991	760.8
December 1992	788.4

Bibliography

Aberbach, Joel D., Putnam, Robert D., and Rockman Bert A. *Bureaucrats and Politicians in Western Democracies*. Cambridge: Harvard University Press, 1981.

Adams, William J., and Stoffaë S, Christian, eds. *French Industrial Policy*. Washington: Brookings Institution, 1986.

Aghevli, Bijan B., and Marquez-Ruarte, Jorge. 'A Case of Successful Adjustment: Korea's Experience during 1980-84.' *IMF Occasional Paper* (No. 39 1985).

Ahn, Chung-si. 'Korean Politics in Transition.' Prepared for Conference on 'The Changing Shape of Government in the Asian Pacific Region,' the Institute for Research on Public Policy, Victoria, British Columbia, Canada, June 19-21, 1987.

Ahn, Dong-Il. 'The True Character of Reform Legislation: Activities of the Legislative Council for National Security.' *Monthly Chosun* (April 1988) (in Korean).

Alam, M. Shahid. *Governments and Markets in Economic Development Strategies: Lessons from Korea, Taiwan, and Japan*. New York: Praeger, 1989.

Alavi, Hamza. 'The State in Post-Colonial Societies - Pakistan and Bangladesh.' *New Left Review* (July-August 1972).

Alexander, Herbert E., ed. *Comparative Political Finance in the 1980s*. Cambridge: Cambridge University Press, 1989.

Almond, Gabriel A. 'The Return to the State.' *American Political Science Review* 82 (No. 3 1988).

Alt, James E., and Shepsle, Kenneth A., eds. *Perspective on Positive Political Economy*. Cambridge: Cambridge University Press, 1990.

Amirahamadi, Hooshang. 'Development Paradigms at a Crossroad and the South Korean Experience.' *Journal of Contemporary Asia* 19 (No. 2 1989).

Amsden, Alice H. *Asia's Next Giant: South Korea and Late Industrialization*. Oxford: Oxford University Press, 1989.

Amsden, Alice H. 'Third World Industrialization: "Global Fordism" or a New Model?' *New Left Review* 182 (July/August 1990).

Amsden, Alice H. 'The State and Taiwan's Economic Development.' In

Peter B. Evans, et al., eds., *Bring the State Back in*. Cambridge: Cambridge University Press, 1985.

Amsden, Alice H. 'The South Korean Economy: Is Business-Led Growth Working?' In Donald N. Clark, ed., *Korea Briefing, 1992*. Boulder: Westview Press, 1992.

Angell, Allen. 'Inflation, Stabilization, and Attempted Redemocratization in Peru, 1975-79.' *World Development* 10 (No. 1 1982).

Aoki, Masahiko, Gustafsson, Bo, and Williamson, Oliver E., eds. *The Firm as a Nexus of Treaties*. Sage Publications, 1990.

Appelbaum, Richard P., and Henderson, Jeffrey, eds. *States and Development in the Asian Pacific Rim*. Newbury Park: Sage Publications, 1992.

Arrow, Kenneth J. *Social Choice and Individual Values*. New Haven: Yale University Press, 1963.

Ashford, Douglas E. *Policy and Politics in France: Living with Uncertainty*. Philadelphia: Temple University Press, 1982.

Atkinson, Michael M., and Coleman, William D. 'Strong States and Weak States: Sectoral Policy Networks in Advanced Capitalist Economies.' *British Journal of Political Science* 19 (1989).

Bae, Byung-Hyu. 'Is the Daewoo Group in Good Shape?' *Sin Dong-A* (March 1981) (in Korean).

Bae, Kyuhan. 'Labor Strategy for Industrialization in South Korea.' *Pacific Affairs* 62 (Fall 1989).

Baek, Kwang-Il, et al. *The Dilemma of Third World Defense Industries: Supplier Control or Recipient Autonomy?* Boulder: Westview Press, 1989.

Bahry, Donna L., and Moses, Joel C., eds. *Political Implications of Economic Reform in Communist Systems: Communist Dialectic*. New York: New York University Press, 1990.

Balassa, Bela. 'Structural Adjustment Policies in Developing Economies.' *World Bank Staff Working Papers* (No. 464 1981).

Balassa, Bela, et al. *Development Strategies in Semi-Industrial Economies*. Baltimore: the Johns Hopkins University Press, 1982.

Baldwin, David A. *Paradoxes of Power*. New York: Basil Blackwell, 1989.

Ball, Nicole. *Security and Economy in the Third World*. Princeton: Princeton University Press, 1988.

Barrow, Clyde W. *Critical Theories of the State: Marxist, Neo-Marxist, Post-Marxist*. Madison: University of Wisconsin Press, 1993.

Barletta, Nicolas, Blejer, Mario I., and Landau, Luis, eds. *Economic Liberalization and Stabilization Policies in Argentina, Chile, and Uruguay*. Washington: World Bank, 1983.

Barzel, Yoram. *Economic Analysis of Property Rights*. Cambridge: Cambridge University Press, 1989.

Bates, Robert H. *Markets and States in Tropical Africa: The Political Basis of Agricultural Policies*. Berkeley: University of California Press, 1981.

Bates, Robert H., ed. *Toward a Political Economy of Development: A Rational Choice Perspective*. Berkeley: University of California Press, 1988.

Bates, Robert H. *Beyond the Miracle of the Market: The Political Economy of Agrarian Development in Kenya*. Cambridge: Cambridge University Press, 1989.

Bates, Robert H. 'Macropolitical Economy in the Field of Development.' In James E. Alt and Kenneth A. Shepsle, eds., *Perspective on Positive Political Economy*. Cambridge: Cambridge University Press, 1990.

Bates, Robert H. 'Contra Contractarianism: Some Reflections on the New Institutionalism.' *Politics and Society* 16 (No. 2-3 1988).

Bates, Robert H. 'Institution as Investments.' *Duke University Program in Political Economy* Working Paper No. 133, 1990.

Bates, Robert H. 'Social Dilemmas and Rational Individuals: An Essay on the New Institutionalism.' *Duke University Program in Political Economy* Working Paper No. 164, 1992.

Bauchet, Pierre (Daphne Woodward, trans.). *Economic Planning: The French Experience*. New York: Praeger Publishers, 1964.

Bauchet, Pierre. *Le Plan Dans L'Economie Française*. Paris: Economica, 1986.

Bennett, Douglas C., and Sharpe, Kenneth E. *Transnational Corporations versus The State: The Political Economy of the Mexican Auto Industry*. Princeton: Princeton University Press, 1985.

Benjamin, Roger, and Elkin, Stephan L. *The Democratic State*. Lawrence: University of Kansas Press, 1985.

Bennett, John T. 'The South Korean Economy: Recovery Amidst Uncertainty and Anguish.' In Donald N. Clark, ed., *Korea Briefing, 1991*. Boulder: Westview Press, 1991.

Berger, Peter L., and Hsiao, Hsin-Huang Michael, eds. *In Search of an East Asian Development Model*. New Brunswick: Transaction Books, 1988.

Berger, Suzanne. 'Lame Ducks and National Champions: Industrial Policy in the Fifth Republic.' In William G. Andrews and Stanley Hoffmann, *The Fifth Republic at Twenty*. Albany: State University of New York Press, 1981.

Berglo'f, Erik. 'Capital Structure as a Mechanism of Control: a Comparison of Financial Systems.' In Masahiko Aoki, et al., eds., *The Firm as a Nexus of Treaties*. Sage Publications, 1990.

Bermeo, Nancy. 'Rethinking Regime Change.' *Comparative Politics* (April 1990).

Bianchi, Robert. 'Interest Group Politics in the Third World.' *Third World Quarterly* (April 1986).

Bianchi, Robert. *Unruly Corporatism: Associational Life in Twentieth-Century Egypt*. Oxford: Oxford University Press, 1989.

Bianco, William T., and Bates, Robert H. 'Cooperation by Design: Leadership, Structure, and Collective Dilemmas.' *American Political Science Review* 84 (March 1990).

Birnbaum, Pierre. 'The State versus Corporatism.' *Politics and Society* 11 (No. 4 1982).

Block, Fred. *Revising State Theory*. Philadelphia: Temple University Press, 1987.

Block, Fred. *Postindustrial Possibilities: A Critique of Economic Discourse*. Berkeley: University of California Press, 1990.

Block, Fred. 'The Ruling Class Does Not Rule: Notes on the Marxist Theory of the State.' *Socialist Review* 33 (1977).

Block, Fred. 'Beyond Relative Autonomy: State Managers as Historical Subjects.' *The Socialist Register* (1980).

Bognanno, Mario F. 'Korea's Industrial Relations at the Turning Point.' *KDI Working Paper* 8816 (December 1988).

Boone, Catherine. 'State Power and Economic Crisis in Senegal.' *Comparative Politics* (April 1990).

Bottomore, Tom, and Brym, Robert J. *The Capitalist Class: An International Study.* New York: New York University Press, 1989.

Bowles, Samuel, and Gintis, Herbert. 'Contested Exchange: New Microfoundations for the Political Economy of Capitalism.' *Politics and Society* 18 (June 1990).

Bowman, John R. *Capitalist Collective Action: Competition, Cooperation and Conflict in the Coal Industry.* Cambridge: Cambridge University Press, 1989.

Brand, Donald Robert. *Corporatism and the Rule of Law: A Study of the National Recovery Administration.* Ithaca and London: Cornell University Press, 1988.

Bruno, Michael, et al., eds. *Inflation Stabilization: The Experience of Israel, Argentina, Brazil, Bolivia, and Mexico.* Cambridge: the MIT Press, 1988.

Buchanan, James M. 'Rent-Seeking and Profit-Seeking.' In James M. Buchanan, et al., eds., *Toward a Theory of the Rent-Seeking Society.* College Station: Texas A & M University Press, 1980.

Bull, Martin J. 'Structural versus Rational Choice Determinants in Corporatism: Theoretical and Empirical Lessons from Italy.' Prepared for Delivery at the 1990 Annual Meeting of the American Political Science Association, San Francisco, August 30-September 2, 1990.

Calder, Kent E. *Crisis and Compensation: Public Policy and Political Stability in Japan, 1949-1986.* Princeton: Princeton University Press, 1988.

Callaghy, Thomas M. *The State-Society Struggle: Zaire in Comparative Perspective.* New York: Columbia University Press, 1984.

Callaghy, Thomas M. 'Lost between State and Market.' In Joan M. Nelson, ed., *Economic Crisis and Policy Choice: The Politics of Adjustment in the Third World.* Princeton: Princeton University Press, 1990.

Callaghy, Thomas M. 'Toward State Capability and Embedded Liberalism in the Third World.' In Joan M. Nelson, et al., *Fragile Coalitions: The Politics of Economic Adjustment.* Washington: Overseas Development Council, 1989.

Callaghy, Thomas M. 'State, Choice, and Context: Comparative Reflections on Reform and Intractability.' Unpublished Paper, 1990.

Callaghy, Thomas M. 'Political Passions and Economic Interests: Comparative Reflections on Political and Economic Logics in Africa.' Prepared for Delivery at the 1990 Annual Meeting of the American Political Science Association, San Francisco, August 30, 1990.

Cammack, Paul. 'Review Article: Bring the State Back in?' *British Journal of Political Science* 19 (1989).

Camp, Roderic A. *Entrepreneurs and Politics in Twentieth-Century Mexico.* Oxford: Oxford University Press, 1989.

Campbell, John L. *Collapse of an Industry: Nuclear Power and The Contradictions of U.S. Policy.* Ithaca: Cornell University Press, 1988.

Caporaso, James A., and Levine, David P. *Theories of Political Economy.* Cambridge: Cambridge University Press, 1992.

Cardoso, Fernando Henrique, and Faletto, Enzo. *Dependency and Development in Latin America.* Berkeley: University of California Press, 1979.

Cargill, Thomas F., and Royama, Shoichi. *The Transition of Finance in Japan and the United States: A Comparative Perspective.* Stanford: Hoover Institution Press, Stanford University, 1988.

Cerny, Philip G., and Schain, Martin A., eds. *Socialism, the State and Public Policy in France.* New York: Methuen, Inc., 1985.

Cerny, Philip G. 'From Dirigism to Deregulation?: The Case of Financial Markets.' In Paul Codat, ed., *Policy-Making in France: From de Gaulle to Mitterrand.* London and New York: Pinter Publishers, 1989.

Cerny, Philip G. *The Changing Architecture of Politics: Structure, Agency, and the Future of the State.* Sage Publications, 1990.

Chang, Dal-Joong. 'Industrialization and Interest Groups.' *The Korean Political Science Association* 19 (1985) (in Korean).

Chang, Dal-Joong. *Economic Control and Political Authoritarianism: The Role of Japanese Corporations in Korean Politics 1965-1979.* Seoul: Sogang University Press, 1985.

Chang, Paek-San. 'A Vibrant Democratic Mass Movement Erupts in South Korea.' *AMPO* 17 (No. 1 1985).

The Changwon Machinery Industry Corporation. *The Five-Year History of the Changwon Complex.* Seoul: 1979 (in Korean).

Chaudry, Kiren Aziz. 'The Myths of the Market and the Common History of Late Developers.' *Politics and Society* 21 (No. 3 September 1993).

Chen, Edward K. Y. *Hyper-Growth in Asian Economics: A Comparative Study of Hong Kong, Japan, Korea, Singapore and Taiwan.* New York: Macmillian, 1979.

Cheng, Tun-jen, and Haggard, Stephan. *Newly Industrializing Asia in Transition: Policy Reforms and American Response*, Policy Paper No. 31. Berkeley: Institute of International Studies, University of California, Berkeley, 1987.

Cheng, Tun-Jen. 'The Politics of Industrial Transformation: The Case of the East Asian NICs.' *Ph.D. Diss.*, University of California, Berkeley, 1987.

Cho, Dong-Sung. *A Study on Korean Jaebols.* Seoul: Maeil Kyungje News Press, 1990 (in Korean).

Cho, Gap-Je. *Yugo (Accident)*, Vols. 1 and 2. Seoul: Hangil Press, 1987 (in Korean).

Cho, Gap-Je. 'The Integrated Investigation Headquarters' Conspiracy for Political Power.' *Monthly Chosun* (July 1990) (in Korean).

Cho, Gap-Je. 'The Plan of Regime.' *Monthly Chosun* (November 1990) (in Korean).

Cho, Jae-Hong. 'Post-1945 Land Reforms and Their Consequences in South Korea.' *Ph.D. Diss.*, Indiana University, 1964.

Cho, Sung-Joon. 'Scenes of Labor Disputes.' *Sin Dong-A* (June 1980) (in Korean).

Cho, Yong-Bum, et al. *Korea's Monopoly Capital and Jaebols.* Seoul: Pool Bit Press, 1984 (in Korean).

Cho, Yoon Je, and Khatkhate, Deena. 'Lessons of Financial Liberalization in Asia: A Comparative Study.' *World Bank Discussion Papers* (No. 50 1989).

Cho, Yoon Je, and Cole, David C. 'The Role of the Financial Sector in Korea's Structural Adjustment.' *KDI Working Paper* (December 1986).

Choi, Byung-Sun. 'Institutionalizing a Liberal Economic Order in Korea: The Strategic Management of Economic Change.' *Ph.D. Diss.*, Harvard University, 1987a.

Choi, Byung-Sun. 'The Structure of the Economic Policy-Making Institutions in Korea and the Strategic Role of the Economic Planning Board (EPB).' *The Korean Journal of Policy Studies* 2 (1987b).

Choi, Jang-Jip. 'The Strong State and Weak Labor Relations in South Korea: The Historical Determinants and Bureaucratic Structures.' In Kyong-dong Kim, ed., *Dependency Issues in Korean Development.* Seoul: Seoul National University, 1987.

Choi, Jang-Jip. 'Interest Conflict and Political Control in South Korea.' *Ph.D. Diss.*, University of Chicago, 1983.

Choi, Jang-Jip, ed. *Korean Capitalism and the State.* Seoul: Hanwool Press, 1985 (in Korean).

Choi, Nak-Dong. 'The Inside Story of the Machinery Industrial Circle.' *Sin Dong-A* (April 1980) (in Korean).

Choi, Sang-Hyun. 'Quasi-Taxes on Jaebols and Behind-the-Scenes of Privileges.' *Monthly Kyunghyang* (December 1988) (in Korean).

Choi, Wan-kyu. 'A Politico-Economic Analysis of the Emergence of an Authoritarian Regime: The Case of the Yushin System.' *Korea and World Politics* 3 (Summer 1987) (in Korean).

Chong, Dennis. *Collective Action and the Civil Rights Movement.* Chicago: University of Chicago Press, 1991.

Choue, Inwon. 'The Politics of Industrial Restructuring: South Korea's Turn toward Export-Led Heavy and Chemical Industrialization, 1964-74.' *Ph.D. Diss.*, the University of Pennsylvania, 1988.

Chu, Yun-han. 'State Structure and Economic Adjustment of the East Asian Newly Industrializing Countries.' *International Organization* 43 (Autumn 1989).

Chun, Bum-Sung. *Chung Joo-Young* (Biography). Seoul: Su Moon Dang Press, 1984 (in Korean).

Chun, Bum-Sung. *Kim Woo Joong* (Biography). Seoul: Su Moon Dang Press, 1987 (in Korean).

Chung, Joo-Young. 'FKI Chairman Chung's Special Speech.' *The Korean Business Review* 53 (November 1979).

Chung, Joo-Young. *Fluttering with a New Hope This Morning: A Collection of Chung Joo-Young's Speeches.* Seoul: Samsung Press, 1986 (in Korean).

Chungsa Press. *70s' Korean Chronology.* Seoul: 1984 (in Korean).

Clark, Rodney. *The Japanese Company.* New Haven and London: Yale University Press, 1979.

Cline, William, and Weintrab, Sidney, eds. *Economic Stabilization in Developing Countries.* Washington: Brookings Institute, 1981.

Clough, Ralph N. *Embattled Korea: The Rivalry for International Support.* Boulder: Westview Press, 1987.

Coase, Ronald H. *The Firm the Market and the Law.* Chicago: University of Chicago Press, 1988.

Coase, Ronald H. 'The New Institutional Economics.' *Journal of Theoretical and Institutional Economics* 140 (No. 1 1984).

Codat, Paul, ed. *Policy-Making in France: From de Gaulle to Mitterrand.* London and New York: Pinter Publishers, 1989.

Cohen, Stephen S. *Modern Capitalist Planning: The French Model.* Berkeley: University of California Press, 1977.

Cohen, Stephen S. 'Informed Bewilderment: French Economic Strategy and the Crisis.' In Stephen S. Cohen and Peter Gourvitch, eds., *France in the Troubled World Economy.* London and Boston: Butterworths Scientific, 1982.

Cohen, Stephen S., Galbraith, James, and Zysman, John. 'Rehabbing the Labyrinth: The Financial System and Industrial Policy in France.' In Stephen S. Cohen and Peter A. Gourevitch, *France in the Troubled World Economy.* London and Boston: Butterworths Scientific, 1982.

Colburn, Forrest D., ed. *Everyday Forms of Peasant Resistance.* Armonk: M. E. Sharpe, Inc., 1989.

Cole, David C., and Park, Yung Chul. *Financial Development in Korea.* Cambridge: Harvard University Press, 1983.

Cole, Robert E. *Strategies for Learning: Small-Group Activities in American, Japanese, and Swedish Industry.* Berkeley: University of California Press, 1989.

Coleman, James S. *Foundations of Social Theory.* Cambridge: Harvard University Press, 1990.

Commons, John R. *Institutional Economics: Its Place in Political Economy,* Vols. 1 and 2. New Brunswick: Transaction Publishers, 1990.

The Consultation Council of Academic Groups. *1980s' Korean Society and Ruling Structure.* Seoul: Pul Bit Press, 1989 (in Korean).

Cook, Karen Schweers, and Levi, Margaret, eds. *The Limits of Rationality.* Chicago: University of Chicago Press, 1990.

Corbo, Vittono, Krueger, Anne O., and Ossa, Fernando, eds. *Export-Oriented Development Strategies: The Success of Five Newly Industrializing Countries.* Boulder: Westview Press, 1985.

Cowhey, Peter F. 'The International Telecommunications Regime: The Political Roots of Regimes for High Technology.' *International Organization* 44 (Spring 1990).

Cumings, Bruce. 'The Legacy of Japanese Colonialism in Korea.' In Ramon H. Myers and Mark R. Peattie, eds., *The Japanese Colonial Empire, 1895-1945.* Princeton: Princeton University Press, 1984.

Cumings, Bruce. 'The Origins and Development of the Northeast Asian Political Economy: Industrial Sectors, Product Cycles, and Political Consequences.' *International Organization* 38 (Winter 1984).

Cumings, Bruce. 'The Abortive Abertura: South Korea in the Light of Latin American Experience.' *New Left Review* 173 (January/February 1989).

Curtis, Gerald L. 'Big Business and Political Influence.' In Ezra F. Vogel, ed., *Modern Japanese Organizations and Decisionmaking*. Berkeley: University of California Press, 1975.

Curtis, Gerald L. *The Japanese Way of Politics*. New York: Columbia University Press, 1988.

Czada, Roland M., and Windhoff-Heritier, Adrienne, eds. *Political Choice: Institutions, Rules and the Limits of Rationality*. Boulder: Westview Press, 1991.

Dahl, Robert A., and Linblom, Charles E. *Politics, Economics, and Welfare: Planning and Politic-Economic Processes resolved into Basic Social Processes*. New York: 1953.

Dee, Philippa S. *Financial Markets and Economic Development: The Economics and Politics of Korean Financial Reform*. Tubingen: Mohr, 1986.

Dessler, David. 'What's at Stake in the Agent-Structure Debate?' *International Organization* 43 (Summer 1989).

Deyo, Frederic C. 'Coalitions, Institutions, and Linkage Sequencing: Toward a Strategic Capacity Model of East Asian Development.' In Frederic C. Deyo, ed., *The Political Economy of the New Asian Industrialism*. Ithaca and London: Cornell University Press, 1987.

Deyo, Frederic C. *Beneath The Miracle: Labor Subordination in the New Asian Industrialism*. Berkeley: University of California Press, 1989.

Diamond, Larry, et al., ed. *Democracy in Developing Countries: Asia Vol. 3*. Boulder: Lynne Rienner, 1988.

Domhoff, G. William. *The Power Elite and the State: How Policy is Made in America*. New York: Aldine De Gruyter, 1990.

The Dongkwang Press. *Wind and Clouds: Economic Inside Stories about High Growth*. Seoul: 1986 (in Korean).

Dore, Ronald. *Flexible Rigidities: Industrial Policy and Structural Adjustment in the Japanese Economy 1970-80*. Stanford: Stanford University Press, 1986.

Dore, Ronald. *Taking Japan Seriously: A Confucian Perspective on Leading Economic Issues*. Stanford: Stanford University Press, 1987.

Dugger, William M., ed. *Radical Institutionalism: Contemporary Voices*. New York: Greenwood Press, 1989.

Eads, George C., and Yamamura, Kozo. 'The Future of Industrial Policy.' In Kozo Yamamura and Yasukichi Yasuba, *The Political Economy of Japan Vol. 1: The Domestic Transformation*. Stanford: Stanford University Press, 1987.

Ecclestan, Bernard. *State and Society in Post-War Japan*. Cambridge: Basil Blackwell Inc., 1989.

The Economic Planning Board (EPB). *White Paper on Foreign Direct Investment*. Seoul: 1981 (in Korean).

The Economic Planning Board. *Economic Policy of the Development Period: Twenty Years' History of the EPB*. Seoul: 1982 (in Korean).

The Economic Planning Board. *White Paper on the Economy*. Seoul: 1980 (in Korean).

The Economic Planning Board. *White Paper on Foreign Debt*. Seoul: 1986 (in Korean).

Eggertsson, Thrainn. *Economic Behavior and Institutions*. Cambridge: Cambridge University Press, 1990.

Eguren, Alberto. 'Adjustment with Growth in Latin America.' *EDI Policy Seminar Report* No. 22 (Washington: World Bank, 1990).

Elster, Jon. *Making Sense of Marx*. Cambridge: Cambridge University Press, 1985.

Elster, Jon, ed. *Rational Choice*. New York: New York University Press, 1986.

Elster, Jon, and Hylland, Aanund, eds. *Foundations of Social Choice Theory*. Cambridge: Cambridge University Press, 1986.

Elster, Jon. *Nuts and Bolts: For the Social Sciences*. Cambridge: Cambridge University Press, 1989.

Elster, Jon. *Solomonic Judgements: Studies in the Limitations of Rationality*. Cambridge: Cambridge University Press, 1989.

Elster, Jon. *The Cement of Society: A Study of Social Order*. Cambridge: Cambridge University Press, 1989.

Encarnation, Dennis J. *Dislodging Multi-Nationals: India's Strategy in Comparative Perspective*. Ithaca and London: Cornell University Press, 1989.

Epstein, Edward C. 'Antiinflation Policies in Argentina and Chile: or, Who Pays the Cost.' *Comparative Political Studies* 11 (No. 2 1978).

Evans, Peter. *Dependent Development*. Princeton: Princeton University Press, 1978.

The Federation of Korean Industries (FKI). *A Survey of the Korean Economic Development*. Seoul: the FKI, 1987 (in Korean).

The Federation of Korean Industries (FKI). *Twenty Years' History of the FKI*. Seoul: FKI, 1983 (in Korean).

The FKI. *Korea's Economic Policies (1945-1985)*. Seoul: FKI, 1987.

The FKI. *The FKI's Annual Reports*. Seoul: FKI (in Korean).

Ferguson, Yale H., and Mansbach, Richard W. *The State, Conceptual Chaos, and the Future of International Relations Theory*. Boulder: Lynne Rienner Publishers, 1989.

Fiels, Karl J. 'Trading Companies in South Korea and Taiwan: Two Policy Approaches.' *Asian Survey* 29 (November 1989).

Fong, Glan R. 'State Strength, Industry Structure, and Industry Policy: American and Japanese Experiences in Microelectronics.' *Comparative Politics* (April 1990).

Foxley, Alejandro, Mcpherson, Michael S., and O'Donnell, Guillermo, eds. *Development, Democracy, and the Art of Trespassing: Essays in Honor of Albert O. Hirschman*. Notre Dame: University of Notre Dame Press, 1986.

Foxley, Alejandro, and Whitehead, Laurence. 'Economic Stabilization in Latin America: Political Dimensions - Editor's Introduction.' *World Development* 8 (1980).

Frank, Charles R., et al. *Foreign Trade Regimes and Economic Development: South Korea*. New York: Columbia University Press, 1975.

Freeman, John R. *Democracy and Markets: The Politics of Mixed Economics*. Ithaca and London: Cornell University Press, 1989.

Frieden, Jeff. 'Third World Indebted Industrialization: International Finance and State Capitalism in Mexico, Brazil, Algeria, and South Korea.' *International Organization* 35 (No. 3 1981).

Friedman, David. *The Misunderstood Miracle: Industrial Development and Political Change in Japan.* Ithaca and London: Cornell University Press, 1988.

Friman, H. Richard. *Patchwork Protectionism: Textile Trade Policy in the United States, Japan, and West Germany.* Ithaca: Cornell University Press, 1990.

Galenson, Water, ed. *Economic Growth and Structural Change in Taiwan.* Ithaca: Cornell University Press, 1979.

Gereffi, Gary, and Wyman, Donald L., eds. *Manufacturing Miracles: Paths of Industrialization in Latin America and East Asia.* Princeton: Princeton University Press, 1990.

Gershenkron, Alexander. *Economic Backwardness in Historical Perspective.* Cambridge: Harvard University Press, 1962.

Gilpin, Robert. 'The Politics of Transnational Economic Relations.' In Robert Keohane and Joseph S. Nye, eds., *Transnational Relations and World Politics.* Cambridge: Harvard University Press, 1972.

Gleysteen, William H., and Romberg, Alan D. 'Korea: Asian Paradox.' *Foreign Affairs* 65 (Summer 1987).

Gold, Thomas. *State and Society in the Taiwan Miracle.* Armonk: M. E. Sharpe Inc., 1986.

Goldstein, Judith, and Lenway, Stefanie Ann. 'Interests or Institutions: An Inquiry into Congressional-ITC Relations.' *International Studies Quarterly* 33 (1989).

Gourevitch, Peter. *Politics in Hard Times: Comparative Responses to International Economic Crises.* Ithaca: Cornell University Press, 1986.

The Government of the Republic of Korea. *The Revised Fifth Economic and Social Development Plan, 1984-86.* Seoul: 1983 (in Korean).

Gowa, Joanne. 'Public Goods and Political Institutions: Trade and Monetary Policy Processes in the United States.' *International Organization* 42 (No. 1 1988).

Gowa, Joanne. 'Rational Hegemons, Excludable Goods, and Small Groups.' *World Politics* (April 1989).

The Graduate School of Public Administration at the Seoul National University, ed. *A Collection of Policy Cases in South Korea.* Seoul: Bub Moon Press, 1989 (in Korean).

The Graduate School of Public Administration at the Seoul National University. *A Research on Cases of Policy Implementation.* Seoul: Seoul National University, 1983 (in Korean).

Grafstein, Robert. *Institutional Realism: Social and Political Constraints on Rational Actors.* New Haven and London: Yale University Press, 1992.

Grant, Wyn, ed. *The Political Economy of Corporatism.* Macmillan: 1985.

Grieco, Joseph M. *Cooperation among Nations: Europe, America, and Non-Tariff Barriers to Trade.* Ithaca: Cornell University Press, 1990.

Grindle, Merilee S. 'The New Political Economy: Positive Economics and Negative Politics.' In Gerald M. Meier, ed., *Politics and Policy Making in Developing Countries: Perspectives on the New Political Economy.* San Francisco: ICS Press, 1991.

Guerin, Daniel. *Fascism and Big Business.* New York: Monad Press, 1973.

Ha, Young-Sun. *Nuclear Proliferation, World Order and Korea*. Seoul: Seoul National University Press, 1983.

Haggard, Stephan, and Moon, Chung-in. 'The South Korean State in the International Economy: Liberal, Dependent, or Mercantile?' In John Ferard Ruggie, *The Antinomies of Interdependence*. New York: Columbia University Press, 1983.

Haggard, Stephan, and Cheng, Tun-jen. 'State Strategies, Foreign and Local Capital in the East Asian NICs.' In Fred Deyo, ed., *The Political Economy of the New Asian Industrialism*. Ithaca: Cornell University Press, 1987.

Haggard, Stephan, and Kaufman, Robert R. 'The Politics of Stabilization and Structural Adjustment.' In Jeffrey D. Sachs, ed., *Developing Country Debt and World Economy*. Chicago: University of Chicago Press, 1989.

Haggard, Stephan. 'The Politics of Adjustment: Lessons from the IMF's External Fund Facility.' In Miles Kahler, ed., *The Politics of International Debt*. Ithaca: Cornell University Press, 1986.

Haggard, Stephan, and Moon, Chung-in. 'Institutions and Economic Policy: Theory and a Korean Case Study.' *World Politics* (January 1990).

Haggard, Stephan, and Moon, Chung-in. *Pacific Dynamics: The International Politics of Industrial Change*. Boulder: Westview Press, 1989.

Haggard, Stephan, Kim, Byung-Kook, and Moon, Chung-in. 'The Transition to Export-Led Growth in South Korea, 1954-66.' *The World Bank Working Paper* (November 1990).

Haggard, Stephan. 'The Politics of Industrialization in Korea and Taiwan.' In Helen Hughes, ed., *Achieving Industrialization in East Asia*. Cambridge: Cambridge University Press, 1988.

Haggard, Stephan. *Pathways from the Periphery: The Politics of Growth in the Newly Industrializing Countries*. Ithaca: Cornell University Press, 1990.

Haggard, Stephan, and Kaufman, Robert R. 'The Economic Adjustment and the Prospects for Democracy.' In Stephan Haggard and Robert R. Kaufman, eds., *The Politics of Economic Adjustment: International Constraints, Distributive Conflicts, and the State*. Princeton: Princeton University Press, 1992a.

Haggard, Stephan, and Kaufman, Robert R. 'The State in the Initiation and Consolidation of Market-Oriented Reform.' In Louis Putterman and Dietrich Rueschemeyer, eds., *State and Market in Development: Synergy or Rivalry?* Boulder: Lynne Rienner Publishers, 1992b.

Hall, John A., and Ikenberry, G. John. *The State*. Minneapolis: University of Minnesota Press, 1989.

Hall, Peter. *Governing the Economy: The Politics of State Intervention in Britain and France*. Oxford: Oxford University Press, 1986.

Hall, Peter A., ed. *The Political Power of Economic Ideas: Keynesianism across Nations*. Princeton: Princeton University Press, 1989.

Halliday, Jon. *A Political History of Japanese Capitalism*. New York: Pantheon Books, 1975.

Hamada, Koichi, and Horiuchi, Akiyoshi. 'The Political Economy of the Financial Market.' In Kozo Yamamura and Yasukichi Yasuba, eds., *The*

Political Economy of Japan Vol. 1: The Domestic Transformation. Stanford: Stanford University Press, 1987.

Han, Sang-Jin. *The Korean Society and Bureaucratic Authoritarianism.* Seoul: Moonhackwa Jisung Press, 1988 (in Korean).

Han, Sung-joo. 'Political Institutionalization in South Korea, 1961-84.' In Robert A. Scalapino and Jusuf Wanandi, *Asian Political Institutionalization.* Berkeley: Institute of East Asian Studies, University of California, 1986.

Han, Sung-joo. 'South Korea: Politics in Transition.' In Larry Diamond, Juan J. Linz, and Seymour Martin Lipset, *Democracy in Developing Countries*, Vol. 3. Boulder: Lynne Rienner Publishers, Inc., 1989.

Handelman, Howard, and Baer, Werner, eds. *Paying the Costs of Austerity in Latin America.* Boulder: Westview Press, 1989.

Hardin, Russell. *Collective Action.* Baltimore: Johns Hopkins University Press, 1982.

The Hapdong News Agency. *Korea Annual: 1981.* Seoul: 1981.

Harrison, Seligs. 'Dateline South Korea: A Divided Seoul.' *Foreign Policy* (Summer 1987).

Hart, Jeffrey A. *Rival Capitalists: International Competitiveness in the United States, Japan, and Western Europe.* Ithaca: Cornell University Press, 1992.

Hartlyn, Jonathan, and Morley, Samuel A., eds. *Latin American Political Economy: Financial Crisis and Political Change.* Boulder: Westview Press, 1986.

Hasan, Parvez. 'Adjustment to External Shocks: Why East Asian Countries Have Fared Better than other LDCs.' *Finance and Development* 21 (1984).

Hecher, Michael, ed. *The Microfoundations of Macrosociology.* Philadelphia: Temple University Press, 1983.

Heijdra, Ben J., Lowenberg, Anton D., and Mallick, Robert J. 'Marxism, Methodological Individualism, and the New Institutional Economics.' *Journal of Institutional and Theoretical Economics* 144 (April 1988).

Henderson, Gregory. *Korea: The Politics of the Vortex.* Cambridge: Harvard University Press, 1968.

Hicks, Alexander. 'National Collective Action and Economic Performance: A Review Article.' *International Studies Quarterly* 32 (1988).

Hinton, Harold C. *Korea under New Leadership.* New York: Praeger Press, 1983.

Hodgson, Geoffrey M. *Economics and Institutions: A Manifesto for a Modern Institutional Economics.* Philadelphia: University of Pennsylvania Press, 1988.

Hollerman, Leon. *Japan, Disincorporated: The Economic Liberalization Process.* Stanford: Hoover Institution Press, Stanford University, 1988.

Hollifield, James F. 'Immigration and the French State: Problems of Policy Implementation.' *Comparative Political Studies* 23 (April 1990).

Horne, James. 'Politics and the Japanese Financial System.' In J.A.A. Stockwin, et al., *Dynamic and Immobilist Politics in Japan.* Honolulu: University of Hawaii Press, 1988.

Hrebenar, Ronald J. *The Japanese Party System: From One-Party to Coalition Government*. Boulder: Westview Press, 1986.

The Hyundai Motor Company. *Twenty Years' History of the Hyundai Motor Company* (in Korean).

The Hyundai Sahoe Research Institute. *The Korean Social Change and a Study on the Role of the State*, Research Report '85-12. Seoul: 1985 (in Korean).

Ikenberry, G. John. 'The Irony of State Strength: Comparative Responses to the Oil Shocks.' *International Organization* (Winter 1986).

Ikenberry, G. John. 'Conclusion: An Institutional Approach to American Foreign Economic Policy.' *International Organization* 42 (Winter 1988).

Ikenberry, G. John. *Reasons of State: Oil Politics and The Capacities of American Government*. Ithaca: Cornell University Press, 1988.

Im, Hyug Baeg. 'The Rise of Bureaucratic Authoritarianism in South Korea.' *World Politics* (January 1987).

Inoguchi, Takashi. 'The Political Economy of conservative Resurgence under Recession: Public Policies and Political Support in Japan, 1977-83.' In T. J. Pempel, ed., *Uncommon Democracies: The One-Party Dominant Regimes*. Ithaca: Cornell University Press, 1990.

Irwin, Alexander. 'Real Wages and Class Struggle in South Korea.' *Journal of Contemporary Asia* 17 (No. 4 1987).

James, William E., Naya, Seji, and Meier, Gerald M. *Asian Development: Economic Success and Policy Lessons*. Madison: University of Wisconsin Press, 1989.

Jankowski, Richard. 'Preference Aggregation in Firms and Corporatist Organizations: The Enterprise Group as a Cellular Encompassing Organizations.' *American Journal of Political Science* 33 (November 1989).

Jenkins, Rhys. *Transnational Corporations and the Latin American Automobile Industry*. Pittsburgh: University of Pittsburgh Press, 1987.

Johnson, Chalmers. *MITI and the Japanese Miracle: The Growth of Industrial Policy*. Stanford: Stanford University Press, 1982.

Johnson, Chalmers. 'Japan: Who governs? An Essay on Official Bureaucracy.' *Journal of Japanese Studies* 2 (Fall 1975).

Johnson, Chalmers. 'The Institutional Foundations of Japanese Industrial Policy.' *California Management Review* 27 (Summer 1985).

Johnson, Chalmers. 'Political Institutions and Economic Performance: The Government-Business Relationship in Japan, South Korea, and Taiwan.' In Frederic C. Deyo, ed., *The Political Economy of the New Asian Industrialism*. Ithaca: Cornell University Press, 1987.

Johnson, Chalmers, Tyson, Laura D'Andrea, and Zysman, John, eds. *Politics and Productivity: How Japan's Development Strategy Works*. Ballinger Publishing Company, 1989.

Jones, Leroy P. 'Jaebul and the Concentration of Economic Power in Korean Development: Issues, Evidence, and Alternatives.' In Il Sakong, ed., *Macroeconomic Policy and Industrial Development Issues*. Seoul: Korea Development Institute, 1987.

Jones, Leroy P. and Sakong, Il. *Government, Business and Entrepreneurship in Economic Development: The Korean Case.* Cambridge: Harvard University Press, 1980.

Joo, Jong-Whan. *A Study on Jaebol Economy.* Seoul: Jung Eum Press, 1985 (in Korean).

Jun, Jong Sup. 'The Paradoxes of Development: Problems of Korea's Transformation.' In Bun Woong Kim, David S. Bell, Jr., and Chong Bum Lee, eds., *Administrative Dynamics and Development: The Korean Experience.* Seoul: Kyobo Publishing Inc., 1985.

Jung, Kwan-Young. 'The Characteristics of the Korean State in the Heavy and Chemical Industrial Policy.' In the Korean Industrial Society Council. *Today's Korean Capitalism and the State.* Seoul: Hangil Press, 1988 (in Korean).

Kahler, Miles. 'Orthodoxy and Its Alternatives: Explaining Approaches to Stabilization and Adjustment.' In Joan M. Nelson, ed., *Economic Crisis and Policy Choice: The Politics of Adjustment in the Third World.* Princeton: Princeton University Press, 1990.

Kang, Kyung-Sik. *Beyond Economic Stability.* Seoul: the Korean Economic Daily News Press, 1987 (in Korean).

Kang, Min. 'The Korea-Typed Emergence of Bureaucratic Authoritarianism.' *The Korean Political Science Association* 17 (1983) (in Korean).

Kaplan, Eugene J. *Japan: The Government-Business Relationship.* U.S. Department of Commerce, 1972.

Katzenstein, Peter J. *Small States in World Markets.* Ithaca: Cornell University Press, 1985.

Katzenstein, Peter J. *Corporatism and Change.* Ithaca: Cornell University Press, 1984.

Katzenstein, Peter J. *Between Power and Plenty: Foreign Economic Policies of Advanced Industrial States.* Madison: University of Wisconsin Press, 1978.

Katzenstein, Peter J. 'The Small European States in the International Economy: European Dependence and Corporatist Politics.' In John G. Ruggie, *The Antinomies of Interdependence.* New York: Columbia University Press, 1983.

Katzenstein, Peter J. 'Japan, Switzerland of the Far East?' In Takashi Inoguchi and Daniel I. Okimoto, eds., *The Political Economy of Japan: The Changing International Context, Vol. 2.* Stanford: Stanford University Press, 1988.

Kaufman, Robert R. 'Stabilization and Adjustment in Argentina, Brazil, and Mexico.' In Joan M. Nelson, ed., *Economic Crisis and Policy Choice: The Politics of Adjustment in the Third World.* Princeton: Princeton University Press, 1990.

Kaufman, Robert R. 'Democratic and Authoritarian Responses to the Debt Issue: Argentina, Brazil, and Mexico.' In Miles Kahler, ed., *The Politics of International Debt.* Ithaca: Cornell University Press, 1986.

Kaufman, Robert R. *The Politics of Debt in Argentina, Brazil, and Mexico: Economic Stabilization in the 1980s.* Berkeley: Institute of International Studies, University of California, Berkeley, 1988.

Kawai, Tadahiko. 'An Analysis of Business-Government Relations in

Japan: The Case of The Federation of Economic Organizations.' *Ph.D. Diss.*, University of California, Berkeley, 1986.

Kee, Woo Sik. 'The Evolution of Korean Macroeconomic Management and Industrial Policies.' In Robert A. Scalapino and Hong Koo Lee, eds., *Korea-U.S. Relations: The Politics of Trade and Security.* Berkeley: Institute of East Asian Studies, University of California, Berkeley, 1988.

Keohane, Robert O. *International Institutions and State Power: Essays in International Relations Theory.* Boulder: Westview Press, 1989.

Keohane, Robert O., and Nye, Joseph S., Jr. 'Power and Interdependence Revisited.' *International Organization* 41 (Autumn 1987).

Kester, W. Carl. *Japanese Takeovers: The Global Contest for Corporate Control.* Boston: Harvard Business School Press, 1991.

Kihl, Young Whan. *Politics and Policies in Divided Korea.* Boulder: Weatview Press, 1984.

Kim, Bong-sik. 'Decision Rules and Economic Policy in Korea: Socio-Political Analysis.' In Se-Jin Kim and Chi-won Kang, eds., *Korea: A Nation in Transition.* Seoul: Research Center for Peace and Unification, 1978.

Kim, Bun Woong, and Rho, Wha Joon. *Korean Public Bureaucracy.* Seoul: Kyobo Publishing, Inc., 1982.

Kim, Byung-Kook. 'Bringing and Managing Socioeconomic Change: The State in Korea and Mexico.' *Ph.D. Diss.*, Harvard University Press, 1988.

Kim, Byung Kook. 'State Capacity for Reforms: The State in Korea and Mexico.' *The Korean Journal of Policy Studies* 3 (1988).

Kim, C.I. Eugene. 'Significance of Korea's 10th National Assembly Elections.' *Asian Survey* (May 1979).

Kim, Dae-Whan. 'The Change of International Economic Environment and Heavy and Chemical Industrialization.' In Hyun-Chae Park, et al., eds., *A Study on the Korean Economy.* Seoul: Kachi Press, 1987 (in Korean).

Kim, Eui-Kyun. 'The Inside Story of the Heavy and Chemical Industrial Investment Adjustments.' *Sin Dong-A* (December 1980) (in Korean).

Kim, Eui-Kyun. 'Hyundai and Daewoo.' *Sin Dong-A* (November 1980) (in Korean).

Kim, Eun Mee. 'From Dominance to Symbiosis: State and Chaebol in the Korean Economy, 1960-1985.' *Ph.D. Diss.*, Brown University, 1987.

Kim, Gyun. 'The Way and Result of State Intervention in the Korean Heavy and Chemical Industrial Process.' In the Korean Industrial Society Research Council, *Today's Korean Capitalism and the State.* Seoul: Hangil Press, 1988 (in Korean).

Kim, Hyung-Kook. 'The Political Economy of Industrial Adjustment Strategies in South Korea: A Comparative Study of the Textile, Steel and Semiconductor Industries.' *Ph.D. Diss.*, Duke University, 1988.

Kim, Hyung-Kook, and Geisse, Guillermo. 'The Political Economy of Outward Liberalization: Chile and South Korea in Comparative Perspective.' *Asian Perspective* 12 (No. 2 1988).

Kim, Ilpyong J., and Kihl, Young Whan. *Political Change in South Korea.* New York: the Korea PWPA, Inc., 1988.

Kim, Jai-Myung. 'The Godfather of the TK (Taegu City and Kyung Sang North Province) Corps.' *Monthly Chosun* (November 1988) (in Korean).

Kim, Jang-Han, et al. *80s' History of Korean Labor Movement*. Seoul: Jogook Press, 1989 (in Korean).

Kim, Ji Hong. 'Korean Industrial Policies for Declining Industries.' *KDI Working Paper* 8910 (January 1989).

Kim, Jin. *The Blue House's Secretariat (the Presidential Secretariat)*. Seoul: Joongang Daily News, 1992 (in Korean).

Kim, Joong-Woong. 'Economic Development and Financial Liberalization in Korea: Policy Reforms and Future Prospects.' *KDI Working Paper* 8514 (December 1985).

Kim, Jung-Ryum. *The Thirty Years History of Korea's Economic Policy: Memoirs*. Seoul: Joongang Daily News, 1990 (in Korean).

Kim, Kwan S. 'The Korean Case: Culturally Dominated Interactions.' In Lee A. Tavis, ed., *Mutinational Managers and Host Government Interactions*. Notre Dame: University of Notre Dame Press, 1988.

Kim, Kwang Suk, et al. 'The Japanese and Korean Experience in Managing Development.' *World Bank Staff Working Papers* (No. 574 1983).

Kim, Kihwan. *The Korean Economy: Past Performance, Current Reforms, and Future Prospects*. Seoul: Korea Development Institute, 1985.

Kim, Myoung Soo. 'The Making of Korean Society: The Role of the State in the Republic of Korea.' *Ph.D. Diss.*, Brown University, 1987.

Kim, Seok-Ki. 'Business Concentration and Government Policy: A Study of the Phenomenon of Business Groups in Korea, 1945-85.' *D.B.A.*, Harvard University, 1987.

Kim, Soo-Kil. 'Kim Jai-Ik and Moon Hee Kap: Presidential Economic First Secretaries of the Fifth and Sixth Republics.' *Monthly Joong"Ang* (September 1989) (in Korean).

Kim, Suk Joon. *The State, Public Policy and NIC Development*. Seoul: Dae Young Moonwha Press, 1988.

Kim, Suk-Whan. 'The Collapse of the Korean Shipping Corporation and Political Maneuvering.' *Monthly Joong-Ang* (January 1989) (in Korean).

Kim, Yong-Ho. 'Authoritarian Leadership and Party Dynamics: The Rise and Fall of the Democratic Republican Party in South Korea, 1962-1980.' *Ph.D. Diss.*, University of Pennsylvania, 1989.

Kim, Yong-Jung. 'The Inside Story of the Companies's Quasi-Taxes to Be Transferred to the Consumer.' *Sin Dong-A* (January 1987) (in Korean).

Kim, Young-Rae. 'A Focus on Corporatist Perspective.' In the Korean Political Science Association, *Modern Korean Politics and the State*. Seoul: Bub moon Press, 1987 (in Korean).

Kim, Young-Rae. 'A Corporatist Analysis of Korean Interest Groups: The FKTU and the FKI.' *Ph.D. Diss.*, Yunsei University, 1986 (in Korean).

Klapp, Merrie Gilbert. *The Sovereign Entrepreneur: Oil Policies in Advanced and Less Developed Capitalist Countries*. Ithaca: Cornell University Press, 1987.

Knight, Jack. *Institutions and Social Conflict*. Cambridge: Cambridge University Press, 1992.

Kobrin, Stephen J. 'Testing the Bargaining Hypothesis in the Manufacturing Sector in Developing Countries.' *International Organization* 41 (Autumn 1987).

Koo, Bon-Ho. 'The Korean Economy: Structural Adjustment for Future Growth.' In Chong-sik Lee, ed., *Korea Briefing, 1990.* Boulder: Westview Press, 1991.

The Korea Development Bank (KDB). *Japan's Industrial Adjustment Policy.* Seoul: KDB, 1981 (in Korean).

Korea Development Institute (KDI). *Collection of Documents and Study Reports related to Economic Stabilization Policies, Vols. 1 and 2.* Seoul: KDI, 1981 (in Korean).

Korea Development Institute (KDI). *Development Orientation of the Automobile Industry and Policy,* Research Report 81-03. Seoul: KDI, 1981 (in Korean).

Korea Development Institute. *Basic Problems of Industrial Policy and the Policy Orientation for Support Measures.* Seoul: KDI, 1982 (in Korean).

Korea Development Institute. *Private-Public Interaction toward Economic Development: Seminar Papers for 14th IDEP (international development exchange program) Policy Forum*, April 10-17, 1989. Seoul: KDI, 1989.

The Korea Exchange Bank. 'Adjustment of Korea's Heavy and Chemical Industry Investment.' *Monthly Review* (December 1980).

The Korea Institute for Economics & Technology (KIET). *Industrial Policies and Practices of the United States and Japan.* Seoul: KIET, 1985 (in Korean).

The Korea Institute for Economics & Technology (KIET). *Problems of the Korean Heavy Machinery Industries and Policy Orientation*, Research Report (in Korean).

The KIET. *Problems of the Automobile Industry and Promotion Orientation*, Special Analysis 23. Seoul: KIET, 1982 (in Korean).

The Korean Chamber of Commerce and Industry (KCCI). *Reflections and Lessons of the Korean Twenty Years Economy.* Seoul: KCCI, 1982 (in Korean).

The Korean Chamber of Commerce and Industry. *Heavy and Chemical Industrial Construction, and Capital Mobilization.* Seoul: KCCI, 1975 (in Korean).

The Korean Council of Christian Churches. *Labor Site and Testimony: 1970s.* Seoul: Pul Bit Press, 1984 (in Korean).

The Korean Political Science Association, ed. *Modern Korean Politics and the State.* Seoul: Bum Moon Press, 1987 (in Korean).

The Korean Political Science Association, ed. *A Study on Modern Korean Politics.* Seoul: Bum Moon Press, 1986 (in Korean).

The Korean Politics Research Council. *A Study on Korean Politics.* Seoul: Baeck San Press, 1989 (in Korean).

The Korean Society Research Institute. *A Study on Organization of Labor Unions.* Seoul: Baeck San Press, 1989 (in Korean).

The Korean Society Research Institute. *A Study on Workers in the Korean Society I and II.* Seoul: Baeck San Press, 1989 (in Korean).

The Korean Workers' Welfare Council. *The History of Y.H. Labor Union.* Seoul: Hyungsung Press, 1984 (in Korean).

Kosai, Yutaka. *The End of High-Speed Growth: Notes on the Postwar Japanese Economy.* Tokyo: University of Tokyo Press, 1986.

Kosai, Yutaka. 'The Politics of Economic Management.' In Kozo Yamamura and Yasukichi, eds., *The Political Economy of Japan Vol. 1: The Domestic Transformation.* Stanford: Stanford University Press, 1987.

Kosai, Yutaka, and Harada, Yutaka. 'Economic Development in Japan: A Reconsideration.' In Robert A. Scalapino, Seizaburo Sato, and Jusuf Wanandi, eds., *Asian Economic Development--Present and Future.* Berkeley: Institute of East Asian Studies, University of California, 1985.

Krasner, Stephen D. *Defending the National Interest.* Princeton: Princeton University Press, 1978.

Krasner, Stephen D. 'Approaches to the State: Alternative Conceptions and Historical Dynamics.' *Comparative Politics* (January 1984).

Krasner, Stephen D. 'United States Commercial and Monetary Policy: Unravelling the Paradox of External Strength and Internal Weakness.' In Peter Katzenstein, ed., *Between Power and Plenty: Foreign Economic Policies of Advanced Industrial States.* Madison: University of Wisconsin Press, 1978.

Krasner, Stephen D. 'Sovereignty: An Institutional Perspective.' *Comparative Political Studies* 21 (No. 1 1988).

Krause, Lawrence B., and Kim, Kihwan., eds. *Liberalization in the Process of Economic Development.* Berkeley: University of California Press, 1991.

Krauss, Ellis S. 'Politics and the Policymaking Process.' In Takeshi Ishida and Ellis S. Krauss, eds., *Democracy in Japan.* Pittsburgh: University of Pittsburgh Press, 1989.

Krauss, Ellis S., and Pierre, Jon. 'The Decline of Dominant Parties: Parliamentary Politics in Sweden and Japan in the 1970s.' In T. J. Pempel, ed., *Uncommon Democracies: The One-Party Dominant Regimes.* Ithaca: Cornell University Press, 1990.

Krueger, Anne O. *The Development of the Foreign Sector and Aid.* Cambridge: Harvard University Press, 1979.

Krueger, Anne O. 'The Political Economy of the Rent-Seeking Society.' *American Economic Review* 64 (June 1974).

Kuisel, Richard F. *Capitalism and the State in Modern France: Renovation and Economic Management in the Twentieth Century.* Cambridge: Cambridge University Press, 1981.

Kuo, Shirley, et al. *The Taiwan Success Story: Rapid Growth with Improved Distribution in the Republic of China, 1952-79.* Boulder: Westview Press, 1981.

Kurth, James R. 'Industrial Change and Political Change: A European Perspective.' In David Collier, ed., *The New Authoritarianism in Latin America.* Princeton: Princeton University Press, 1979.

Kuznets, Paul W. *Economic Growth and Structure in the Republic of Korea.* New Haven: Yale University Press, 1977.

Kuznets, Paul W. 'The Dramatic Reversal of 1979-80: Contemporary Economic Development in Korea.' *Journal of Northeast Asian Studies* 1 (No. 3 1982).

Kwack, Sung Y., and Chung, Un Chan. 'The Role of Financial Policies and Institutions in Korea's Economic Development Process.' In Hang-Sheng Cheng, ed., *Financial Policy and Reform in Pacific Basin Countries*. Lexington: Lexington Books, 1986.

Kwack, Taewon. 'Industrial Restructuring Experience and Policies in Korea in the 1970s.' *KDI Working Paper* (84-08 1984).

Kwack, Young-Kil. 'Lee Won-Cho and the Suspicious Disposal of the Korean Shipping Corporation.' *Monthly Chosun* (March 1989) (in Korean).

Kwon, Soon-Jik. 'The Inside Story in the Disposals of Financially Weak Firms.' *Sin Dong-A* (May 1988) (in Korean).

Lau, L. J., ed. *Models of Development: A Comparative Study of Economic Growth in South Korea and Taiwan*. San Francisco: Institute for Contemporary Studies, 1986.

Lauber, Volkmar. *The Politics of Economic Policy: France 1974-82*. New York: Praeger, 1983.

Lauber, Volkmar. *The Political Economy of France: From Pompidou to Mitterrand*. New York: Praeger, 1983.

Launius, Michael A. 'The State and Industrial Labor in South Korea.' *Bulletin of Concerned Asian Scholars* 16 (Oct-December 1984).

Laux, Jeanne Kirk, and Molot, Maureen Appel. *State Capitalism: Public Enterprise in Canada*. Ithaca: Cornell University Press, 1988.

Layman, Thomas A. 'Financing Growth and Development in Asia.' In Robert A. Scalapino, Seizaburo Sato, Jusuf Wanandi, and Sung-joo Han, eds., *Pacific-Asian Economic Policies and Regional Interdependence*. Berkeley: Institute of East Asian Studies, University of California, Berkeley, 1988.

Lazonick, William. *Business Organization and the Myth of the Market Economy*. New York: Cambridge University Press, 1991.

Lee, Chae-Jin, and Sato, Hideo. *U.S. Policy toward Japan and Korea*. New York: Praeger Publishers, 1982.

Lee, Chong-sik. *Japan and Korea: The Political Dimension*. Stanford: Hoover Institution, Stanford University, 1985.

Lee, Chong-sik. 'South Korea 1979: Confrontation, Assassination, and Transition.' *Asian Survey* 20 (No. 1 1980).

Lee, Chong-sik. 'South Korea 1980: The Emergence of a New Authoritarian Order.' *Asian Survey* 21 (No. 1 1981).

Lee, Dukhoon. 'The Role of Financial Markets in Korea's Economic Development.' *KDI Working Paper* 8801 (January 1988).

Lee, Hye-Man. 'The Bankruptcy of Tong Myung Timber.' *Sin Dong-A* (July 1980) (in Korean).

Lee, Jang-Kyu. 'Anti-Democratic Government Organizations.' *Monthly Joong-Ang* (March 1988) (in Korean).

Lee, Jang-Kyu. *You are Economic President: The Inside Economic Story of Chun's Regime*. Seoul: Joongang Daily News, 1991 (in Korean).

Lee, Jin-Sup. 'Pan Ocean's Mystery.' *Monthly Chosun* (June 1987) (in Korean).

Lee, Jong-Nam. *Jaebols: Necessary Good or Evil for Economic Growth?* Seoul: Hyunje Press, 1985 (in Korean).

Lee, Jung-Bock. 'Industrialization and the Change of Political System.' *The Korean Political Science Association* 19 (1985) (in Korean).

Lee, Kyu-Uck. 'Recent Development in Industrial Organizational Issues in Korea.' *KDI Working Paper* 8609 (1986).

Lee, Man-Hee. *Did the EPB Achieve a Miracle?: The Ideal and Reality of Korea's Industrial Policy.* Seoul: Haedoji Press, 1993 (in Korean).

Lee, Manwoo. *The Odyssey of Korean Democracy: Korean Politics, 1987-1990.* New York: Praeger, 1990.

Lee, Won-Young. 'Direct Foreign Investment in Korea: Pattern, Impacts, and Government Policy.' *KDI Working Paper* 8706 (June 1987).

Lee, Young-Se. *Plans for Efficiency of Industrial Financial Policy.* Seoul: KIET, 1987 (in Korean).

Lehmbruch, Gerhard. 'Concertation and the Structure of Corporatist Networks.' In John H. Goldthorpe, ed., *Order and Conflict in Contemporary Capitalism.* Oxford: Oxford University Press, 1984.

Levi, Margaret. *Of Rule and Revenue.* Berkeley: University of California Press, 1988.

Levi, Margaret. 'A Logic of Institutional Change.' In Karen Schweers Cook and Margaret Levi, eds., *The Limits of Rationality.* Chicago: University of Chicago Press, 1990.

Levine, Daniel H. 'Paradigm Lost: Dependence to Democracy.' *World Politics* (April 1988).

Libecap, Gary D. *Contracting for Property Rights.* Cambridge: Cambridge University Press, 1989.

Lieberman, Ira W. 'Industrial Restructuring: Policy and Practices.' *Policy and Research Series* No. 9 (Washington: World Bank, 1990).

Lim, Hyun-Chin. *Dependent Development in Korea 1963-1979.* Seoul: Seoul National University Press, 1985.

Lim, Jin-Sook. 'State-Capital Relationships in Peripheral Capitalism: The Korean Policy of Heavy and Chemical Industrialization.' *M.A. Thesis*, Seoul National University, 1985 (in Korean).

Lim, Myo-Min. 'Jaebols and Power.' *Sin Dong-A* (April 1983) (in Korean).

Lim, Myo-Min. 'Conflicts of Jaebols.' *Sin Dong-A* (March 1983) (in Korean).

Lim, Youngil. *Government Policy and Private Enterprise: The Korean Experience with Industrialization.* Berkeley: Institute of East Asian Studies, University of California, Berkeley, 1981.

Lin, Ching-yuan. 'East Asia and Latin America as Contrasting Models.' *Economic Development and Cultural Change*, Supplement to Vol. 36 (No. 3 1988).

Lincoln, Edward J. *Japan: Facing Economic Maturity.* Washington: Brookings Institution, 1988.

Lindblom, Charles E. *Politics and Markets.* New York: Basic Books, 1977.

Lindblom, Charles E. 'The Market as Prison.' *Journal of Politics* 44 (May 1982).

Linz, Juan J., and Stepan, Alfred. *The Breakdown of Democratic Regimes: Latin America.* Baltimore: the Johns Hopkins University Press, 1978.

Lockwood, William W., ed. *The State and Economic Enterprise in Japan:*

Essays in the Political Economy of Growth. Princeton: Princeton University Press, 1965.

Loriaux, Michael. 'States and Markets: French Financial Interventionism in the Seventies.' *Comparative Politics* (January 1988).

Luedde-Neurath, Richard. 'State Intervention and Export-Oriented Development in South Korea.' In Gorden White and Robert Wade, eds., *Developmental Studies in East Asia.* Institute for Development Studies, Research Report 16, 1985.

Luedde-Neurath, Richard. *Import Controls and Export-Oriented Development: A Reassessment of the South Korean Case.* Boulder: Westview Press, 1986.

Lutz, Vera. *Central Planning for the Market Economy: An Analysis of the French Theory and Experience.* London and Harlow: Longmans, 1969.

Lynn, Leonard H., and McKeown, Timothy J. *Organizing Business: Trade Associations in America and Japan.* Washington: American Enterprise Institute for Public Policy Research, 1988.

Machado, Kit G. 'Japanese Transnational Corporations in Malaysia's State Sponsored Heavy Industrialization Drive: The HICOM Automobile and Steel Projects.' *Pacific Affairs* 62 (Winter 1989-90).

March, James G., and Olsen, Johan P. 'The New Institutionalism: Organizational Factors in Political Life.' *American Political Science Review* 78 (September 1984).

March, James G., and Olsen, Johan P. *Rediscovering Institutions: The Organizational Basis of Politics.* New York: Free Press, 1989.

Marin, Bernd, and Mayntz, Renate, eds. *Policy Networks: Empirical Evidence and Theoretical Considerations.* Boulder: Westview Press, 1991.

Markoff, John. 'Economic Crisis and Regime Change in Brazil: The 1960s and the 1980s.' *Comparative Politics* (July 1990).

Martin, Cathie Jo. 'Business Influence and State Power: The Case of U.S. Corporate Tax Policy.' *Politics and Society* 17 (June 1989).

Maxfield, Sylvia. *Governing Capital: International Finance and Mexican Politics.* Ithaca: Cornell University Press, 1990.

McArthur, John H., and Scott, Bruce R. *Industrial Planning in France.* Boston: Harvard University Press, 1969.

McCormack, Gavan. 'Beyond Economism: Japan in a State of Transition.' In Gavan McCormack and Yoshio Sugimoto, eds., *Democracy in Contemporary Japan.* Armonk: M.E. Sharpe, Inc., 1986.

McCubbins, Mathew D., and Sullivan, Terry, eds. *Congress: Structure and Policy.* Cambridge: Cambridge University Press, 1987.

McEachern, Doug. 'Combining Democracy with Growth.' In Gavan McCormack and Yoshio Sugimoto, eds., *Democracy in Contemporary Japan.* Armonk: M. E. Sharpe, Inc., 1986.

Michalet, Charles-Albert. 'France.' In Raymond Vernon, ed., *Big Business and the State: Changing Relations in Western Europe.* Cambridge: Harvard University Press, 1974.

Migdal, Joel S. *Strong Societies and Weak States: State-Society Relations and State Capabilities in the Third World.* Princeton: Princeton University Press, 1988.

Milanovic, Branko. *Liberalization and Entrepreneurship: Dynamics of Reform in Socialism and Capitalism*. Armonk: M. E. Sharpe, Inc., 1989.

Milner, Helen V. *Resisting Protectionism: Global Industries and the Politics of International Trade*. Princeton: Princeton University Press, 1988.

The Ministry of Labor. *The Labor Statistics Yearbook*. Seoul: 1987 (in Korean).

Mitchell, Neil J. *The Generous Corporation: A Political Analysis of Economic Power*. New Haven: Yale University Press, 1989.

Moon, Chung-in. 'U.S. Third Country Arms Sales Regulation and the South Korean Defense Industry: Supplier Control and Recipient Dilemma.' In Manwoo Lee et al., *Alliance Under Tension: The Evolution of South Korean-U.S. Relations*. Boulder: Westview Press, 1988.

Moon, Chung-in. 'South Korea: Between Security and Vulnerability.' In James Everett Katz, *The Implication of Third World Military Industrialization: Sowing the Serpents' Teeth*. Lexington Books, 1986.

Morris, Felipe, et al. 'Latin America's Banking Systems in the 1980s: A Cross-Country Comparison.' *World Bank Discussion Papers* (No. 81 1990).

Moser, Paul K., ed. *Rationality in Action: Contemporary Approaches*. Cambridge: Cambridge University Press, 1990.

Mueller, Dennis C. *Public Choice II: A Revised Edition of Public Choice*. Cambridge: Cambridge University Press, 1989.

Muramatsu, Michio, and Krauss, Ellis S. 'Bureaucrats and Politicians in Policy Making: The Case of Japan.' *American Political Science Review* 78 (No. 1 1984).

Muramatsu, Michio, and Krauss, Ellis S. 'The Conservative Policy Line and the Development of Patterned Pluralism.' In Kozo Yamamura and Yasukichi Yasuba, eds., *The Political Economy of Japan Vol. 1: The Domestic Transformation*. Stanford: Stanford University Press, 1987.

Muramatsu, Michio, and Krauss, Ellis S. 'The Dominant Party and Social Coalitions in Japan.' In T. J. Pempel, ed., *Uncommon Democracies: The One-Party Dominant Regimes*. Ithaca: Cornell University Press, 1990.

Myhrmann, John. 'The New Institutional Economics and the Process of Economic Development.' *Journal of Institutional and Theoretical Economics* 145 (March 1989).

Myrdal, Gunnar. *Asian Drama: An Inquiry into the Poverty of Nations*. New York: Pantheon, 1968.

Nakamura, Takafusa (Robert A. Feldman, trans.). *Economic Growth in Prewar Japan*. New Haven and London: Yale University Press, 1983.

Nam, Koon Woo. *South Korean Politics: The Search for Political Consensus and Stability*. Washington: University of America, 1989.

Nam, Sang-Woo. 'Korea's Stabilization Efforts since the Late 1970s.' In Joong-woong Kim, ed., *Financial Development Policies and Issues*. Seoul: Korea Development Institute, 1986.

The National Assembly Records. *The 4th Session of the Commerce and Industry Committee in the 101th National Assembly Meeting*. Seoul: 1979 (in Korean).

The National Assembly Records. *The 5th Session of the Economic and*

Science Committee in the 101th National Assembly Meeting. Seoul: 1979 (in Korean).

The National Assembly Records. *The 2nd Session of the Commerce and Industry Committee in the 102nd National Assembly Meeting.* Seoul: July 30, 1979 (in Korean).

The National Assembly Records. *The 9th Session of the Commerce and Industry Committee in the 103rd National Assembly Meeting.* Seoul: February 1980 (in Korean).

The National Assembly Records. *Special Hearings on the Kwangju Incident.* Seoul: 1989 (in Korean).

The National Assembly Records. *Special Hearings on the Measures of Purging Journalists and Merging Newspapers and Broadcasting Stations.* Seoul: 1989 (in Korean).

The National Assembly Records. *Special Hearings on the Ilhae Foundation.* Seoul: 1989 (in Korean).

Nelson, Joan M. 'The Politics of Stabilization.' In Richard E. Feinberg and Valeriana Kallab, eds., *Adjustment Crisis in the Third World.* New Brunswick: Transaction Books, 1984.

Nelson, Joan M., et al. *Fragile Coalitions: The Politics of Economic Adjustment.* Washington: Overseas Development Council, 1989.

Nelson. Joan M. 'The Politics of Economic Transformation: Is Third World Experience Relevant in Eastern Europe?' *World Politics* (April 1993).

Nolan, Janne E. *Military Industry in Taiwan and South Korea.* New York: St. Martin's Press, 1986.

North, Douglass C. 'The New Institutional Economics.' *Journal of Theoretical and Institutional Economics* 142 (No. 1 1986).

North, Douglass C. 'Institutions, Transaction Costs, and Economic Growth.' *Economic Inquiry* 25 (July 1987).

North, Douglass C. *Structure and Change in Economic History.* New York: W. W. Norton & Company, 1981.

North, Douglass C. *Institutions, Institutional Change and Economic Performance.* Cambridge: Cambridge University Press, 1990.

O'Donnell, Guillermo. 'State and Alliance in Argentina, 1956-76.' *Journal of Development Studies* 15 (October 1978).

O'Donnell, Guillermo. *Modernization and Bureaucratic "Authoritarianism.* Berkeley: University of California Press, 1979.

O'Donnell, Guillermo. 'Reflections on the Patterns of Change in the Bureaucratic Authoritarian State.' *Latin American Research Review* 13 (No. 1 1978).

O'Donnell, Guillermo. 'Tensions in the Bureaucratic-Authoritarian State and the Question of Democracy.' In David Collier, ed., *The New Authoritarianism in Latin America.* Princeton: Princeton University Press, 1979.

O'Donnell, Guillermo. *Bureaucratic Authoritarianism: Argentina, 1966-1973, in Comparative Perspective.* Berkeley: University of California Press, 1988.

O'Donnell, Guillermo, Schmitter, Philippe C., and Whitehead, Laurence.

Transitions from Authoritarian Rule Vols. 1, 2, 3, and 4. Baltimore: the Johns Hopkins University Press, 1986.

Offe, Claus. *Contradictions of the Welfare State.* Cambridge: the MIT press, 1984.

Offe, Claus. 'The Theory of the Capitalist State and the Problem of Policy Formation.' In Leon N. Lindberg, et al., eds., *Stress and Contradiction in Modern Capitalism.* Lexington Books, 1975.

Offe, Claus. 'The Attribution of Public Status to Interest Groups: Observations on the West German Case.' In Suzanne D. Berger, ed., *Organizing Interests in Western Europe: Pluralism, Corporatism, and the Transformation of Politics.* Cambridge: Cambridge University Press, 1981.

Offe, Claus. 'Two Logics of Collective Action.' In Claus Offe (John Keane, ed.), *Disorganized Capitalism: Contemporary Transformations of Work and Politics.* Cambridge: MIT Press, 1985.

The Office of the Presidential Secretariat (the Republic of Korea). *Collection of President Park's Speeches* (in Korean).

Okimoto, Daniel I. *Between MITI and Market: Japanese Industrial Policy for High Technology.* Stanford: Stanford University Press, 1989.

Okimoto, Daniel I., Sugano, Takuo, and Weinstein, Franklin B., eds. *Competitive Edge: The Semiconductor Industry in the U.S. and Japan.* Stanford: Stanford University Press, 1984.

Okimoto, Daniel I., and Rohlen, Thomas P., eds. *Inside the Japanese System: Readings on Contemporary Society and Political Economy.* Stanford: Stanford University Press, 1988.

Olsen, Edward A. 'Korea, Inc.: The Politics Impact of Park Chung Hee's Economic Miracle.' In Tae-Whan Kwak, ed., *The Two Koreas in World Politics.* Seoul: The Institute for Far Eastern Studies, Kyungnam University, 1983.

Olson, Mancur. *The Logic of Collective Action: Public Goods and the Theory of Groups.* Cambridge: Harvard University Press, 1965.

Opp, Karl-Dieter. *The Rationality of Political Protest: A Comparative Analysis of Rational Choice Theory.* Boulder: Westview Press, 1989.

Ordeshook, Peter C. *Game Theory and Political Theory: An Introduction.* Cambridge: Cambridge University Press, 1986.

Ostrom, Elinor. *Governing the Commons: The Evolution of Institutions for Collective Action.* Cambridge: Cambridge University Press, 1990.

Oye, Kenneth A. 'Explaining Cooperation under Anarchy: Hypotheses and Strategies.' In Kenneth A. Oye, ed., *Cooperation Under Anarchy.* Princeton: Princeton University Press, 1986.

Packenham, Robert A. 'The Politics of Economic Liberalization: Argentina and Brazil in Comparative Perspective.' Prepared for Delivery at the 1992 Annual Meeting of the American Political Science Association, 1992.

Park, Byung-Yun. 'Wild Currents in the Business Circle in 1978.' *Sin Dong-A* (December 1978) (in Korean).

Park, Byung-Yun. 'The Inside Story of the Automobile Industry.' *Sin Dong-A* (December 1979) (in Korean).

Park, Byung-Yun. *Jaebols and Politics*. Seoul: Hankook Yangsu Press, 1982 (in Korean).

Park, Byung-Yun. 'The Inside Story of Heavy and Chemical Industries.' *Sin Dong-A* (May 1980) (in Korean).

Park, Chung Hee. *Korea Reborn: A Model for Development*. Englewood Cliffs: Prentice-Hall, Inc., 1979.

Park, Hyo-Chong. 'Development and State Autonomy: South Korea.' *Ph.D. Diss.*, Indiana University, 1986.

Park, Jong-Joo. 'Korean Modernization and State Corporatist Control: The Third and Fourth Republics.' *Ph. D. Diss.*, Seoul National University, 1986 (in Korean).

Park, Jong-Ryul. 'The Fifth Republic's Political Funds.' *Sin Dong-A* (January 1989) (in Korean).

Park, Jong-Ryul. 'The Ilhae Foundation.' *Sin Dong-A* (October 1988) (in Korean).

Park, June-Sik. 'Labor Movement around 1980 and State Intervention.' in the Korean Industrial Society Research Council, ed., *Today's Korean Capitalism and the State*. Seoul: Hangil Press, 1988 (in Korean).

Park, Keun-Ho. 'A Study on the Korean Administrative Reform.' *M.A. Thesis*, Dong-Kook University, 1985 (in Korean).

Park, Moon Kyu. 'Interest Representation in South Korea: The Limits of Corporatist Control.' *Asian Survey* (August 1987).

Park, Sang-Sup. *A Study on the Capitalist State: Modern Marxist Political Theories*. Seoul: Han wool Press, 1985 (in Korean).

Park, Sang-Sup. 'Poulantzas' Theory and the Third World.' *Hyundai Sahoe* (Winter 1984) (in Korean).

Park, Se-Hoon. 'The Fifth Republic's Collusive State-Business Coalition.' *Monthly Chosun* (December 1988) (in Korean).

Park, Young Chul. 'Financial Repression, Liberalization and Development in Developing Countries.' *KDI Working Paper* (No. 8704 May 1987).

Patrick, Hugh and Rosovsky, Henry, eds. *Asia's a New Giant*. Washington: Brookings Institution, 1976.

Paul, Samuel. 'Institutional Reforms in Sector Adjustment Operations: The World Bank's Experience.' *World Bank Discussion Papers* (No. 92 1990).

Pauly, Louis W. *Opening Financial Markets: Banking Politics on the Pacific Rim*. Ithaca: Cornell University Press, 1988.

Pempel, T. J. *Policy and Politics in Japan: Creative Conservatism*. Philadelphia: Temple University Press, 1982.

Pempel, T. J. 'Japanese Foreign Economic Policy.' In Peter Katzenstein, ed., *Between and Power and Plenty*. Madison: University of Wisconsin Press, 1978.

Pempel, T. J. 'Corporatism without Labor?: The Japanese Anomaly.' In Philippe C. Schmitter and Gerhard Lehmbruch, eds., *Trends toward Corporatist Intermediation*. Sage Publishers, 1979.

Perkins, Dwight H., and Roemer, Michael. *Reforming Economic Systems in Developing Countries*. Cambridge: Harvard Institute for International Development, 1991.

The Planning Office of the Heavy and Chemical Industry Promotion

Committee (HCIPC). *The Conference Records of the Heavy and Chemical Industry Promotion Committee.* Seoul: 1980 (in Korean).

The Planning Office of the HCIPC. *An Investigative Study on the Development of Korean Industrialization: The Behind-the-Scenes History of the Policy-Making Process.* Seoul: 1979c (in Korean).

The Planning Office of the HCIPC. *The Heavy and Chemical Industry Promotion Plan.* Seoul: June 1973 (in Korean).

The Planning Office of the HCIPC. *An Investigative Study on the Development of Korean Industrialization: The Heavy and Chemical Industrial Policy History.* Seoul: 1979b (in Korean).

The Planning Office of the HCIPC. *An Investigative Study on the Development of Korean Industrialization: The Heavy and Chemical Industrial Development History.* Seoul: 1979a (in Korean).

Polanyi, Karl. *The Great Transformation: The Political and Economic Origins of Our Time.* Boston: Beacon Press, 1944.

Popkin, Samuel L. *The Rational Peasant: The Political Economy of Rural Society in Vietnam.* Berkeley: University of California Press, 1979.

Porter, Michael E. *The Competitive Advantage of Nations.* New York: Free Press, 1990.

Poulantzas, Nicos. 'The Problem of the Capitalist State.' *New Left Review* 58 (1969).

Przeworski, Adam. 'Material Interest, Class Compromise, and the Transition to Socialism.' *Politics and Society* (No. 2 1980).

Przeworski, Adam. *Democracy and the Market: Political and Economic Reforms in Eastern Europe and Latin America.* New York: Cambridge University Press, 1991.

Quirk, Paul J. 'The Cooperation Resolution of Policy Conflict.' *American Political Science Review* 83 (September 1989).

Reich, Simon. *The Fruits of Fascism: Postwar Prosperity in Historical Perspective.* Ithaca: Cornell University Press, 1990.

Rhee, Hang Yul. 'The Economic Problem of the Korean Political Economy.' In Ilpyong J. Kim and Young Whan Kihl, *Political Change in South Korea.* New York: the Korea PWPA, Inc., 1988.

Rhee, Sung Sup. 'Current State and Policy Issues of Declining Industries in Korea.' In Korea Development Institute, *Joint Conference on Structural Adjustment and Industrial Policy Issues in Korea and Germany.* Seoul: December 5-6, 1985.

Rhee, Sung Sup. 'Policy Reforms of the Eighties and Industrial Adjustments in Korean Economy.' *KDI Working Paper* 8708 (1987).

Rhee, Young Whee. 'Instruments for Export Policy and Administrative Lessons from the East Asian Experience.' *The World Bank Working Paper* (No. 725 1985).

Ro, Jae-Hyun. *The Blue House's Secretariat (the Presidential Secretariat) 2.* Seoul: Joongang Daily News, 1993 (in Korean).

Rockman, Bert A. 'Minding the State – or A State of Mind?: Issues in the Comparative Conceptualization of the State.' *Comparative Political Studies* 23 (April 1990).

Roe, Alan R. 'Industrial Restructuring: Issues and Experience in Selected Developed Economies.' *The World Bank Technical Paper* (No. 21 1984).

Roe, Alan, and Popiel, Paul A. 'The Restructuring of Financial Systems in Latin America.' *EDI Policy Seminar Report* No. 25 (Washington: World Bank, 1990).

Roemer, John, ed. *Analytical Marxism.* Cambridge: Cambridge University Press, 1986.

Rogowski, Ronald. *Commerce and Coalitions: How Trade Affects Domestic Political Alignments.* Princeton: Princeton University Press, 1989.

Rosenau, James N. 'The State in an Era of Cascading Politics: Wavering Concept, Widening Competence, Withering Colossus, or Weathering Change?' *Comparative Political Studies* 21 (No. 1 1988).

Rosenbluth, Frances McCall. *Financial Politics in Contemporary Japan.* Ithaca: Cornell University Press, 1989.

Rothchild, Donald, and Chazan, Naomi, eds. *The Precarious Balance: State & Society in Africa.* Boulder: Westview Press, 1988.

Rueschemeyer, Dietrich, and Evans, Peter. 'The State and Economic Transformation: Toward an Analysis of the Conditions Underlying Effective Intervention.' In Peter Evans, et al., eds., *Bring the State Back In.* Cambridge: Cambridge University Press, 1985.

Saburo, Zushi. 'Case Study: How to Go Bankrupt and Still Stay Afloat (the Ataka Affair).' In Murakami Hyoe and Johannes Hirschmeier, *Politics and Economics in Contemporary Japan.* New York: Kodansha International Ltd., 1983.

Safran, William. *The French Polity* (Third Edition). New York: Longman, 1991.

Sakong, Il, ed. *Macroeconomic Policy and Industrial Development Issues.* Seoul: KDI, 1987.

Samuels, Richard J. *The Business of the Japanese State: Energy Markets in Comparative and Historical Perspective.* Ithaca: Cornell University Press, 1987.

Saul, John. 'The State in Post-Colonial Societies: Tanzania.' *Socialist Register* (1974).

Saxonhouse, Gary. 'Industrial Restructuring in Japan.' *Journal of Japanese Studies* 5 (No. 2 1979).

Schmitter, Philippe C. 'Path to Political Development in Latin America.' In Douglas A. Chalmers, ed., *Changing Latin America: New Interpretations of Its Politics and Society.* New York: Academy of Political Science, Columbia University, 1972.

Schmitter, Philippe C. 'Corporatism is Dead – Long Live Corporatism.' *Government and Opposition* 24 (Winter 1989).

Schonfield, Andrew. *Modern Capitalism: The Changing Balance of Public and Private Power.* Oxford: Oxford University Press, 1965.

Schultze, Charles L. 'Industrial Policy: A Dissent.' *Brookings Review* (Fall 1983).

Schweitzer, Arther. *Big Business in the Third Reich.* Bloomington: Indiana University Press, 1964.

Scott, James C. *Weapons of the Weak: Everyday Forms of Peasant Resistance.* New Haven: Yale University Press, 1985.

Scott, James C. *Domination and the Arts of Resistance: Hidden Transcripts.* New Haven: Yale University Press, 1990.

The Secretariat for the President (the Republic of Korea). *The 1980s Meeting a New Challenge Vol. 1: Selected Speeches of President Chun Doo Hwan.* Seoul: the Korea Textbook Co., 1981.

Shepherd, Geoffrey, and Duchène, François, and Saunders, Christopher. *Europe's Industries: Public and Private Strategies for Change.* Ithaca: Cornell University Press, 1983.

Shin, Ryung-In. *Labor Laws and Labor Movement.* Seoul: Ilwulsugak Press, 1987 (in Korean).

Shorrock, Tim. 'The Struggle for Democracy in South Korea and the Rise of Anti-Americanism.' *Third World Quarterly* 8 (October 1986).

Shorrock, Tim. 'South Korea: Chun, the Kims and the Constitutional Struggle.' *Third World Quarterly* 10 (January 1988).

Sikkink, Kathryn. 'Development Ideas and Economic Policy in Latin America.' Prepared for Delivery at the 1990 Annual Meeting of the American Political Science Association, San Francisco, August 30 September 2, 1990.

Sin, Sang-Min. 'The Background of the Establishment of the Fair Trade Act.' *Sin Dong-A* (December 1980) (in Korean).

Sin, Sang-Min. 'Business Concentration as a Result of the Disposals of Financially Weak Firms.' *Sin Dong-A* (November 1986) (in Korean).

Skidmore, Thomas E. 'Politics and Economic Policy-Making in Authoritarian Brazil, 1937-71.' In Alfred Stepan, ed., *Authoritarian Brazil: Origins, Policies, and Future.* New Haven: Yale University Press, 1973.

Skidmore, Thomas E. 'The Politics of Economic Stabilization in Postwar Latin America.' In James M. Malloy, ed., *Authoritarianism and Corporatism in Latin America.* Pittsburgh: University of Pittsburgh Press, 1977.

Skidmore, Thomas. *The Politics of Military Rule in Brazil 1964-85.* Oxford: Oxford University Press, 1988.

Skocpol, Theda. 'Political Response to Capitalist Crisis: Neomarxist Theories of the State and the Case of the New Deal.' *Politics and Society* 10 (No. 2 1980).

Skocpol, Theda. *State and Social Revolutions.* Cambridge: Cambridge University Press, 1979.

Skocpol, Theda. 'Bring the State Back In.' In Peter Evans, et al., eds., *Bring the State Back In.* Cambridge: Cambridge University Press, 1985.

Skully, Michael T., and Viksnins, George J. *Financing East Asia's Success: Comparative Financial Development in Eight Asian Countries.* New York: St. Martin's Press, 1987.

Skyrms, Brian. *The Dynamics of Rational Deliberation.* Cambridge: Harvard University Press, 1990.

Slote, Michael. *Beyond Optimizing: A Study of Rational Choice.* Cambridge: Harvard University Press, 1989.

Smith, B. C. *Bureaucracy and Political Power.* New York: St. Martin's Press, 1988.

Smith, W. Rand. 'Nationalizations for What? Capitalist Power and Public Enterprise in Mitterrand's France.' *Politics and Society* 18 (March 1990).

Smith, William C. *Authoritarianism and the Crisis of the Argentine Political Economy.* Stanford: Stanford University Press, 1989.

Snidal, Duncan. 'Public Goods, Property Rights, and Political Organizations.' *International Studies Quarterly* 23 (December 1979).

Song, Byung-Nak. *The Rise of the Korean Economy.* Oxford: Oxford University Press, 1990.

Spalding, Rose J. 'State Power and Its Limits: Corporatism in Mexico.' *Comparative Political Studies* 14 (July 1981).

The Special Committee for National Security Measures. *White Paper on the Special Committee for National Security Measures.* Seoul: 1980 (in Korean).

Spivey, W. Allen. *Economic Policies in France 1976-1981: The Barre Program in a West European Perspective*, Michigan International Business Studies No. 18. Ann Arbor: Division of Research Graduate School of Business Administration, University of Michigan, 1982.

Stallings, Barbara. 'International Lending and the Relative Autonomy of the State: A Case Study of Twentieth-Century Peru.' *Politics and Society* 14 (No. 3 1985).

Stallings, Barbara, and Kaufman, Robert R. *Debt and Democracy in Latin America.* Boulder: Westview Press, 1988.

Staniland, Martin. *What is Political Economy?* New Haven: Yale University Press, 1985.

Steers, Richard M., Shin, Yoo Keun, and Ungson, Gerardo R. *The Chaebol: Korea's New Industrial Might.* New York: Harper & Row, Publishers, 1989.

Stein, Arthur A. *Why Nations Cooperate: Circumstance and Choice in International Relations.* Ithaca and London: Cornell University Press, 1990.

Steinmo, Sven. 'Political Institutions and Tax Policy in the United States, Sweden, and Britain.' *World Politics* (July 1989).

Stepan, Alfred. *The State and Society: Peru in Comparative Perspective.* Princeton: Princeton University Press, 1978.

Stepan, Alfred. *The Military in Politics: Changing Patterns in Brazil.* Princeton: Princeton University Press, 1971.

Stepan, Alfred. *Rethinking Military Politics.* Princeton: Princeton University Press, 1988.

Stepan, Alfred, ed. *Democratizing Brazil: Problems of Transition and Consolidation.* Oxford: Oxford University Press, 1989.

Stinchcombe, Arthur L. *Constructing Social Theories.* Chicago: University of Chicago Press Edition, 1987.

Stoffa's, Christian. 'Industrial Policy and the State: From Industry to Enterprise.' In Paul Codt, ed., *Policy-Making in France: From de Gaulle to Mitterrand.* London and New York: Printer Publishers, 1989.

Stoleru, Lionel. *L'Imperatif Industriel.* Paris: Seuil, 1969.

Streeck, Wolfgang, and Schmitter, Philippe, eds. *Private Interest Government: Beyond Market and State.* Sage Publications, 1985.

Streeten, Paul. 'Structural Adjustment: A Survey of the Issues and Options.' *World Development* 15 (No. 12 1987).

Subcommittee on Economic Growth and Stabilization of the Joint Economic Committee in the Congress of the United States (95th Congress

1st Session). *Recent Developments in French Planning: Some Lessons for the U.S.*. Washington: U.S. Government Printing Office, 1977.

Suh, Jae Jean. 'Capitalist Class Formation and the Limits of Class Power in Korea.' *Ph.D. Diss.*, University of Hawaii, 1988.

Suh, Sang-Mok. 'Economic Growth and Change in Income Distribution: The Korean Case.' *KDI Working Paper* 8508 (1985).

Suleiman, Ezra N. *Private Power and Centralization in France: The Notaires and the State*. Princeton: Princeton University Press, 1987.

Suleiman, Ezra N., ed. *Bureaucrats and Policymaking*. New York: Holmes & Meier, 1984.

Sun, Kyung-Sik. 'The Special Committee for National Security Measures.' *Monthly Joong-Ang* (March 1988) (in Korean).

Suzuki, Yoshio, ed. *The Japanese Financial System*. Oxford: Clarendon Press, 1989.

Swenson, Peter. *Fair Shares: Unions, Pay, and Politics in Sweden and West Germany*. Ithaca: Cornell University Press, 1989.

Tavis, Lee A. 'The Role of Multinational Corporations in the Third World.' In Lee A. Tavis, ed., *Multinational Managers and Host Government Interactions*. Notre Dame: University of Notre Dame Press, 1988.

Taylor, Michael. 'Structure, Culture and Action in the Explanation of Social Change.' *Politics and Society* 17 (June 1989).

Taylor, Michael, ed. *Rationality and Revolution*. Cambridge: Cambridge University Press, 1988.

Taylor, Michael. *The Possibility of Cooperation*. Cambridge: Cambridge University Press, 1987.

The Tokyo University Press Council, ed. *A Study on Japan's Industrial Policy*. Seoul: Korea Institute for Economics & Technology, 1986 (in Korean).

Torre, Juan Carlos. 'The Politics of Economic Crisis in Latin America.' *Journal of Democracy* (January 1993).

Trezise, Philip H. 'Industrial Policy is not the Major Reason for Japan's Success.' *Brookings Review* (Spring 1983).

Tsebelis, George. *Nested Games: Rational Choice in Comparative Politics*. Berkeley: University of California Press, 1990.

Turner, Jonathan H. *A Theory of Social Interaction*. Stanford: Stanford University Press, 1988.

Uekusa, Masu. 'Industrial Organization: The 1970s to the Present.' In Kozo Yamamura and Yasukichi Yasuba, eds., *The Political Economy of Japan Vol. 1: The Domestic Transformation*. Stanford: Stanford University Press, 1987.

Vernon, Raymond., ed. *Big Business and the State: Changing Relations in Western Europe*. Cambridge: Harvard University Press, 1974.

Vogel, David. *National Styles of Regulation: Environmental Policy in Great Britain and the United States*. Ithaca: Cornell University Press, 1986.

Vogel, David. *Fluctuating Fortunes: The Political Power of Business in America*. New York: Basic Books, Inc., 1989.

Vogel, Ezra. *Japan as Number One: Lessons for America*. New York: Harper & Row, 1979.

Wade, Robert. 'East Asian Financial Systems as a Challenge to Economics: Lessons from Taiwan.' *California Management Review* 27 (Summer 1985).

Wade, Robert. 'The Role of Government in Overcoming Market Failure: Taiwan, Republic of Korea and Japan.' In Helen Hughes, ed., *Achieving Industrialization in East Asia*. Cambridge: Cambridge University Press, 1988.

Wade, Robert. *Governing The Market: Economic Theory and the Role of Government in East Asian Industrialization*. Princeton: Princeton University Press, 1990.

Wade, Robert. 'State Intervention in Outward-Looking Development: Neoclassical Theory and Taiwanese Practices.' In Gorden White and Robert Wade, eds., *Developmental Studies in East Asia*. Institute for Development Studies, Research Report 16, 1985.

Waligorski, Conrad P. *The Political Theory of Conservative Economists*. Lawrence: University Press of Kansas, 1990.

Wartenberg, Thomas E. *The Forms of Power: From Domination to Transformation*. Philadelphia: Temple University Press, 1990.

Watanabe, Toshio. 'Heavy and Chemical Industrialization and Economic Development in the Republic of Korea.' *The Developing Economies* 16 (December 1978).

Weatherford, M. Stephen, and Fukui, Haruhiro. 'Domestic Adjustment to International Shocks in Japan and the United States.' *International Organization* 43 (Autumn 1989).

Weaver, R. Kent. *The Politics of Industrial Change: Railway Policy in North America*. Washington: Brookings Institution, 1985.

Weaver, R. Kent, and Rockman, Bert A., eds. *Do Institutions Matter?: Government Capacities in the United States and Abroad*. Washington, D.C.: Brookings Institution, 1993.

Wendt, Alexander E. 'The Agent-Structure Problem in International Relations Theory.' *International Organization* 41 (Summer 1987).

Westphal, Larry E. 'The Republic of Korea's Experience with Export-Led Industrial Development.' *World Development* 6 (No. 3 1976).

Westphal, Larry E., et al. 'Korean Industrial Competence: Where It Came From.' *World Bank Staff Working Papers* (No. 469 1981).

Whang, In-Joung. 'Korea's Economic Management for Structural Adjustment in the 1980s.' *KDI Working Paper* 8606 (December 1986).

Williamson, Oliver E. *The Economic Institutions of Capitalism: Firms, Markets, Relational Contracting*. New York: Free Press, 1985.

Williamson, Oliver E. *Economic Organization: Firms, Markets and Policy Control*. New York: New York University Press, 1986.

Williamson, Oliver E. 'A Comparison of Alternative Approaches to Economic Organization.' *Journal of Institutional and Theoretical Economics* 146 (March 1990).

Williamson, Peter J. *Corporatism in Perspective: An Introductory Guide to Corporatist Theory*. London: Sage Publications, 1989.

Wilsford, David. 'Tactical Advantages versus Administrative Heterogeneity: The Strengths and Limits of the French State.' *Comparative Political Studies* 21 (April 1988).

Wilson, Frank L. 'French Interest Group Politics: Pluralist or Neocorporatist.' *American Political Science Review* 77 (December 1983).

Wilson, Frank L. *Interest-Group Politics in France*. New York: Cambridge University Press, 1987.

Wilson, Graham K. *Interest Groups*. Oxford: Basil Blackwell, 1990.

Wilson, Graham K. *Business and Politics*: A Comparative Introduction, 2nd Edition. Chatham: Chatham House Publishers, Inc., 1990.

Wolf, Charles, Jr. *Markets or Governments: Choosing between Imperfect Alternatives*. Cambridge: MIT Press, 1988.

Woo, Jung-en. *Race to the Swift: State and Finance in Korean Industrialization*. New York: Studies of the East Asian Institute, Columbia University, 1991.

The World Bank. *Korea: Development in a Global Context*. Washington: World Bank, 1984.

The World Bank. *Korea: Managing the Industrial Transition*, Vols. 1 and 2. Washington: World Bank, 1987.

The World Bank. *Korea: The Management of External Liabilities*. Washington: 1988.

The World Bank, *Argentina: Reforms for Price Stability and Growth*, A World Bank Country Study. Washington: World Bank, 1990.

Woronoff, Jon. *Korea's Economy: Man-Made Miracle*. Seoul: the Si-Sa-Young-A-Sa Publishers, 1983.

Wright, Maurice. 'Policy Community, Policy Network and Comparative Industrial Policies.' *Political Studies* 36 (December 1988).

Wrong, Dennis H. *Power: Its Forms, Bases, and Uses*. Chicago: University of Chicago Press Edition, 1988.

Yanaga, Chitoshi. *Big Business in Japanese Politics*. New Haven: Yale University Press, 1968.

Yarbrough, Beth, and Yarbrough, Robert M. 'International Institutions and the New Economics of Organization.' *International Organization* 44 (Spring 1990).

Yasuda, Ryuji. 'Politics of Industrial Financing Policy: Korea and Japan.' *Ph.D. Diss.*, University of California, Berkeley, 1979.

Yoo, Hoon. *A Study on Government-Business Relations*. Seoul: Bub Moon Press, 1989 (in Korean).

Yoshino, M. Y., and Lifson, Thomas B. *The Invisible Link: Japan's Sogo Shosha and the Organization of Trade*. Cambridge: MIT Press, 1986.

Young, Soogil. 'Import Liberalization and Industrial Adjustment in Korea.' *KDI Working Paper* 8613 (1986).

Young, Soogil. 'New Challenges to the Korean Economy and Their International Implications.' *KDI Working Paper* 9004 (1990).

Yu, Mizushima. 'A Close Encounter with the Korean Democratic Movement.' *AMPO* 17 (No. 1 1985).

Yun, Suk-Woong. 'Large Firms' Fund War.' *Sin Dong-A* (December 1978) (in Korean).

Zeigler, Harmon. *Pluralism, Corporatism, and Confucianism: Political Association and Conflict Regulation in the U.S., Europe, and Taiwan*. Philadelphia: Temple University Press, 1988.

Zukin, Sharon, and Dimaggio, Paul, eds. *Structures of Capital: The Social*

Organization of the Economy. Cambridge: Cambridge University Press, 1990.

Zysman, John. *Governments, Markets and Growth: Financial Systems and the Politics of Industrial Change.* Ithaca: Cornell University Press, 1983.

Zysman, John. 'The Interventionist Temptation: Financial Structure and Political Purpose.' In William G. Andrew and Stanley Hoffmann, *The Fifth Republic at Twenty.* Albany: State University of New York Press, 1981.

Zysman, John, and Tyson, Laura. *American Industry in International Competition.* Ithaca: Cornell University Press, 1983.

Newspapers, Magazines, and Government Documents:

Business Korea
The Chosun Daily News
The Dong-A Daily News
Far Eastern Economic Review
The Federation of Korean Trade Unions
Government Documents from the Economic Planning Board, the Ministry of Commerce and Industry, the Ministry of Finance, the Bank of Korea, and the Special Committee for National Security Measures
The Hankook Daily News
The Hyundai Kyungje (Korea Economic) Daily News
The Joong-Ang Daily News
The Korea Herald
The Korean Business Review
The Kyunghyang Daily News
The Maeil Kyungje Daily News
New York Times
The Seoul Daily News

Index